While it is yet Day

The Story of Elizabeth Fry

by Averil Douglas Opperman

Orphans

First published in Great Britain in 2015 by
Orphans Publishing
an imprint of Orphans Press Ltd
3 Arrow Close, Leominster Enterprise Park, Herefordshire HR6 0LD
www.orphanspublishing.co.uk

ISBN 978-1-90-336014-9 (Hardback edition)

Orphans Publishing supports the Forest Stewardship Council® (FSC®), the
leading international forest-certification organisation. Our books carrying
the FSC label are printed on FSC®- certified paper.

RECYCLED
Made from
recycled material
FSC   FSC® C010720
www.fsc.org

Cover illustration by Adam Fisher from an original painting of Elizabeth Fry
reading to prisoners by Jerry Barrett, 1863, held in the British Museum.

Typeset in Adobe Garamond Pro 11pt / 15pt

Designed, printed and bound in Great Britain by Orphans Press Ltd

"Come what come may,
Time and the hour runs
through the roughest day"

(Wm. Shakespeare, *Macbeth* Act 1, Sc. 3)

In memory of
Senator James Green Douglas and
J. Harold Douglas

Author's Note

The quotes from Elizabeth's diaries and letters include her original spelling, grammar and punctuation. Quakers used the pronouns 'thee' and 'thou' to show that everyone was equal in the eyes of God. These terms were usually used for family and inferiors and the more polite 'you' used for superiors. Years ago strict Quakers were regarded as 'plain' because of their solemn dress and speech. Those who continued to enjoy music and dancing were termed 'gay'. Also Quakers did not use the names of the months regarding them as heathen. They used numbers instead e.g. first month 28th first day [Sunday].

The title, *While It Is Yet Day,* was one of Elizabeth Fry's mantras. She took it from the Bible: St John 9.4 *'I must work the works of him that sent me, while it is day…'* Hopefully, you will see how fitting this is as you read the book.

Contents

Family Trees   *I*

Prologue   *III*

Childhood   1

Quaker Family   11

Awakenings   17

An American Friend   21

Trip to London   29

Subtle Changes   37

Resolute Admirer   51

Blushing Bride   65

Visitors   77

Motherhood   89

Love and Death   109

Plashet   125

A Spell in Prison   145

Prison Life   153

Domestic Change	159
Anguish & Loneliness	165
Return to Newgate	171
Family Interlude	185
Further Reform	189
Convict Ships	197
Capital Punishment	207
Reluctant Celebrity	215
Letter from Down Under	221
Changing Times	229
Inner Reflection	235
Return to Domesticity	245
Coastguards and Shepherds	251
Gathering Clouds	255
The Storm Approaches	263
Adapting to Change	269
Royalty and Reform	277
Visiting the Continent	283
Wider Horizons	295
Fry's Nursing Sisters	299
The King of Prussia	307
A Sad Farewell	313
Inspiration for *While it is yet Day*	325
What Is Quakerism?	327
A Brief History of Quakerism	329
Acknowledgements	333

John & Catherine Gurney's 12 Children

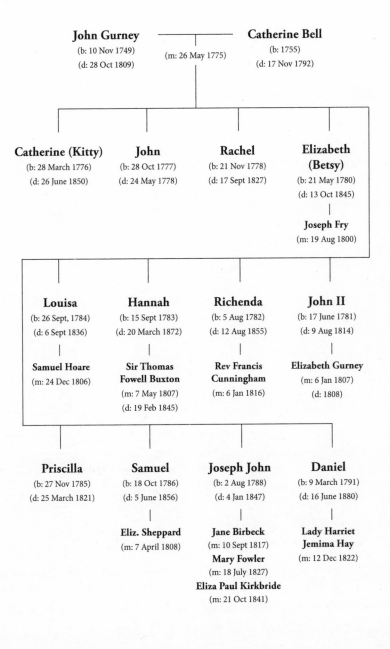

Joseph & Elizabeth Fry's 11 Children

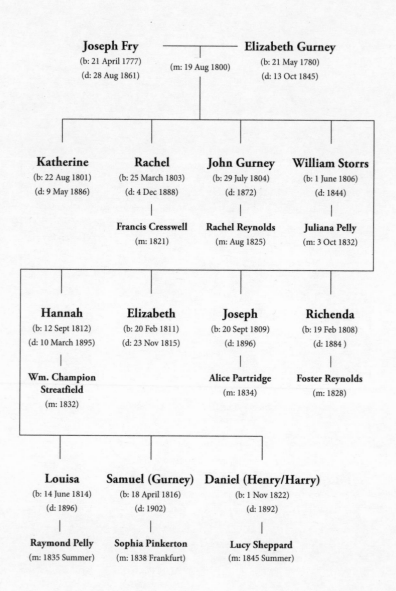

Joseph Fry
(b: 21 April 1777)
(d: 28 Aug 1861)

(m: 19 Aug 1800)

Elizabeth Gurney
(b: 21 May 1780)
(d: 13 Oct 1845)

Katherine
(b: 22 Aug 1801)
(d: 9 May 1886)

Rachel
(b: 25 March 1803)
(d: 4 Dec 1888)

Francis Cresswell
(m: 1821)

John Gurney
(b: 29 July 1804)
(d: 1872)

Rachel Reynolds
(m: Aug 1825)

William Storrs
(b: 1 June 1806)
(d: 1844)

Juliana Pelly
(m: 3 Oct 1832)

Hannah
(b: 12 Sept 1812)
(d: 10 March 1895)

Wm. Champion
Streatfield
(m: 1832)

Elizabeth
(b: 20 Feb 1811)
(d: 23 Nov 1815)

Joseph
(b: 20 Sept 1809)
(d: 1896)

Alice Partridge
(m: 1834)

Richenda
(b: 19 Feb 1808)
(d: 1884)

Foster Reynolds
(m: 1828)

Louisa
(b: 14 June 1814)
(d: 1896)

Raymond Pelly
(m: 1835 Summer)

Samuel (Gurney)
(b: 18 April 1816)
(d: 1902)

Sophia Pinkerton
(m: 1838 Frankfurt)

Daniel (Henry/Harry)
(b: 1 Nov 1822)
(d: 1892)

Lucy Sheppard
(m: 1845 Summer)

Prologue

It was January 1817 and in the gloomy hall outside the women's yard at Newgate prison, two guards argued with a strangely dressed lady. It was cold and grey but the lady was obstinate and stood her ground. She had a permit from the Governor and would not be deterred.

As they argued a woman prisoner rushed wildly out of a doorway in the yard beyond them and with shrieks of furious laughter snatched off the caps and headgear of every woman she could reach.

'And she wouldn't stop at doing that to you, Ma'am. Tear off your things – scratch and claw you – that's what they'd do, Ma'am,' warned one of the turnkeys. The guards felt it would be inappropriate to describe all that could be done by these harpies to a lady who ventured alone into their midst. They never went in alone, always in pairs; even the Governor himself was well protected when he visited.

The lady smiled, gave the men a little money and talked to them with unconscious authority. 'I am going in – and alone. I thank you for your kind intentions, but you are not to come with me.'

They begged her to at least leave behind the gold watch chain which glittered on the simplicity of her dress.

'Oh, no, I thank you. My watch goes with me everywhere. I am not afraid. Open the gate for me, please!'

With trepidation the turnkeys pressed open the gate against the noisy, surging crowd and the lady went inside. Instantly there was silence. Then every woman in the yard pushed forward and suddenly she was surrounded and the guards could no longer protect her.

Childhood

T HE HORSES first alerted the Norwich coachman that something was wrong. Raising their heads, they arched their necks and pricked their ears in interest. Their step lightened as they trotted up the sloping road towards Lynn. The coachman, adjusting his hold on the reins, peered into the distance. Suddenly his young companion called out, arousing the passengers inside from their travel stupor: 'My faith, what's that? That red thing – like a ribbon across the road'.

Hugging his overcoat around him against the bitter March wind, the coachman growled: 'T'wont be there long! Soon see it busted when my leaders breast it'.

But he was wrong because the red ribbon strung across the road turned out to be a row of frisking girls. Defiantly they stood, arms linked firmly, red cloaks flying in the breeze. There were seven of them; the three tallest in the middle, the four younger ones arranged two on either flank. The centre three were steady and grave as goddesses but the younger four were giggling and excited, their feet skipping to keep warm and in delight at this early spring madness. Their ages ranged from ten to twenty and their bright auburn, golden and flaxen hair flew out from beneath their scarlet hoods.

The coachman was outraged that such flibbertigibbets should plot to stop the London Mail and make him look a fool. He flourished his whip and lashed the horses to a gallop. 'Out o' the way, ye hussies! I'll show ye! I'll run ye down! Out o' the way there!'

The guard sounded the horn, somewhat shakily as he choked with laughter. The young man on the box shouted through cupped hands: 'Two to one on the girls!' A clergyman leaned out of the coach and shook his fists. 'Break up! Break up! You bad young ladies!' Then he gasped in surprise. 'I know you. You're the Gurneys of Earlham. Your father's my banker. Make way or I'll tell your father – I'll tell your Uncle Joseph! Stop the coach, would you? Out of the way! Get you into your home!'

But the wind blew back his words. The girls tightened their linked arms, braced themselves together and set their feet firm. Defiantly they threw up their heads in the face of danger with a flash of white teeth and sparkling eyes. They were laughing! One of the younger girls put out her tongue with a quick, impish gesture. All of them were horsewomen and knew that the four great horses, prancing and snorting, would not run them down so long as they maintained their unbroken front.

With stomping hooves and a rustle of harness, the coach stopped. The scarlet line broke into units, dancing in momentary triumph around the conquered, captured coach. Two of them produced apples for the horses. The smallest girl threw a placating kiss to the scowling coachman which was promptly returned by the delighted young man at his side. And then they swooped like a flock of birds into an avenue of budding limes and disappeared towards the mellow red-brick front of a stately house in the background.

'Twas the prettiest adventure I ever encountered,' exclaimed the young man, enraptured. 'For all the world like an unbelievably natural and spontaneous corps de ballet!'

'Shocking, quite shocking,' said the clergyman, shaking his head. For these young ladies were Quakers.

—

Up at Earlham Hall, John Gurney, a wealthy woollen manufacturer and banker, and a member of a notable Norwich Quaker family, was unaware of his daughters' mischievous prank. He was a widower and found caring for his spirited girls and their brothers quite a challenge. He had eleven children and he loved them all but he was a busy man. Catherine, Rachel and Elizabeth were the elder three. Then came John, Richenda, Hannah, Louisa, Priscilla, Samuel, Joseph John and Daniel. They were a lively, handsome and energetic brood.

John Gurney's wife, Catherine Bell, had died in 1792 when baby Daniel was a toddler. Her namesake Catherine, being the eldest daughter, became head of the household four months before her seventeenth birthday. Dutifully she raised her siblings helped by various governesses, tutors, and by stern Uncle Joseph. Poor Catherine, or Kitty as she was known, found the responsibility great –

> 'A continual weight and pain which wore my
> health and spirits. I never again had the joy and
> glee of youth.'

Nonetheless it was a joyful household full of fun and happiness even if, like any other, it had its moments.

Sometimes the children would take to the fields and make a fire and roast potatoes; or ride into Norwich and drink syllabubs through straws; or listen enthralled to the military band. One evening a blind fiddler came to the house and they danced to his music, becoming increasingly raucous. The house itself was ideal for hide and seek with its many rooms and passages, cupboards and corners. On another occasion, led by the high-spirited Richenda, the younger four went to the high road intent on being cheeky to passers-by.

> 'I do think being rude is most pleasant sometimes,' the unrepentant ringleader tells her diary.

Like so many in the eighteenth century, the children spent hours recording in their often introspective diaries the daily minutiae of their early years. It was a time of change in Britain. One form of civilisation had reached its peak and unaware that, like a ripe fruit, it was about to fall, looked forward to further steady progress along the old familiar path. But there had been considerable growth in the population over two generations which had led to over-crowding in the cities. Unemployment spiralled, particularly when huge numbers of troops returned from war in the American colonies. The authorities struggled to apply old rules to communities which no longer conformed to old patterns.

In this setting, the early journals of the Gurney girls reflected life in the heart of their family in 1797 and provided a wonderful insight into these young people.

> 'I must not mump [be sullen] when my sisters are liked and I am not,' Elizabeth wrote in her secret book.

With seven sisters, there was bound to be competition and Elizabeth was neither commanding like Catherine, nor beautiful like Rachel. She belonged to their group as one of the three elder sisters, yet felt in her sensitive heart that two was company and three a crowd.

Often she felt out of it and Betsy, as they called her, was not always a first choice for the other girls' confidences. She was the delicate one, kindly but temperamental. Her volatile spirit caused her profound unhappiness and she was capable of subtle self-analysis. Besides, she harboured three fears – the dark, death and the sea. As a small child, night after night she sobbed herself to sleep in terror for the want of a night light in her room. Day after day on holiday she trembled in terror when grabbed and ducked time and again in the icy waves of the sea, only to be released shivering, gasping, choking and, to her mind, half drowned. The fear of death frightened her so much that often in the night she would creep up to her delicate and beautiful sleeping mother and listen anxiously to be sure she was still breathing. As if to confirm her worst fears, her mother died when she was only twelve and she and the whole family missed her terribly.

Surprisingly, Elizabeth could bounce back in style from the depths and shine just as brightly as the others. She was anxious to please although this desire was never fully satisfied in her mind. Her serious side battled constantly against her love of gaiety. Her sisters found it so easy to please; even her little brothers, Joseph John and Sam, promised to grow into charming men. Elizabeth felt that superficial pleasing, the charming of people at a tea or a dance, was worthless. It was exciting at the time but afterwards in her journal – that mirror of her soul – she despised it.

'My mind feels very flat after this storm of pleasure.'

Of the four younger girls, Louisa was tall and attractive and at the age of twelve received an 'intentional' kiss from the young man who would be her future husband. She considered Richenda, or 'Chenda', to be far the most pleasing character of the younger four.

'All those by whom I should most wish to be
admired prefer her', she complained to her diary.

The sisters were certainly the sensation of Norfolk at the time.
Indeed some of their unruly behaviour may have rubbed off on
brother Sam. He was only six when his mother died and grew
to be so strong-willed that he was sent away to school at eight
instead of twelve. His seven sisters accompanied him for the
first stage of his journey. Then, after being almost crushed to
death by their embraces, he took his solitary place in the coach
bound for London. This was the boy who grew up to be the
Gurney of Overend, Gurney & Co, the 'banker's banker', one
of the greatest financiers of a critical age.

Sam's brothers, John, the eldest, and the good-looking Joseph
John were also away at school. Just young Daniel was at
home with his sisters. And he was too young to appreciate
the excitement when Prince William, the Duke of Gloucester,
nephew and later son-in-law of King George III came to stay.

'I like him vastly. There was amazing fuss made
about his coming,' wrote Louisa.

The girls had a 'gay and bustling' time and Elizabeth received
a proposal from one of the officers which Louisa found most
'droll'. The prince was stationed at Norwich with his regiment
and was attracted to Earlham Hall by word of seven young
maidens in their early bloom with lively, free yet well-bred
manners and a simplicity not to be found in the houses of
fashion at that time.

The first time he called on them he kept his carriage waiting for
two hours while he sat enchanted by their singing. On another
visit, livelier mischief was afoot. On some challenge of his, the
prince was swept by the girls up to Elizabeth's room, away from

the great parlour and the danger of discovery and rebuke. Once safe, they staged a Quaker Meeting for him with Rachel acting as a preacher. The fifteen-year-old Richenda recalled:

> 'I never saw anything so droll as it was to see the prince and all of us locked up in Betsy's room, and Rachel preaching to him, which she did in her most capital manner, giving him a good lesson in the Quaker's strain.'

When the prince left after a sociable dinner, the household, still humming with excitement, took to the floor. Richenda remembered it as the finest dance ever:

> 'All joined, single and married, old and young, little and great. I had no idea that gay company could be as pleasant as it was.'

The arrival of the military and royalty had quickened the pace in Norwich. There were three or four parties a week and Richenda adored it all.

> 'We danced from seven to twelve. I don't know when I enjoyed dancing so much, there were such beaux, so superior to the bank boys [clerks from her father's bank]. What a surprising difference rank and high life make in a person's whole way and manner; it is most pleasant being with people who have been brought up that way.'

It was not only the prince who was attracted to this cheerful, alluring household. The 'bank boys' were soon surpassed by officers and admirers from rank and high life. The military might only have existed in the country towns of England for the sake of providing dancing partners and disturbing maidenly meditation with their admiring stares. Besides, they were all officers!

These were young men of the Gurneys' own world, friends, comrades and, if permitted, serious suitors. There was Louisa's Sam Hoare; James Lloyd who was almost engaged to Elizabeth; the romantic, passionate and fascinating Henry Enfield; and John Pitchford, a young Roman Catholic whose chivalry passed every test – for a time. Both Henry and John were in love with the beautiful Rachel.

The young men found every excuse to be at Earlham Hall. John Pitchford recorded a day which he would 'ever remember with delight'. It was 27 July 1797:

> 'I have spent 17 hours with my seven most enchanting friends. I rose at 4 am and walked slowly to Earlham as I did not wish to disturb them too soon. I had partly made up my mind not to throw pebbles at their windows (the pre-concerted signal of my arrival) till six, but I found them already risen. The morning was clear and brilliant. Rachel saw me first and knocked at the window. Then Richenda and Louisa came down and soon all the rest except Betsy who does not rise as soon on account of her health. After a short walk, the four were sent to the schoolroom to do their lessons.'

Kitty and Rachel sat in the shade while John read to them from *Peregrinus Proteus*. Elizabeth joined them for breakfast after which the little group headed into the kitchen garden to eat fruit. Selecting a shady spot on the grass where the whole party reclined on a haycock, John read to them from his diary

'Omitting certain passages which avowed my attachment to Rachel'.

Rachel read some tracts from Henry Enfield's diary which he sent her regularly; Elizabeth read hers, bravely acknowledging all her faults, and finally Kitty read hers.

Afterwards the group joined hands and promised eternal friendship. They discussed the frequency of John's visits, feeling that once a week was good but that to limit his visits to once a fortnight might be better. While the girls dressed for dinner, John browsed in the library. Later he and Rachel practised some songs at the piano.

> 'I taught her the *Stabat Mater,* which she much liked,' he recalled. 'We then went in the boat and had some most interesting conversation and after tea chose a delightful spot in the garden facing the setting sun, where Kitty read the poetry of *The Monk,* and I, the *Deserted Village.* Then we went to the village church where I read *Gray's Elegy* by twilight with great effect. Kitty said: 'We will be your seven sisters.' When we got to the riverside, we again had enchanting singing, finishing by *Poor John is Dead* and, as we returned, promised each other that any of us in danger of death should be visited by the rest. Then we extended our views beyond the grave and enthusiastically sang till we reached the house *In Heaven for ever dwell.* It was with difficulty that I tore myself away after supper. It was a day ever to be remembered with transport.'

The day was one which they might all have recalled with bitter-sweet memory. For it was the climax of the Gurney youth.

Never again would they gather on the sunny lawns at Earlham with nothing to divide heart from heart, sharing each other's journals, swearing eternal friendship, full of hope, gaiety and warmth.

By the following summer, dawning maturity had wrought its inevitable changes, more drastic than usual. John Pitchford and Henry Enfield were discouraged from visiting Earlham too often because of their respective religions. And Enfield broke Rachel's heart. John Gurney, at his strict brother Joseph's insistence, had reluctantly sent Enfield packing because he was a Unitarian. Both men, while charming as friends, might mislead maturing minds with their views and Uncle Joseph viewed them as inappropriate suitors. Enfield's departure had such a serious effect on Rachel that after a year, during which time he continued to send her regular excerpts from his diary, they were allowed to meet. No one knows what happened between them but it must have been a stormy encounter because Enfield rode away in a passion. After a few weeks, John Gurney sent a servant on horseback to Enfield's house with a relenting letter from himself to be delivered only if the circumstances seemed to warrant it. To everyone's astonishment, Enfield had already married another.

Quaker Family

J OHN GURNEY was what was known at the time as a 'gay' Quaker. Easy-going, he enjoyed open-house hospitality and the romps and music of his girls. He admired their scarlet cloaks and felt he had done his duty when he took his bevy to Meeting for Worship, the Quaker equivalent of a church service; besides, they brightened up the place. Basically 'gay' Quakers were much like other people, except for their disapproval of inter-marriage outside the faith. Unusually at the time, many Quakers encouraged their women to get an education and to speak freely.

'Plain' Quakers, like John's brother Joseph, disapproved of music and dancing and preferred not to mix with general society. They chose plain clothes and a simple life rather than the aristocratic affectation of the time.

Norwich in the eighteenth century was the centre of the woollen trade, a city of the middle class. With its cathedral spire and the remains of the old castle, its citizens proudly boasted of their 'city in an orchard or an orchard in a city'. All around was open country, the flat, sparse meadows and sea-deserted marches of Norfolk with wide skies which could be so cheerful or bleak in turn.

The Gurneys were among the wealthiest of the woollen manufacturers and had added banking to their various enterprises. Theirs was the chief bank of Norwich, with a branch in the neighbouring town of Lynn, or King's Lynn as it is now. John's wife Catherine had been, on her mother's side, a member of the Barclay banking family in London.

Changing fortunes saw three of the most attractive estates in the area fall from the hands of impoverished country gentry into those of enterprising merchants. Keswick Hall, near the village of Earlham, with its heronry, rookery, gardens, woods and sixteen summer-houses, was bought by John Gurney's father and later inherited by his eldest brother, Richard.

His brother Joseph bought The Grove nearby and John moved his young family three miles from Norwich centre along the gently rising slope to the beautiful estate of Earlham Hall. The house was entailed on the Bacon family and could not be sold but was held by the Gurneys on so long a lease that more than five generations of them were able to live there. John added 60 acres of adjoining land to the estate and his family loved every brick, bush and tree on the place.

The eighteenth century proved the heyday of the private banks which all issued their own notes. Gurney notes were currency wherever the name held good. The science of banking was in its infancy and was to go through violent convulsions before attaining international stability. But for the moment it paid very well. John Gurney of Earlham walked through Norwich with a brisk step and a face which betrayed a man of happy life. Rumour had it that on state occasions the bishop borrowed his striking team of four matched black horses for the Episcopal coach, sending his inferior bays to Earlham to convey the Gurney family to Meeting.

So one way or another the Gurneys had an air, a sort of dashing grace that appeared aristocratic. No wonder the 'plain' Quakers in Norwich were respectful of John Gurney's birth, wealth and standing. They tolerated his fun-loving behaviour but as his family grew, they became concerned by the family's close friendship with the Enfields and the Pitchfords. Uncle Joseph, an elder of the Friends' Meeting House in Goats Lane which they attended, took it upon himself to air this concern. John Gurney conceded, although at great pain to himself, his girls and their young friends.

The Earlham girls only remembered they were Quakers on Sundays when their father took them to Meeting. They sat fidgeting in their 'gay' attire throughout the two hours. Nowadays, Meeting is usually an hour long but the format of silence interspersed with occasional prayers, thoughts or readings continues. The girls, in their diaries, referred to it as 'Goats' describing it as 'disgusting', or 'dis' for short. When illness prevented attendance, they thanked their stars.

> 'We have been blessed with staying at home lately because of our coughs.' Elizabeth was the most fortunate in this regard. Her sister Louisa wrote in her diary: 'Sometimes I think I will make better use of my time at Goats but when I get there I seldom think of anything else but when it will be over, unless perhaps some little foolish circumstance happily engages my attention'.

Somehow the girls did not feel morally benefited after Meeting. Richenda, who grew up to join the Church of England and marry a vicar, wrote:

> 'I had a truly uncomfortable cloudy sort of Meeting. It was real bliss to hear the clock strike twelve. What an impatient disposition of mine!

> I sometimes feel so extremely impatient for
> Meeting to break up that I cannot, if you would
> give me all the world, sit still. Oh, how I long to
> get a broom and bang all the old Quakers who
> do look so triumphant and disagreeable'.

Their amiable father did not suspect what sceptical hearts beat so violently under those scarlet cloaks. Even in the afternoon, when home from Meeting in the spacious luxury of Earlham, the girls would still be irritable or 'rather goatified and cross'. If he attempted a little religious education now and then, remembering that his children had no mother, it was unwelcome. As Louisa recalled:

> 'I read half a Quaker's book through with my
> father before Meeting. I am quite sorry to see
> him grow so Quakerly.'

Their own reading was quite different – Rousseau, Voltaire, William Godwin, Tom Paine they discussed happily with their non-Quaker friends. If the scandalised old Quakers, including stern Uncle Joseph, had only realised, it was actually the girls' friend John Pitchford, soon to be banished as unsuitable, who provided the most genuine religious influence in the girls' lives. He was a sincere Catholic but chivalry and good breeding prevented him from forcing his religious views on others. Yet religion to him was too real and important to be ignored so he spontaneously and simply turned the thoughts of his seven lovely friends towards God as his own turned there. They admired him and were affected by him – up to a point. Catherine especially felt her conscience stirred and made spasmodic efforts to do her duty to the younger ones as she felt, like her father, their mother might have done.

Everywhere they went, the girls were exposed to free, lively and speculative talk. John Wesley was nearing the end of his life, his personality and teachings reaching every corner of England. The Bastille had fallen in 1789 filling people with further ideas of freedom, the ideal life and what might be the perfect State. Restrictions of any sort, religious, political or social were seen by the young as cramping vigorous personal growth. The poet Coleridge at Cambridge University was revelling in the flood of new ideas as was his friend, Wordsworth:

> *'Bliss was it in that dawn to be alive*
> *But to be young was very heaven!'*

Not for everyone, though. At Earlham, one young lady's head was filled with torment and conflict. The first of the family to seriously question where life was going was the person who forged the Gurneys into the prosperous, cultivated annals of the nineteenth century. It was the delicate Elizabeth.

Awakenings

T HE AFFECTION of James Lloyd had a profound effect on Elizabeth. Whereas her sisters were used to constant admirers, she was not. So his attentions when she was only fifteen left a deep impression on her. The son of a large Quaker family in Birmingham, his father was the founder of Lloyds Bank. Their home, Bingley Hall, reminded Elizabeth of Earlham but was more scholarly with Wordsworth, Coleridge, Robert Southey and Charles Lamb among their regular visitors. James entered Elizabeth's life, fired her quick blood, stirred her vanity and awakened her heart. There was what amounted to an engagement between the two young people. Then suddenly it ended and James left.

Elizabeth appeared to recover quickly but she had been hurt and something within her changed. A touch of bitterness, disillusion crept in almost causing a nervous breakdown. She felt life was hollow at the core and struggled to get back feelings of reality and satisfaction at living. How did people achieve the good life? She was hungry for the real secret of happiness.

An impulse towards religion may be prompted by the desire to escape from pain or by a need to escape from mystery and to find a comfortable and reassuring explanation to this daunting universe. The development of every person of genius requires a period, or periods, of solitude. If circumstances or education do not provide it, the growing spirit must be protected in some other way from the constant pressure of the commonplace and the magnetism of more aggressive personalities. Elizabeth's protection lay in her physical delicacy.

Neither Elizabeth nor her sisters had the slightest suspicion that she possessed that uncommon extra quality, that mysterious something more which achieves greatness. But she needed room to grow. In the late eighteenth century the need of a healthy person to be alone occasionally had not been recognised; and a room of one's own was rare. A quarter of a century later young Florence Nightingale would complain about having no time or space to herself. And the girl heir to the English throne grew up in the stuffy safety of her mother's bedroom only to make one of her first commands as Queen Victoria in 1837: 'Then may I be alone for half an hour?'

Elizabeth shared a bedroom with three other sisters; she was seldom alone for a moment, day or night, in that abundant family circle. But there were excursions which she could not share when she was unwell. On those long Sunday mornings when everyone else had been driven reluctantly to Goats, she could experience the delight and the rest, the mental and spiritual stretch, of solitude. Assuming, of course, that she was not suffering too much pain from neuralgia.

On her seventeenth birthday, Elizabeth reflected over the past year hoping that she had become a better person and striving to be even better next year.

> 'I hope to be quite an altered person, to have
> more knowledge, to have my mind in great order;
> and my heart too, that wants to be put in order
> as much, if not more, than any part of me, it is

in such a fly-away state.' She considered herself a
'contemptible fine lady – all outside, no inside.'

She feared she was all frippery, vain, proud and conceited and she
was determined to strengthen herself mentally and physically.
Even night brought little respite because she continued to suffer
from dreadful dreams, of dying in the sea with the terrible tide
rising higher and higher until the waves beat upon her and
she struggled fiercely but was submerged. This dream recurred
night after dark night and each morning she would wake in an
agony of sweating and shaking and longing for the comfort of
her mother.

By day, she would bounce back, her common sense wrestling
with her demons and forcing her out of depression. 'In a valley',
she called her moods of dejection. 'Off my centre', she called
her moods of wild gaiety but constantly she tried to be of 'good
mind'. It was during 1797 that a possible solution came to her.

> 'If I had some religion, I should be superior to
> what I am.'

She thought perhaps it would be delightful to depend upon a
higher power for all that was good.

> 'It is at least always having the bosom of a friend
> open to us, to rest all our cares and sorrows upon,
> and what must be our feelings to imagine that
> friend perfect, and guiding all and everything as
> it should be guided. I think anybody who has
> real faith could never be unhappy.'

But she had no real faith in any sort of religion at this time.
As January set its dreary grip upon the landscape, Elizabeth
struggled with herself and the will to believe. Pushing back her

fair hair, she looked out the window at the leafless trees, the
bare lawns, the dead garden and she meditated upon death. The
winter gloom was depressing.

> 'I don't feel any religion,' she agonised. 'I should
> think those feelings impossible to obtain, for
> even if I thought all the Bible was true, I do not
> think I could make myself feel it.'

Her sense of need deepened. She was aware of 'that dim
capacity for wings' that stirred beneath the restricting female
dress: full rustling skirts, frills, flounces, ribbons and lace. The
hampering female life highlighted her ambitious nature and her
present futility. Being a young lady stultified her. She was not
of a studious or academic nature yet dreaded her days drifting
by in a futile struggle with privileged lifestyle and aimless
occupation. Her days comprised gentle walks, sewing, being
read to or reading oneself. Indolence and dissipation ate up her
time and she had desperate moments.

> 'I am a bubble, without reason, without beauty
> of mind or person: I am a fool... I am now 17
> and if some kind and great circumstance does not
> happen to me, I shall have my talents devoured
> by moth and rust.'

Little did she know that the catalyst for her future development
was just around the corner. A 'kind and great circumstance' was
indeed about to happen and 1798 proved a definitive year in
her life.

An American Friend

S UNDAY MORNING arrived and Elizabeth was not feeling great but decided she had better go to Goats Lane with the family. Her Uncle Joseph was beginning to protest at her frequent absences and a famous American Friend was to be there who might provide some welcome distraction.

There was a strong Quaker link with America after the famous English Quaker, William Penn, left England and founded Pennsylvania in 1681 as a refuge from religious persecution.

The Gurney girls crowded into the carriage and presently bustled colourfully into Meeting eager to see the visiting American. They sat in the front row, facing the ministers' gallery, Elizabeth showing off her new boots – purple, laced with scarlet. The girls nudged each other and smiled before settling into their usual decorous fidget. Two hours of Goats! Ah me! How disgusting! How 'dis'!

William Savery, a prosperous 48-year-old from Philadelphia, sat thoughtfully beside Uncle Joseph and other 'plain' Friends in the gallery. He had observed already that few of the 200 Friends present were wearing strict Quaker garb – simple clothes in sober shades without adornment. But he was profoundly shocked by the arrival of the bright row just beneath him. It was true that as a rule he felt more inspired to preach in the company of non-Quakers, but these were not non-Quakers, they were 'pretend' Quakers. They had thrown off the traditions of their fathers. Not ignorant of the Truth, but indifferent to it, they selfishly and indolently came to Meeting out of a habit they did not care to break.

As a visitor travelling in the ministry, Savery knew that he was expected to speak at Meeting but, strangely, never felt compelled to do so and often remained silent. On this occasion, would it have mattered if he had maintained his customary silence? Would it have made any difference to these 'gay' people in the end? As it turned out, his need to address them guaranteed his place in history.

To 'travel in the ministry' is a term used by Friends to describe someone who has a 'calling' to visit Friends in other places. Mostly they pay their own expenses but often they receive generous hospitality – board, lodgings and meals – with Friends along the way. Savery's first visits were in his own country among the Indian tribes. His knowledge of French and German may have sparked his urge to visit Europe and he travelled extensively in France, Germany, Holland and Ireland before arriving in Britain.

Elizabeth sat quietly, her head bowed. She appeared all the fairer between the warm auburn colouring of Rachel and Louisa. Her head might have been lowered in prayer but in fact she was looking at her pretty boots, turning her foot gently this way and that in a purr of girlish vanity.

Suddenly the dull silence was broken, not by the usual drone of preaching, but by a voice resonant and musical with something definite to say and great feeling in saying it. 'Your Fathers, where are they, and the Prophets, do they Live Forever?' Elizabeth's head shot up and her concentration sharpened.

She was transfixed by Savery's words and oblivious to the fact that Meeting was prolonged due to this late outburst by their distinguished visitor. In the waves of emotion which enveloped her, she struggled to keep calm as they left Meeting and joined a large party in Savery's honour at Uncle Joseph and Aunt Jane's house. Elizabeth was a sceptical Gurney and was not going to submit to a lightning conversion, displaying all the dreaded qualities of 'enthusiasm' which could vanish as quickly as they came.

Her uncle however, observing her sensitive state, later sent her alone with Savery to an evening Meeting at Gildencroft. Whereas Goats Lane Meeting House was surrounded by houses, Gildencroft – the Flemish name for a meadow of golden buttercups – provided a green oasis in the city and a gracious resting place for generations of Quakers. It was used mostly for large, special occasions and on this occasion it was open to the public.

According to a local paper report at the time, Savery addressed 2,000 people for two and a half hours. He spoke of Christianity and pacifism and of the need for peace without self-glory in those troubled times. But he was also concerned by the gaiety of the Norwich Friends. Although he was aware that he might have made an impression upon one of them as they travelled together to and from Meeting, he hardly dared hope that the seed could take root amongst so many other distractions.

The morning Meeting which had caught Elizabeth's imagination at Goats had lasted almost three hours in all. But during the evening Meeting at Gildencroft, she had been distracted. She admired Savery's 'excellent' sermon but felt very low.

> 'I could not help considering how near my
> mother was in the burying-ground, which led me
> to think of death,' she wrote. 'When I got home

I mixed too much the idea of growing religious
and growing the Quaker. I had a painful night.
I dreamt nor thought of anything but this man
and what had passed.'

The following morning, in a collected frame of mind, Elizabeth
slipped quietly into the anteroom at Earlham, often called
'Betsy's room' because it was one of her favourite places. There
she sat and wrote her diary analysing and recording the events
of the previous day, her thoughts, emotions, hopes, fears and
the extraordinary experience through which she had passed.

She described William Savery as kind and pleasing.

'Today [4 February 1798] much has passed of
a very serious nature. I have had a faint light
spread over my mind; at least I believe it is
something of that kind owing to having been
much with and heard much excellence from one
who appears to me a true Christian. It has caused
me to feel a little religion,' she records. 'I have
felt there is a GOD. I have been devotional and
my mind has been led away from the follies that
it is mostly wrapped up in. I loved the man as if
almost he were sent from heaven. We had much
serious conversation, in short what he said and
what I felt was like a refreshing shower upon
parch'd earth that had been dried up for ages. It
has not made me unhappy. I have felt ever since
humble. I have longed for virtue. I hope to be
truly virtuous, to let sophistry fly from my mind,
not to be enthusiastic and foolish, but only to
be so far religious as will lead to virtue. There is
nothing seems so little understood as religion.'

Savery arrived at Earlham for breakfast the next morning and Elizabeth found him kind and affectionate. When he left, she was thoughtful. Was her experience real and lasting or would it wear off? Was it just an 'enthusiasm'? Only time would tell. With the return to daily routine on Tuesday, the first doubts crept in.

> 'I rode to town and had a very serious ride but meeting someone and being star'd [stared] at with apparent admiration by some officers brought on vanity, and I rode home as full of the world as I had ridden to town full of heaven.'

> She continued: 'My feelings toward friend S. are unintelligible – a strong and odd impression he made upon me. I could almost have gone to America with him. I felt no fear, not the least, in his company as I do with most plain Friends. I loved him as a messenger of glad tidings. He felt as if he overflowed with true religion and was so humble, yet a man of great abilities and he having been gay and unbelieving only a few years ago made him better acquainted with the heart of one in the same situation. If I were to grow like him a preacher, I should be able to preach to the gay and unbelieving better than to any others for I should feel more sympathy for them and know their hearts better than any others.'

A week later and the girls were back at Goats – without the distraction of a distinguished speaker. Dis!

> 'Today I have felt all my old irreligious feelings,' wrote Elizabeth. 'What little religion I have felt

has been owing to my giving way quietly and humbly to my feelings; but the more I reason upon it, the more I get into a labyrinth of uncertainty, and my mind is so much inclined to both scepticism and enthusiasm, that if I argue and doubt, I shall be a total sceptic. If, on the contrary, I give way to my feelings and as it were, wait for religion, I may be led away.' She added: '...at all events, religion, true and uncorrupted, is of all comforts the greatest; it is the first stimulus to virtue; it is a support under every affliction.'

A family so affectionate, outspoken and united as the Gurneys could not fail to notice the turmoil of mind of one of its members. Uncle Joseph had his opinion – of hope; the sisters had theirs – of apprehension. John Gurney felt that, for good or ill, his daughter needed a change. It was time for Elizabeth to go to London and see the world.

Her excitement was captured clearly in her diary.

'My mind is in a whirl. In all probability I shall go to London. Many, many are the sensations I feel about it.'

London might well have seemed the world; but at that moment London was also William Savery. What a challenge – Savery and all the plain Quakers to the right; glamorous balls and the theatre to the left. How would she cope with such temptation?

'One will, I do not doubt, balance against the other; I must be careful not to be led away; I must not overdo myself. I dare say,' she warned herself, with a flash of insight, 'it will not be half so pleasant as the Earlham heartfelt gaieties in the Prince's time. I must be careful not to get vain or silly, for I fear I shall. Be independent, and do not follow those I am with, more than I think right. Do not make dress a study, even in London.'

She added: 'But if I see William Savery, I shall not, I doubt, be over fond of gaieties.'

Trip to London

J OHN GURNEY and Elizabeth set off for London on a bright, frosty morning. There was a tearful farewell with the six remaining sisters bustling into the hall to watch as their sister waved from the chaise. It was their first major separation and as Elizabeth wistfully reminded herself, they were 'sisters formed after my own heart'.

In no time the excitement of travel took over and her spirits restored. The chaise bumped along over the frosty ruts but it was well-sprung and cushioned so the occupants were comfortable. It was lined with fawn-coloured watered silk and contained large pockets for books, drinks and snacks. The carpet-covered steps were folded up inside the carriage. Elizabeth and her father and a companion were well wrapped up with a warm sheepskin rug over their feet which rested on tins of hot water.

Elizabeth used a mitten occasionally to rub away the condensation on the inside of the window and looked out at the wintery scene. She saw bare trees with a bud here and there, flocks of birds grubbing for feed in the fields while hints of green appeared in the hedgerows promising the appearance soon of spring and a transformation of the landscape.

Soon it was time to stop and rest. They had arrived at the White
Hart Inn at Thetford. Here their own horses would be rested
and fed and for the remainder of the journey they would hire
both horses and armed postilions. But first a welcome stretch
in front of a roaring fire. The low-ceilinged parlour was bright
with candles and firelight. Elizabeth and her father enjoyed their
cheerful tete-a-tete meal of broiled chicken, a plover, a plate of
sturgeon, tart, mince-pies and jellies – all for the princely sum
of eighteen-pence a head. They drank beer with their meal and
then had coffee by the fire.

As he watched his daughter's lithe grace while she carefully
brought over the brimming coffee cup, John Gurney was filled
with admiration and pride. Her flaxen hair was parted simply
on the brow and arranged in a high knot behind. Muff, cloak
and poke bonnet put aside, she wore a simple white muslin
dress cut low in the neck, with a pale blue sash running under
the armpits. It was a fashion unsuited to the billowing outlines
of middle age, or to the angular, flat-chested woman, but ideal
for enhancing the beauty of rounded, long-limbed, supple
youth.

They were a striking pair. His red hair was hardly touched with
grey and his handsome figure was well set off by the current
fashion of knee-breeches and stockings, light waistcoat, dark
buff tail-coat, and a high white stock, camouflaging any
signs of a double chin. He smiled at his daughter then gazed
thoughtfully into the glow of the fire. He had more than one
iron in the fire on this trip to London. He was secretly of the
opinion that if a young person of either sex of a certain age
showed signs of serious disturbance, marriage was the best
remedy. And watching Elizabeth now, her features enhanced
by the firelight, he told himself with fatherly pride that she was
eminently marriageable.

Relaxing now, replete and becoming sleepy, he talked to Elizabeth, as he often did, about her mother remembering the dark beauty he married for love [she had no dowry] and whose magical Gainsborough's canvas would keep forever young. Before long, the dreamy talk and the warmth and food had their effect. Gurney lit a candle for his daughter and Elizabeth said goodnight and went upstairs to lavender-scented sheets made snug with a warming-pan.

> 'My father has been truly kind to me as he always
> is, but sometimes a little attention from him is
> quite delightful, he does it in so nice a way.'

The following day they passed numerous towns and villages and more travellers upon the road until at last, just as the sun set and the rain started, they entered the hurly-burly of London. The lamplighters were doing their rounds, running quickly up and down the ladders and lighting the oil-lamps which made London the best-lit, as it was the best-paved, city in Europe. All the main thoroughfares were flagged and had kerbs. The side-streets were paved with cobblestones but unlike the main streets had no sewers with gratings as outlets for the rain. The sedan-chair men were plying a lively trade and a few sturdy women clicked past stiffly on pattens – shoes or clogs with either raised soles or set on an iron ring for walking in the rain or mud.

The Gurneys were welcomed by Cousin Barclay in his solid and comfortable mansion where warmth and food lessened the strangeness of arrival for shy Elizabeth. Later she fell asleep to the unfamiliar cry of the watch – 'Ten o'clock! Ten o'clock of a cold, wet night and all's well!'

The following morning, John Gurney left on business and for the first time Elizabeth found herself out on her own with just her maid as a companion. London in 1798 was a strange mixture of elegance and violence. Manners were elaborate and polished but morals could be crude and loose. It was a city of dandies, wits and bluestockings, and the three famous clubs – Brook's, White's and Boodle's. Fashion was led by the Prince of Wales who, because of George III's poor health, became Regent. His friends were the playwright Sheridan and politician Charles James Fox. Beau Brummell, that fashion icon of simple birth, was using his extraordinary social daring to rise to such heights that he could censor the fashion sense of royalty. Brummell's views on the tying of a neck stock or the placing of a button, created an artificial world of comforting trifles for the prince and his circle in which the guns of the French sounded unimportant and the intimate horrors of the Irish rebellion seemed far away.

The King was a man of relatively simple tastes and his prime minister, William Pitt, was austere in his conduct and devotion to his country. War with France was sinking the country deeper into debt and prices were rising daily. But neither the King's example of sobriety nor fear of national disaster could check the extravagance of society.

The turf and the ring were popular. A government lottery encouraged the gambling spirit among the very poor. Cockfighting and bull-baiting were outlets for heavy betting and for the lust of cruelty present in the brutalised, uneducated and underfed lower classes of the time.

Everywhere there was evidence of cruelty and violence. The stocks and the pillory, public hangings and whippings were instruments of order. Both the Army and Navy were notorious for brutal punishments, and harmless men in the lower ranks of life were liable to be kidnapped by their press-gangs.

There were neither factory laws nor trade unions and the industrial revolution was creating its own problems. Long hours, low wages, rising prices and illiteracy were making life miserable for working people who were reduced to a wretched level of existence from which drunkenness was the only relief. Child labour was widespread and both children and adults often worked twelve hours a day in the factories or down the mines. Gin shops in London openly invited people to 'get drunk for a penny, dead drunk for tuppence'. Workhouses, where the poor and destitute got board and lodging in return for work done, and the debtors' prisons, were filled to capacity.

The wealthy appeared unaware of this misery, or ignored it, still sheltered and protected from life's harsh realities although gradually this was changing. Rarely a word of this misery was mentioned in the introspective personal diaries of the time. Poverty meant keeping three servants or less. Even the poets and writers preferred more pleasing subject matter although the words of some, Blake, Wordsworth and others were beginning to penetrate the euphoria.

London for Elizabeth meant social exploration and gaiety. Advised by her fashionable relatives she went to theatres, dances, dinners, routs [large evening parties] and receptions. She had always been fond of dress and it proved impossible not to make fashion a study. Ah, vanity! Make-up was the fashion and Elizabeth submitted to it adding a little powder and rouge. Her mirror approved:

> 'I looked quite pretty, for me!' But to have her hair done in the fashionable Grecian mop of curls with a tall plume or bunch of feathers in front, proved too much. 'My hair was dressed and I felt like a monkey.'

She loved to dance, particularly lively, spirited square dances, but she was shy and her partners were strangers so it was not

as much fun as at home. And she was shocked by the banality
of conversation at evening receptions. To what purpose all this
crowding together and exchange of sharp glances and quite
meaningless remarks? Even the theatre, never her favourite, was
a sad disappointment. Drury Lane and Covent Garden, Hamlet
and Bluebeard, received casual mention in her diary. She gazed
at the hollow glitter of eighteenth century drama with her
serious, sincere young eyes and found herself unimpressed.

> 'I must own I was extremely disappointed. I had
> no other feeling when there than that of wishing
> it over...'

However, there was one evening which thrilled her to the
core. She loved music and was always enthralled by glittering
company so the evening she spent at the opera with her
childhood friend, the writer Amelia Alderson and her fiancé, the
painter John Opie, was magical. The combination of excellent
music and amusing company quite bowled her over – and she
was fascinated by a close view of the Prince of Wales. Perhaps it
was exciting because with Amelia and John she entered a more
glittering circle than when with her Quaker cousins. With her
impending marriage, Amelia's days were a bustle of writing,
preparations for the wedding and forthcoming domesticity,
and social engagements. Elizabeth was caught briefly in this
current, swept along and left again upon the shore.

It was something of a relief to spend a fortnight with her old
friends, the Hoares, the family of Sam, Louisa's beau. Their
home at Hampstead was cheerful and opulent. Its large gardens
were bright with crocuses under the bare branches which
swayed in the March wind and cast shadows across spectacular
views of London. For Elizabeth, it was a second home, familiar
and jolly, and reminded her of life at Earlham. The parties of

young people, cousins and close friends who gathered for her entertainment were just the sort that she was used to and she made many new acquaintances and several good friends. One was a dark-eyed girl of her own age, Hester Savory who, despite the change in family name spelling, was related to William Savery and whose family were the American visitor's principal hosts.

There were admirers too. Principally cousin Hudson Gurney, an attractive man older than Elizabeth with an air of confidence and maturity which appealed to her. The attentions of the duller Frederick Bevan she did not encourage. On her return to the home of Uncle Barclay she begged for a return visit to the opera. It was wonderful, she recalled, when people in the dazzling crowd around her were paying and receiving visits between acts, to have Hudson Gurney approach with the self-possession of a man of the world.

> 'I was charmed to see him: I was most merry.'
> Later she commented: 'I got out of the carriage before we got to the gates and met Hudson. It gave me quite a glow to see him. How very much I do like him, I think I would do anything to make Hudson happy...I always feel so much confidence in him.'

Occasional meetings with William Savery at both Meeting and private homes had, as she anticipated, prevented her from being too fond of gaieties. London was not all glittering company and fun and once again she fell under Savery's spell.

> 'May I never forget the impression William Savery has made on my mind. As much as I can say is, I thank God for having sent at least a glimmering of light through him into my heart,

which I hope with care and keeping it from the many draughts and winds of this life, may not be blown out, but become a large, brilliant flame.'

He was by now quite aware of his young admirer, his 'dear E.G.' She recalled, after hearing him speak at Westminster Meeting:

'He said the Deist and those who did not feel devotion looked at Nature, admired the thunder, the lightning and earthquakes as curiosities; but they looked not up through them to Nature's God…How well he hits the state I have been in.' She hoped she would never lose the little religion she had found. 'But if I cannot feel religion and devotion, I must not despair; for if I am truly warm and earnest in the cause, it will come one day… I feel there is a God and immortality, happy, happy thought. May it never leave me; and if it should, may I remember I have felt there is a God and immortality'.

Soon the time came to return home. Father, daughter and companion resumed their places in the chaise and rattled home to Earlham through the opalescent landscape of mid-April. The experiment was over and unknown to Elizabeth and her father it would have a major impact on her future.

Subtle Changes

O N HER return, Elizabeth was subjected to that close, critical examination which only sisters can supply. But she was too absorbed in her own growing pains to notice their scrutiny. They were satisfied that the trip had improved their sister but were concerned that William Savery's influence over her might not be an entirely good one from their point of view.

Elizabeth's thoughts were confusing; she struggled with mixed emotions and wrote to Savery for advice. Four days after her return, she received a long, supportive letter from him warning her not to be led away by 'gay' companions and holding up before her the ideal of religious peace and power. She commented on this letter:

> 'I feel he gives me a stimulant to virtue; but I fear
> by what I expressed in my letter he suspects I am
> turning plain Quaker.'

Her abhorrence of the 'plain' Quakers and their lack of moderation was very hard to overcome. Even Savery with all his charm had something of the 'totem of Quakers' about him which had put her off at first. Her strong independence came into force even against his powerful influence.

'I must look to One higher than him; and if I feel
my own soul satisfied I need not fear... I must
not despair or grow sceptical if I do not always
feel religious. I felt God, as it were, and I must
seek to find Him again.'

She was glad that Earlham did not seem dull after the bustle of
London; instead she found it

'... a better relish for the sweet innocence and
beauties of Nature. I hope I may say I do look
"through Nature up to Nature's God".'

She fortified her halting faith with a remarkable piece of
pragmatic evidence now confirmed on her return home. Her
terrifying dreams had definitely stopped. On 4 February, she
had dreamed as usual that the sea was coming to wash her away.

'But I was beyond its reach; beyond its powers
to wash me away. Since that night I do not
remember having dreamed that dream. Odd! It
did not strike me at the time so odd; but now it
does... It ought, I think, to make my faith steady;
it may be the work of chance. But I do not think
it is, for it is so odd not having dreamed it since.
What a blessed thought to think it comes from
heaven!'

As time went by, Elizabeth's lively sisters became increasingly
concerned. Was there, could there be, something of the 'totem
of Quakers' appearing about their sister? Was it merely one of
her headaches that made her reluctant to join the dance? Was
it her toothache that made her less eager to sing duets with
Rachel? She had made no marked change in her dress, to be
sure, but she was dressing as plain as she could.

'We all feel about it alike, and are truly sorry
that one of us seven should separate herself in
principles, actions and appearance from the rest.'

On the other hand, there was something appearing in Elizabeth
which was extraordinarily attractive; an increase in vitality as
well as sweetness. The changes were noticeable and admirable:

'In short, if it were not for that serious manner
which Quakerism throws over a person, Betsy
would indeed be a most improved character.'

However, Elizabeth thought about and spoke of William Savery
regularly; and she wrote to him often. This was a man whose
charm the sisters recognised; these frequent references, these
letters – what could they mean but one thing...

They talked among themselves and presently Rachel, Elizabeth's
closest confident, challenged her directly. It was now late June
and the garden at Earlham was filled with the scent of roses.
Elizabeth, rosy herself, turned her startled attention away from
the problems of belief, from 'F.B.' – the dull Frederick Bevan;
from 'H' – the more dashing Hudson; even from the heart-
breaking 'J.L.' – James Lloyd who had recently reclaimed her
attention by becoming seriously ill. She gave her full attention
to her sisters' new and extraordinary idea. Savery was married
and in his journals often referred to letters from 'my dear Sally'.
Indoors, in privacy, Elizabeth put pen to paper to enable clearer
thought.

'*June 23rd* [1798] Rachel has just said she thinks
I am in love with W. Savery. I answer'd I did
not think I was but I own I felt not clear in my
own mind respecting him. I think I may love a
person as I love him without being in love, but

I doubt it. I first loved him for his religion, but
the feelings of human nature are very apt to join
in with the superior feelings of the heart. I don't
think I am in love with him. I should be grieved
to think I was. I think it a wrong suspicion to
enter my mind but I fear I shall never, no never,
see him again.' And she burst into tears.

John Gurney, ever sensitive to the emotions of his seven
daughters, particularly his beloved Betsy, decided once again
that a trip might be a useful distraction. Out came the chariot
and the chaise and they set off to tour the South of England
and Wales. It was, perhaps, no coincidence that Elizabeth was
at William Savery's farewell Meeting at Gracechurch Street in
London in July. Savery, in his journal, recalled numbers coming
to take 'affectionate' leave of him – 'Dear E.G. was much
affected.' Elizabeth gave him a girlish keepsake and felt sad, but
not too sad and wrote in her journal that what she felt for him
was not the same love she felt for a close girlfriend whom she
was 'grieved to part with.' But she longed to know how he liked
the pocketbook she gave him.

Soon the Gurneys were on their travels again and Savery was on
the high seas back to America.

'I think a good deal of W. Savery and I do not
much feel for him though he is on a small and
old vessel,' wrote Elizabeth.

In fact, Savery's staunch pacifism had delayed his departure
to avoid sailing under protection of arms. The un-seaworthy
Washington, although sailing with a convoy, herself carried
no arms. But Elizabeth was right not to worry. No privateers,
icebergs or leaks could have brought that liberal soul to the
bottom. Although their correspondence continued, they never
met again; Savery's work was already done.

The girls were happy and enjoyed the variety of their trip. They stayed at many different places, met friends and relatives, made new acquaintances and had the occasional adventure. On one occasion, Elizabeth almost fainted in terror climbing down steep rocks in Shropshire by the 'Devil's Bridge', the first cast-iron bridge ever built. Spanning 100 feet over the River Severn, it rose 40 feet from the rocky gorge beneath. Another time they arrived, soaked through, at an inn where they were

> 'obliged to put on our dressing-gowns and sit over a fine turf fire in the public house, singing and being sung to by the interesting Welsh inhabitants'.

It was a visit to Coalbrookdale in Shropshire which marked another milestone in Elizabeth's life. She became very friendly with her cousin, Priscilla Gurney and attracted the attention of a distinguished 'plain' Friend, Deborah Darby.

> 'I look upon this as one of the happy and bright seasons of my life,' she wrote.

In this mood – open, confiding, understanding and, more important, understood – she went to Deborah's house and afterwards rated it in importance with Savery's visit to Norwich the previous February.

After an enjoyable evening, the company lapsed into a silence which gradually became a Meeting at which one or two people spoke, most movingly Deborah Darby. Elizabeth recalled afterwards:

> 'I only fear she says too much of what I am to be. After the Meeting, my heart felt really light and as I walked home by starlight I looked through

Nature up to Nature's God. Here I am now in
Cousin Prissy's little room – never to forget this
day while life is in my body. I know now what
the mountain is I have to climb – I am to be a
Quaker.'

As she lifted her pen to consider what she had written, she
realised with some horror what it might entail including, among
other things, the willingness at some point to speak in Meeting.
Alas! Down she fell from the heady heights of high resolve and
exaltation! There were difficulties in the way which she noted
soberly and planned their remedy.

'There is another little matter that I do wish
most hartily I could obtain which is to write and
speak english better. My want of percevearance is
my only objection.'

Many years later, she recalled her early education and its defects:

'I was considered and called very stupid and
obstinate. I certainly did not like learning, nor
did I, I believe, attend to my lessons, partly from
a delicate state of health that produced languor
of mind as well as of body; but I think having
the name of being stupid really tended to make
me so, and discouraged my efforts to learn. I
remember having a poor, not to say low, opinion
of myself, and used to think that I was so very
inferior to my sisters Catherine and Rachel.'

What had Deborah said she would be? Light to the blind,
speech to the dumb, feet to the lame. Was that what being a
Quaker meant? Well, that was exactly what she wanted, what

she had been waiting for – something to do. She thought of ways to put her new experience of religious feeling in touch with the world of reality.

Once the Gurneys were home Elizabeth set to work. She started a course of grammar and serious reading; but self-improvement and self-discipline were not enough. She wanted someone to help, even with her limited qualifications, now, today. She didn't want to wait any longer. And then it hit her. All around her were children without any education. Her very desire to educate herself had taught her the value of such knowledge and the crippled state of life without it.

These poor children all around her could neither read nor write – and neither could their parents. They had no one to tell them stories, to open up to them the world of books. Timidly she approached one little boy and read to him and taught him Bible stories on Sunday evenings. He was delighted and told his friends. Soon more children wanted to come. Elizabeth took the growing brood up to the 'eleven-sided attic' and taught them. Their eagerness touched her and she was thrilled at her success. As the numbers grew, she left the attic and took them into the laundry where they did not need to traipse through the house. From 50 to 70 children of all ages gathered there weekly, some of them already wizened and distorted by work in the factories of Norwich.

Gradually she was drawn into the children's homes where she found hunger and sickness. She administered to both to the best of her untrained ability. As the months went by, increasingly she longed to be able to 'lessen the sorrows of the afflicted'. In December, she wrote:

> 'I have many things rather weighing on my mind
> – first the poor, next my French, next my logic,
> next to write to W. Savery'.

Gradually she was indeed becoming feet to the lame, eyes to the blind and speech to the dumb.

And soon it was February again. Absorbed in her interests she wrote half absently:

> '*Feb. 14th* 1799. It is more than a year since I first knew W. Savery and I think it was through him I first was made acquainted with the doctrines of religion… I have one remark to make – every step I have taken towards Quakerism has given me satisfaction.'

There seemed enough work in her school and in the village and city near her home to keep her busy for the rest of her life. How strange that it had been there all the time and she had never noticed it. Neither had her sisters nor her many friends noticed it. All those neglected children, growing up like 'savages', losing even the little primitive culture of the home as their mothers and fathers were caught up in the new industrialisation and snatched into the factories. Who was caring for these children? Simply, no one – but young Elizabeth Gurney. And she was still only eighteen years of age.

Her sisters called them 'Betsy's Imps' and were glad not to be involved. After all, even if 70 children were learning something here, look at all the thousands who were not. It was a mere drop in the bucket. Reform was necessary, some government measure; new laws. Just what, no one could say. Meanwhile the family gathered cosily in the great parlour with their music and their books in the atmospheric glow of the candlelight and a bright fire. It was forlorn in the laundry. And with all those dirty, ill-fed little bodies – phew, my dear! So they did not offer to help – but neither did they hinder; they respected.

There were other aspects of Elizabeth's new outlook which they resisted with all their might. The 'plain' Quakers had always seemed to Elizabeth and her sisters too drastically severe, absurdly narrow. They wore special Quaker dress, used special Quaker speech, thee and thou, and condemned the four chief social pleasures – dancing, music, cards, and the theatre. Even when first under Savery's spell, Elizabeth had dreaded 'being religious with being the Quaker'. One could be the former in a moderate and pleasing manner without falling into the uncomfortable extremes of the latter.

But as the months passed, she began to see the 'plain' Quakers' point. To see it not only caused her pain, but would, she knew, create friction in the family. What Elizabeth wanted was concentration. She longed to bring her whole life into training, as a musician is constrained to devote herself to her instrument, or a painter to the constant exercise of brush and pencil. She wanted order in her life. She valued religious emotion, but she feared it too. Action was her refuge and her ultimate satisfaction, and she was suspicious of her 'enthusiastic and changeable' feelings. She felt she needed every possible protection and incentive for the living of a good life and was drawn towards the outward and visible signs, the protective habits and manners of the 'plain' Quakers. As if by adopting these outward signs of Quakerism, people would leave her alone to get on with her work.

> 'I still continue my belief that I shall turn "plain"'.
> She did not, however, do it easily, nor did she do
> it quickly. She worried for months about dancing
> and singing: '... so sweet and so pretty do they
> seem. It is not only my giving up these things,
> but I am making the others miserable and laying
> a restraint upon their pleasures.'

After a winter's day had closed with dancing, she wrote:

'If I could make a rule never to give way to
vanity, excitement or flirting, I do not think I
should object to dancing, but it always leads
me into some one of these faults; indeed I never
remember dancing without feeling one, if not a
little of all three and sometimes a great deal. But
as my giving it up would hurt many, it should be
one of those things I part with most carefully.'

For John Gurney, it was frustrating. He liked his girls just as
they were and had taken trouble to restore Elizabeth to the fold.
His displeasure hurt Elizabeth.

'My father not appearing to like all my present
doings has been rather a cloud over my mind this
day…There are few, if any, in the world I love so
well; I am not easy to do what he would not like,
for I think I could sacrifice almost anything for
him, I owe him so much, I love him so much.'

In her private torment, she balanced the good and bad of
dancing and singing.

'Is dancing wrong? It animates the spirits and
produces good effects. I think dancing and music
the first pleasures in life.'

But then she reckoned with her excitable, sensitive temperament:

'The danger of dancing, I find, is throwing me
off my centre; at times when dancing I know that
I have not reason left, but that I do things which
in calm moments I must repent of.' Singing too.
'How much my natural heart does love to sing!
But if I give way to the ecstasy singing sometimes

produces in my mind, it carries me far beyond the centre. It increases all the wild passions and works on enthusiasm.' She added: 'Many say and think that it leads to religion. It may lead to emotions of religion but true religion appears to me to be in a deeper recess of the heart.' However, she could not bear to condemn what was so joyous. 'Music may sometimes be of use; and I think our earthly feelings are made use of, to lead us to better things.'

Gradually the metamorphosis took place, from 'gay' Quaker to 'plain'. Firstly she used 'plain' language, saying 'thee' and 'thou' when addressing people:

'It makes me think before I speak, and avoid the spirit of gaiety and flirting.'

Then, as her wardrobe needed replenishing, she replaced her fashionable gowns with others of a more Quakerly style. Instead of a turban in the day-time and a feathered head-dress for the evenings, she wore at all times a white lawn cap.

Her diaries of 1799 illustrate her prolonged struggle with regard to being 'plain' or not but she never lost her sense of the fundamental unimportance of all these things.

'I used to think, and do now, how very little dress matters.'

She sought greater concentration and the simplification of life; such simple dress reduced the number of decisions to be made. A person who adopted Quaker dress would never be asked to a ball, to the theatre, to a card party, or to the opera. A person would not even be expected to dance or sing. Perhaps it sent similar signals to that of a nun's habit. For Elizabeth, to become 'plain' was not to escape from sin – a word she rarely used – but to prune away the unessential.

The pruning hurt. For everything she removed was bound up with the lives of those most precious to her and their pain doubled hers. She went out of her way to be close to her brothers and sisters:

> 'I should fully express my love for them, and how
> nearly it touches my heart, acting differently to
> what they like.'

In March 1799, John Gurney decided it was time for Elizabeth to visit London again. This time Rachel – the sister with whom as a small child, when their mother was alive, she had shared the pleasures of dolls and of a shell cabinet – came too. Rachel, still recovering from her painful love affair with Henry Enfield, was deeply sympathetic towards her sister's transformation without being entirely approving.

As her father had hoped, London gave Elizabeth huge relief from various strains, although difficult choices still had to be considered – cap, turban, cap, turban! Perhaps Gurney knew this would be a defining moment in his daughter's life. Would she finally appear as a 'plain' Quaker in London, where on her last visit, she had enjoyed such fun and gaiety?

Before appearing in public at a party given by the Hoares', she battled with herself over dress. Cap, turban, cap, turban? It was not just a question of vanity and the dread of being conspicuous and perhaps the centre of attention, but would it embarrass Rachel?

> 'After much uncertainty, I felt most easy to
> appear like a Quaker and wear my cap...'

That settled the matter of the head. But what of the heart?

> 'The Roaches were there, who I admire,
> particularly Benjamin who reminded me of
> William Savery. I think I felt rather too flirty
> with him, partly because I was told he was a flirt,'
> she wrote.

The change in appearance of a young girl who adopted Quaker dress at the turn of the eighteenth century held its own attraction. Instead of a semi-transparent gown with a high waist-line and low neck, she wore a dress of silk or print with a natural waist-line and white kerchief folded softly around her throat. This kerchief was sometimes partly covered with another cross-over in silk or print matching the dress. It was charming in its simplicity, particularly on a shapely young woman, although the Gurneys, including Elizabeth, did not see the beauty of it. Colours could be muted, pastel browns and greys were popular, but brighter, more cheerful colours were worn too.

Perhaps it was a fault of Quakerism at the time that too much fuss was made about details of dress from the point of view of 'mortifying vanity' instead of concentrating on practical religion. To an outside observer of taste, however, Quaker fashion held charm and a Quaker girl could quite easily preserve her womanly power to attract. Unknown to Elizabeth, a shy young admirer was captivated by her new attire. He had carried in his heart for many months the picture of a tall girl in a brown silk dress, the fairness of her hair and skin enhanced by a black lace turban, the lacy ends of which fell gently to one side of her face. To see her now with her white Quaker cap upon her hair made her all the sweeter to him – and more accessible.

Resolute Admirer

F OR MONTHS, Joseph Fry had watched the flowering
Elizabeth with growing interest. He was a friend of her
eldest brother John and had often ridden over to Earlham
from the Norfolk estate of his friend John Holmes. But he was
painfully shy and a 'plain' Quaker and had seen little of the
ladies of the house who were scarcely aware of seeing him at all.
He was more comfortable outdoors and spent his time hunting
and coursing with John Gurney and their friends. Although
well set up, he had not the sort of polished manners which the
Gurney girls admired. He could be withdrawn and had a loud,
hearty laugh that could make him seem uncouth.

Like the Gurneys, the Frys were bankers whose banking
activities arose out of successful business ventures, in their case
importing tea and spices. Their businesses were based at the
family home, St Mildred's Court in London where Joseph lived.
As the son of William Storrs Fry, he was one of the wealthiest
and most eligible bachelors in Quaker circles. He was heir to
the family estate Plashet, near Epping Forest, which William
Savery, when he visited it, described as 'sumptuous'; Savery
believed that riches and Quakerism were an ill-yoked team –
English Friends at the time thought otherwise.

When Elizabeth started to show signs of serious Quakerism, her father had remembered this 'plain' acquaintance and considered him at least one of the irons in the fire on his daughter's first visit to London the previous year. Elizabeth by herself, rather than as one of the bright bevy of sisters, was far less alarming to Joseph. As Hester Savory's friend, as the Hoares' and Bevans' cousin, circles in which Joseph himself was familiar and at ease, he could at least watch her from afar without becoming overwhelmed with blushes. He could even exchange a word or two with her in the course of an evening and he could listen to what she said to other people.

The previous year he had taken note of her favourite subjects and a few months later, in the summer of 1798, had called on the family when he was in Norfolk. When he spoke to her this time he knew how to hold her attention. She recorded in her little book:

> '... this afternoon I have been entertained by an account of animal magnetism by young Fry. J. Fry has been telling me he saw W. Savery not a week ago.'

Joseph might have lacked elegance but he had discernment and a certain sturdy power of making himself felt. Elizabeth rebuked herself later for vanity and for 'being a long time dressing', then quickly forgot his visit. But 'young Fry' had obviously made an impression albeit brief.

Seeing her in Quaker dress in London the following March settled it for him. Four months later, he returned to Earlham seeking John Gurney's permission for his daughter's hand in marriage. His own father had already approved the match. And so started a mighty battle of wills which would last for months.

Elizabeth had hardly given 'young fry' another moment's thought. She was completely embroiled in her new life – her school, her poor, her 'so boring' French lessons. Her knowledge of life had expanded with young friends married, including a former housekeeper at Earlham, Hannah Scarnell, in whose problems she had become involved. Her nineteenth birthday on 21 May had come and gone and she was particularly delighted in her father's new found interest in her 'school'.

John Gurney had, indeed, come to see in 'Betsy's Imps' more than either a passing whim or a sign of ill-health. Looking in now and then at the laundry, he had seen a surprising sight, and a rather lovely one. He began to bring his friends to see it. Elizabeth might have been weak in formal education but she was developing a gift for easy narrative and clear, straightforward expression. She was 'educating' her 'schollers' and in return they were liberally educating her.

And then that 'young Fry', from the very edge of her consciousness, walked right into the middle of her ordered world. Not only was he there, at Earlham, a very solid and inescapable fact, as her father pointed out, but he threatened to disrupt everything. She was so taken by surprise that her initial alarm gave way to girlish curiosity, and a little vanity, as to how and when she would receive the proposal.

He kept her waiting while he found the right moment, then:

> 'This morning Joseph Fry made me an offer in a
> long talk with him. I discouraged the affair but
> fixed not to give him a final answer till 6th day.'

Until the early twentieth century Quakers referred to the months of the year and the days of the week numerically to avoid using their 'heathen' names – hence 6th day meant Friday which in this case was the 27 July 1799.

She turned him down.

'Though I fully see the many good things I give
up in not having him, and perhaps may never
have another chance of marrying so well, yet I
believe all in all I am wise in my determination
of giving it up.'

Joseph Fry left Earlham, the sisters rejoiced and Elizabeth set
herself the task of reading Hume's History of England in her
continuing quest for knowledge and self-improvement. But the
seeds of restlessness had been sown. Joseph Fry, large and solid,
was now right there in the middle of her consciousness. Do
what she would, her thoughts just kept returning to him.

John Gurney resorted to his usual tactics. No time to brood,
he whisked his family away on one of their sudden journeys.
This time it was to the north – from York they travelled to
Newcastle; then they spent some happy days riding on a family
estate on the beautiful banks of the Wanspeck at Sheepwash
– possibly a sheep farm worked in connection with Gurney's
woollen mills at Norwich. Elizabeth, no timid horsewoman,
had her courage tested by an unruly horse but apart from
toothache and a certain 'flatness of mind' loved it all.

They went as far north as Edinburgh before returning to
Earlham by the end of August. It was not quite as easy as usual
to pick up the home threads again. In September, Elizabeth
awoke with 'a cloud over me'. A month later, it was worse:

'I feel in a state of real and true discouragement;
I have little faith and little hope'.

Her happy energy seemed lost. She began to feel flurried with
her home duties, her lessons, her 'schollers', and her poor. By
the end of October, she wrote:

'I feel this morning as I have felt lately, quite in a hurry about what I have to do; and I do not think that that is the way to do it well; it is better to go soberly and quietly to work about it, and not to flurry and bluster... I put some things in proper order, read history and grammar, wrote letters and worked...' But still she felt 'in rather a flat silent state of mind'.

Winter was approaching. The autumn leaves which had swirled colourfully around the lawns at Earlham had been swept up. Unruly rooks' nests appeared in the skeletal trees. The fields were neat and bare and thin ice formed by the edges of the little river Wensum. It was time to ride out in a scarlet cloak and be busy with the poor; it was not a time for thoughts of love.

It was a time of action for Joseph Fry too. It was ideal hunting weather and he returned to Norfolk after more than just foxes. His friends, the Holmes, with whom he stayed occasionally to learn estate management in preparation for future responsibilities, offered the perfect base for a new campaign. He had given his intended time for reflection and now his decisive action proved quite a shock to her. He wrote to her father saying he intended to be in Norfolk the following week.

Elizabeth fretted; those secret thoughts and feelings that had played havoc with her work and her peace of mind were dragged out into the open to be examined thoroughly – in justice to an honest man. In a flurry of anxious thought, she wrote:

'I have, almost ever since I have been a little under the influence of religion, rather thought marriage at this time was not a good thing for me as it might lead my interest and affections from that source in which they should be centred;

and also if I have any active duties to perform in the church (if I really follow as far as I am able the voice of truth in my heart) are they not rather incompatible with the duties of a wife and mother, and is it not safest to wait and see what is the probable course I shall take in this life before I enter into engagements that affect my future life. So I think and so I have thought, but to look on the other side, if truth appears to tell me I may marry, I shall leave the rest and hope whatsoever my duties are, if I am willing I shall be able to perform them.'

Once again she tussled with her perception of right and wrong and wrote, almost prophetically:

'… it is now at this time the prayer of my heart that if ever I should be a mother, I may rest with my children, and realy find my duties lead me to them and my husband; and if my duty ever leads me from my family… it may be in single life…'

The following week, when the girls returned exhilarated and flushed from a ride in the country and in time for their three o'clock dinner, Joseph Fry had arrived. He too was a little highly coloured, awkward in his manner, obviously embarrassed but carried an air of sturdy determination to be himself.

It was a tough ordeal for a rejected suitor, even for a self-confident one which he was not. To be the centre of attention of that lively and curious group was bad enough but to know that they all knew why he had come made it worse. He was painfully aware that he stood publicly at Elizabeth's mercy. But he was stubborn and knew his worth. He could offer any one of the rich Gurney girls a home suitable to her upbringing – other girls had set their caps, even Quaker caps, at him before now – but he knew who he wanted. He had chosen Elizabeth.

He greeted her with determination, perhaps as he might have put his horse at a difficult fence out hunting, and was encouraged to see that she was nervous too. She blushed, was confused and couldn't look him in the eye; it was very loveable. He accepted the astute invitation from her father to stay several days at Earlham. John Gurney had noticed a chink in his daughter's resolve and decided to work on it.

Elizabeth's conflict of heart tormented her. Since his arrival she had suffered an 'agitating' and 'awkward' time and had spent hours of serious discussion with him.

> 'It puts me most in mind of my feelings to James
> Lloyd's affair,' she confided to her diary.

After a long concluding talk, she refused his offer again but this time, timidly, hesitatingly and with regret.

> '… I was not at liberty to say to what the future
> might produce… The day may come that I feel
> willing and at liberty to marry, and whenever
> that is the case I am sure I cannot tell who it may
> be, for at this time I am not inclined to marry
> anybody, and am not in love with any person,'
> she told her diary.

Once again, young Joseph Fry left Earlham a rejected man. But this time he left behind him very different feelings. Elizabeth's sisters were not pleased to see him go, they were sorry. Their views were changing. Although a 'plain' Quaker, his love of music and skill as a performer had made him a welcome addition to the evening circle in the great parlour. Although he was not a great talker, they realised as they got to know him better that this reticence was the result of his upbringing and of shyness and that he had in fact a sharp, informed mind. They discovered that although a Quaker coat did not set off a young man's figure, and Fry had not the grace of build of the Gurney men, he had an admirable seat on a horse. And the two John Gurneys, father and son, were his firm friends.

As for Elizabeth, she was fully aware of the progress he had made. It was true that she was not 'in love with any person' but then she was always justly suspicious of 'enthusiastic' and changeable feelings. During those five days of walks, of riding out together and those long talks, Joseph had quietly drawn close to her. He drew from her, her dawning sense of vocation, her delight in her work, her children, her poor, her half-formed ambitions towards the full use of her powers and abilities in some great, as yet un-classified, cause. She told it all to him, as she had told it to no one before. They discussed marriage from that angle: could a married woman have any other vocation as well as the duties of her home? Joseph said yes, if she were *his* wife.

She shed tears for his pain as he rode away and felt she had lost a precious friend. The following day, the family attended Meeting but Goats offered her little comfort. Her work helped to steady her and she had a satisfactory evening with her children. Monday was better still; she spent much of the morning nursing her friend Hannah Scarnell who was very poorly.

> '... I attended to her and the little baby – a job
> I rather liked.'

Yet when she was not distracted, she was depressed and restless. In her diary for 1 January 1800, she wrote:

'This has not been one of the clear and bright
days of life: little has been done, and that little as
if in a nightmare; not feeling able to get forward,
and discouraged... I had my children and found
them a great burden.'

She tried to discipline herself by confronting her fear of the
dark, forcing herself through sheer will-power to go into dark
rooms in remote parts of the house. She rode to Norwich in
the bitter winter weather to 'pay visits to some in affliction'.
She read her Ackworth grammar, the gift of its author Lindley
Murray. She received a letter from William Savery. But all
efforts to distract herself failed because she had lost her peace
of mind.

One subject only remained firmly in her mind:

'How much the family are altered about Joseph
Fry. All now seem to wish for the connection.'

As ever, her devoted father was watching. He decided another
trip to London might be the answer; the city had never failed
yet to do her good. And besides, if young Fry could just be
patient and use his opportunities as they came...
Joseph was feeling far from patient. The long talks with
Elizabeth had encouraged him and he believed that the time
was right for action. He acted directly but with delicacy; he
persuaded his friend John Gurney, jnr. to write home. Elizabeth
was horrified:

'My father received a letter from John saying
poor Joseph Fry hoped to pay another visit
here... I think he had better not come as I think
of soon being in the neighbourhood of London.'

But then, what to do when she arrived there? 'I
don't quite like the thought of what I am to do
about him in London.'

John Gurney wrote to his son to advise Fry not to come to
Earlham at that time; Elizabeth took what comfort she could
from that. Her sisters were tactful and gentle; they were aware
of her inner torment.

'It is a fine sight to observe their tenderness
towards me and sympathy in my feelings.'

But what she really longed for was solitude, a little time to think
and feel without even the kindest of comments. As luck had
it, everyone went off on an overnight trip to Clare in Suffolk
during March and she was left on her own. She was delighted.

'I intend to sleep alone tonight, which I think I
hardly ever remember doing in the house. It is
lovely to me their being from home, particularly
of an evening being by myself.'

Whatever peace she may have found was short-lived. A week
later Joseph Fry, having received the kindly rebuff from his
friend John, returned again to the attack. He threw aside the
delicacy of the indirect approach and wrote a manly letter of
entreaty to his lady's father. In that letter, Elizabeth again felt
the sturdy shock of his presence.

'My father shewed me a letter from Joseph Fry to
beg he might come. I think that has brought me
to see the affair in a better light.'

Her father had refused the request before showing Elizabeth the
letter. Her visit to London was imminent and she had expressed

herself most clearly and decidedly at the time of her brother John's letter in February concerning Joseph's possible visit. John Gurney had never felt less optimistic as to Fry's prospects than he did that March in 1800. He told the young man to waive all thoughts of a visit to Earlham. While Elizabeth was unable to return his feelings, he felt it would be better for both Elizabeth and Fry not to meet up while she was in London.

Joseph Fry had other ideas. He had seen Elizabeth blush before him, had seen her weep and was convinced to the contrary. During previous visits to London, Fry might hardly have been noticed. Not so now. He brazenly took every advantage of the many opportunities to see Elizabeth while she was in the city. He laid siege to her emotions. At least she would get to know him further, risk or no risk. He had more ardour and determination than tact but perhaps, after all, he was the best judge of his own business.

Elizabeth was tormented; her feelings swung to and fro like a pendulum.

> 'I feel oddly and very changeably toward him, but I know I always feel emotion, either dislike or really like. I cannot well describe how I am with him but now the remembrance of him is very pleasant to me – the other day it was truly disagreeable – so I go on...' One day she was keen to know his family '... an important thing in forming such a connection.' The next she was furious: 'This has once more been a day of absolute trial about Joseph Fry. He came early... vexing to me he stayed so late... I like him as my friend but dislike him as my lover.'

Her vague wish to meet some of his family was granted after Meeting at Gracechurch Street, Moorgate, when she was introduced to Joseph's sister-in-law, Eliza Fry and her father:

> '... and although I longed to have the matter
> ended, I felt a little drawn toward them...' But
> still her feelings were confused. 'Went to Joe
> Bevan's. I was low, tired, nervous, and vexed a
> little when I heard them say Joe Fry was expected
> to supper. I was rather cross with him but as the
> evening advanced I grew more comfortable –
> things brightened and I enjoyed his company.'
> She added: 'I dreamed pleasantly about him. I
> mention that because I think dreaming agreeably
> or disagreeably of a person has its effect in such a
> tossed-about mind as mine.'

When John Gurney returned to London to collect Elizabeth,
he brought his daughters Catherine and Rachel with him. To
promote friendship between the families, William Storrs Fry
invited Gurney and the two girls to Plashet. It was a friendly
and hospitable visit and they enjoyed it, and afterwards the
sisters were enthusiastic in their praise of the house and family
to Elizabeth.

On her return to Earlham, Elizabeth herself received a letter
from Joseph. She returned a kind reply, nothing more. Had
she forgotten her lover's determination? Her note brought him
down to Earlham as fast as horses could make the journey.
And it brought him in a mood of ultimatum. He carried with
him a gold watch. His meeting with Elizabeth that evening in
May 1800 was brief and dramatic. He gave her the watch with
the proviso that if she returned it to him by nine o'clock the
following morning, he would never approach her again. If she
kept it after that hour, he would never receive it back.

Elizabeth's months of torment were reaching their conclusion.

She was restless and uncertain. What should she do? She appeared at breakfast the following morning in a nervous state.

> '... my heart was full. I could hardly keep from crying before them all. I was so oppressed with the weight of the subject before me, natural inclination seemed to long to put the hour of decision afar off, but he gave me the watch last night with this engagement.'

Joseph had studied his love thoughtfully. He was growing to understand her complex character and, finally, his tactics succeeded. Elizabeth could not return the watch.

> 'I did not feel at liberty to return the watch,' she wrote. 'I cryed heartily. Joseph felt much for me.'

It was to him alone that Elizabeth could confide her fears and it was on his comfortable shoulder that she sobbed away her indecision. He had established himself as such a firm friend that she had no other like confidante. She turned to him unconsciously, instinctively, with childlike trust. She had no reserves with him. The honesty of their friendship from the start boded well for their future life together.

Finally, Elizabeth had said 'yes'. But it took her a few days more before she convinced herself that the decision was the correct one.

> 'Last night before I went to bed painful feelings towards Joseph began to enter my mind and this morning I woke with them strongly upon me. I went to him and told him alone what I felt and soon began to recover [from] them, only great trepidation remained which I did not mind in comparison to painful feelings.'

Within days of their engagement, Joseph had the ability to calm her. She trusted him and felt safe with him. Her skies cleared.

> 'My feelings towards Joseph are so calm and pleasant, and I can look forward with so much chearfulness to the connection with him.'

Soon William Storrs Fry arrived at Earlham and marriage arrangements were underway. None of the three men involved favoured a delay; Joseph was already established in business and had an ample house at his command. The wedding was set for August.

Blushing Bride

E LIZABETH PREPARED for her marriage with gentle anticipation. She sorted out her trousseau, cutting, turning and folding the smooth linen, sewing seams, assessing her wardrobe, putting her work in order. All that she had begun with zest and success only three months ago would be left behind forever. She would have to say farewell, not just to her 'imps' but to her family.

> 'The idea of leaving my station at home is to me surprising, as I had not thought that it would have been the case,' she had written when succumbing to Joseph's advances.

She moved about dreamily performing these tasks while outside Earlham basked in the warmth of summer. The scent of roses, which she always loved, wafted once more through the open windows. For a while she had respite from the responsibility of high resolve. She was a spirit, but she was a woman too enjoying peace of mind and body. Some of her stricter friends who noticed this change made her feel she was being a 'lukewarm' Quaker.

'I believe I am in some respects,' she confessed
to her diary, 'because deeply as I feel interested
in the Society and much as I feel some of its
scruples, yet my limits are great and I do not feel
little scruples of that importance as other people
do.'

For example, she wore on her simple Quaker dress a single,
incongruous item – the gold watch on its chain. Uncle Joseph's
reproving eye made her abashed and self-defensive but nothing
would make her remove it. She admitted in her diary that it
was not quite consistent with her dress, almost an unnecessary
ornament but concluded obstinately: 'It has its uses.'

A week before her wedding, she gathered her little 'schollers'
for the last time.

'It was rather a melancholy time to me. After
having enjoyed themselves with playing about, I
took them to the summerhouse and bade them
farewell; there were about 86 of them, many of
them wept... when they went away, I shed my
tears also.'

Bright sunshine greeted the family on 19 August 1800.
Sunbeams filtered through the windows of the old Meeting
house at Goats Lane. It was crowded to capacity for the first
wedding in the Gurney family of Earlham. A profound silence
lay over the gathering. There was an occasional rustle, a gentle
sigh or cough, the quiet tread of a late-comer passing quickly
to a seat. Neither a whisper, nor a glance went from one person
to another. Each sat, if not wrapped in meditation, at least in
silence, men on one side of the aisle, women on the other.

At last the wedding procession arrived, walking slowly and
softly. Joseph Fry, sitting with folded arms in the facing

benches beside his parents, saw them enter and got to his feet with a blush. A slight wave of movement went through the congregation as heads turned, but all remained seated.

The twenty-year-old Elizabeth came up the aisle on her father's arm, pale and tremulous in her quaint Puritan dress, followed by her six sisters and four brothers all fashionably dressed. They took their places in the front benches reserved for them; John Gurney and his eldest daughter Catherine sat with Elizabeth on the facing seats. The bride now sat before the Meeting between her father and her bridegroom; Joseph Fry sat with his mother on his left, his bride on his right.

Silence settled once more over the gathering and seemed to deepen as time passed. Eventually Joseph cleared his throat uneasily. He knew that everything now rested with him. It was he, shy and reserved as he might be, who had to break that profound stillness, to interrupt that silent worship, to start the marriage ceremony. Panic-stricken, he stole a glance at Elizabeth, and saw a tear slip down her cheek. It braced him. The flood of tenderness for her weakness which was at the very heart of her charm for him, coupled with the deep respect he had for her, made him lose his own embarrassment in pity.

He laid his hand firmly on hers. She started, trembled and looked up at him. Had the terrifying moment come? It had, his eyes answered in reassurance. He rose and drew her gently to her feet. The two of them now stood alone before the congregation. She was trembling terribly, the throbbing of her heart vibrating with his, her hand clasping his as if she might drown. He held her fast and said, huskily and hastily:

> 'In the presence of the Lord and of this assembly,
> I take this my friend, Elizabeth Gurney, to be my
> wife, promising by divine assistance to be unto
> her a loving and faithful husband until it shall

please the Lord by death to separate us.'

Silence. Not a sound could be heard as the assembly held its breath. Joseph pressed Elizabeth's hand. She took a deep breath and with a supreme effort her voice came out sweet and clear:

> 'In the presence of the Lord and of this assembly,
> I take this my friend, Joseph Fry, to be my
> husband, promising by divine assistance to be
> unto him a loving and faithful wife until it shall
> please the Lord by death to separate us.'

It was done; they were married. With huge relief, they sat down. There was a rustle of relaxation throughout the Meeting. The tension had been broken. The younger John Gurney and a cousin carried forward a small table spread with the wedding certificate, ink and pens. Joseph Fry signed first, followed by Elizabeth, writing her maiden name for the last time.

The certificate was handed to Uncle Joseph who read it aloud, word for word, including the signatures. It was then returned to the table to be signed after Meeting by all who cared to do so. Quaker weddings still follow this pattern today. Once again the gathering settled into silence. It was broken almost immediately by Uncle Joseph offering a prayer of blessing for the young couple. For a further hour, prayer and exhortation followed from both men and women speaking spontaneously one after the other.

The nervous bride, who had awoken that morning in terror at the prospect before her, sat tearfully through the Meeting noting that her beloved father seemed nearly as overcome as she was. At length, the appointed elders broke up the Meeting by shaking hands, as is still the custom today, and everyone stirred themselves, straightening bonnets and picking up their hats.

Elizabeth, securely on the arm of her husband, led the procession out of the Meeting house into the warm August sunshine. There were carriages waiting and some of 'Betsy's Imps' lined up to throw flowers. It was all such a confusion of faces and bustle. She scarcely knew who travelled with them in the carriage; her father, Kitty, Rachel. Later, she wrote:

> 'The day passed off well... although cold hands
> and a beating heart were often my lot.'

These were mild ailments compared to the misery she experienced leaving Norwich. Driving through the town for the last time as Betsy Gurney, she recalled:

> '... the very stones of the street seemed dear to
> me.'

Leaving Earlham was the most difficult of all. The wedding feast had been eaten; the last farewells exchanged with wise Kitty, with John, with lovely Rachel, with the Four, with handsome Joseph John, dearest Sam, and little Daniel, aged nine. Her father, unable to speak, handed her into the carriage, while servants and guests crowded out on to the gravel sweep to see them go. The carriage moved off down the drive, passed the turn in the avenue, then the lodge and gates, before bowling out and away down the familiar London road. How comforting then to find beside her no dazzling stranger, no formidable bridegroom, but her sturdy friend Joseph with whom she was so at ease? Before him she could if she wished cry 'hartily' and he would patiently dry her tears and sympathise.

The first week of their lengthy honeymoon was spent visiting various relatives as they moved south from Norwich. Then they spent a month with Joseph's parents at Plashet House.

'From continued change of scene, and the great
deal that I am obliged to talk, I seem of late to be
continually letting out, and taking nothing in,'
the bewildered bride confided briefly in her diary.
Even with the delights of Plashet's fishponds and
woods, she found herself homesick.

So Joseph Fry took his bride back home for their final three
weeks and this proved just the tonic she needed. Every man
who married one of the Gurney girls had, in turn, to deal with
the homesickness of his bride and each, without exception,
followed Joseph's example and returned to spend part of the
honeymoon at Earlham Hall. Then, cheered by the feeling that
her old home was still accessible to her as a married woman,
and reassured by her husband's consideration, each bride went
cheerfully forward to establish her new home and create for
herself another centre of happiness.

John Gurney, with his customary insight, sent Joseph and
Elizabeth off to start their married life together in his coach, for
comfort, and accompanied by Nurse Barns who would help the
young bride settle into her new home, and who was to prove
indispensable. For nothing could have prepared Elizabeth fully
for the mammoth task ahead. Joseph had forewarned her that
life at St. Mildred's Court might not be easy but she had no way
of understanding exactly what he meant.

The first months of marriage proved extremely difficult and
were made harder by the continual interference of her husband's
relatives. She could not have imagined what it would mean to
marry the younger son of a great mercantile house and live at
the seat of business. And she had not been associated intimately
enough with the Frys before her marriage to realise the different
standard of behaviour to which they had been bred.

Joseph's elder brother William and his wife Eliza had been living

at Mildred's Court but it had been arranged that the house
and its responsibilities should be handed over to Joseph and his
bride on their marriage. It was typical of pretty Eliza's inability
to cope with her responsibilities that no steps had been taken to
prepare the house for its new mistress. When Elizabeth arrived
on the afternoon of 1 November her joy at being in her new
home was short lived. True, William Fry was on the steps to
welcome them. But domestic matters were not his concern and
he retired to the counting-house as soon as possible and left the
weary and dispirited girl to deal with affairs as best she could.

> 'I felt rather low at the prospect before me,
> and more so when I saw the state of the house;
> confusion in every part.'

Joseph was furious but there was little he could do. This was a
rough start after the order of Earlham and the familiar scattiness
of William's wife struck him more forcibly than usual.

Thank heaven, or rather John Gurney, for Nurse Barns. She
was a source of strength, a lively and bustling liaison officer
between a young, inexperienced mistress and her new domestic
staff. Elizabeth took advice from Nurse, gave orders and they
were carried out. She put a few matters in order immediately,
then went and put herself in order for dinner.

William dined with them and afterwards returned to his wife
Eliza at Plashet leaving the newly-weds on their own at last. It
was cosy to sit together by the fire in a little oasis she had made
amid the muddle.

> 'Joseph and I had a comfortable evening. Both
> I believe, feeling the true comfort, I may say
> blessing, of being at last quiet in our own house.'

It was the quiet before the storm. The following day, being a

Sunday, they went to Gracechurch Street Meeting, proud after all their exhaustion to be on time. It seemed incredible that they should not be allowed to dine alone that day. The Fry family must have been well aware that there had been no time for the new mistress to settle in let alone get the house straight. But Mildred's Court was so conveniently near Gracechurch Street and it had long been the custom to go there for a family Sunday meal. The Frys took it for granted, on this day as on all others. Why not?

Elizabeth's spirits sank when she arrived home.

> '... seeing the freedom of the family in the house
> was rather a trial to me. I think they could not be
> freer if it were their own, and also there was such
> a state of muddle.'

Monday was no better. Elizabeth rose early to do some reading and after breakfast sat down to write her footman's instructions. Soon afterwards, back came the Frys:

> '... after that I had not much quiet... The bustle
> of today's dinner, all the family dining with us in
> spite of all our muddles!'

Gradually, with Nurse Barns' help, order was brought to Mildred's Court. But worse problems bristled under the orderly surface. William Fry commuted to Mildred's Court to work. He often had both breakfast and dinner with Joseph and Elizabeth, just as formerly, Joseph had taken all his meals with his brother and sister-in-law. It did not occur to William that a husband and wife who had been married for some years might adapt themselves more easily to the constant company of a bachelor brother, than a bridal couple to the constant company of a married elder. William was used to behaving as master of the house and found it difficult to relinquish the role to his younger brother. He had no patience with the changes and the new formalities Elizabeth was introducing. He even listened to the complaints of a housekeeper, Jane King, and undermined the new mistress's authority.

But Elizabeth's quiet, shy manners and soft speech combined with her fair, feminine look had misled William. He thought he could manage the young couple with an elder brother's assurance of being in the right and speaking for their own good and keeping them up to the mark in the old ways. He did not want things changed; but a surprise awaited him.

Behind the new Mrs Fry's softness was a firm resistance, a disconcerting dignity. William made his various protests and retired in discomfort. Elizabeth was upset and felt a renewed bout of homesickness for Earlham and 'its beloved inhabitants'. But she tried to be practical:

> 'I should remember that every situation has its trials and I had mine there. What sweet tempers they all have... when my Joseph is try'd, I must endeavour to put on a cheerful face do my part towards making him happy.'

Her determination to be a good wife proved her father right – Elizabeth was made for marriage. It was just her husband's misfortune that in those early, precious and malleable days, he could not have had her more to himself.

The morning after William's protests dawned brightly and Elizabeth felt stronger. The Frys might not be sweet-tempered, but they were honest and good-hearted. William's conscience got the better of him and he apologised to his sister-in-law, receiving an unexpected 'talk' for his trouble:

> 'William came and ask'd my excuse for what he

said yesterday, and then I had a little talk with
him about our present situation with the family.'

It was a step towards understanding, but there was further to
go. Although the Frys were 'plain' Quakers and highly respected
within the Society, they had difficulty accepting Elizabeth as
'plain' despite the pains she had taken with her thoughts and
dress. William secretly considered her one of the stuck up 'gay
Gurneys'. Her natural elegance would not be disguised. The
supple figure that had so loved to dance could only move with
ease and grace. Her daintiness, her fastidious refinement, her
quiet charm and the good manners in which she had been
brought up, made her appear, to her blunt new relatives, like a
woman of fashion.

Polished behaviour seemed to make the Frys feel inferior, and
they resented it. Joseph was persuaded to try and make his wife
conform to the Fry pattern on the grounds of Quaker sincerity.
Although he may have had his doubts about the success of
such a venture, in the interest of family harmony, he spoke to
her. So his first expressed criticism of his wife was one of the
strangest ever made by a bridegroom – that her manners were
too gracious. She was deeply hurt but her temperament and
training helped her deal with it. She contemplated what would
happen if, instead of being gracious, she spoke her mind and
told the whole truth at all times, and concluded: '… it will not
do always to tell our minds.'

Her father-in-law had no such inhibitions. He made it clear that
he would never have allowed his son to marry a 'gay' Gurney
daughter. He had obviously considered Elizabeth 'plain' but
now found her not 'plain' enough. Elizabeth was furious at
even a hint of criticism towards her sisters whose virtues she
cherished. On the rare occasions that she had the courage to
speak out, she felt remorse afterwards and determined to find

peace with her parents-in-law. In time she achieved this and grew to love her mother-in-law:

> '... in whom I see much to admire, although she may want a softness and refinement in her character.'

She dealt more directly with her father-in-law. She asked that he take them on a trip to Richmond Park so she could concentrate on spending time with him. It rained early in the morning and the outing was almost cancelled but Elizabeth insisted, despite being nervous to show authority in his company. He gave in and was rewarded with fine weather and the kindness of his open-hearted daughter-in-law. They both enjoyed the trip immensely and from then on their relationship changed and he grew to love her very much.

Visitors

E LIZABETH SOON discovered that hospitality at Mildred's Court extended beyond just family. Not only was her daily programme shattered by the incursions of invading and pervading Frys from the adjoining tea and spice business, but she soon found that to be mistress there was a career.

Joseph and she hoped that their first house guests would be the eldest and youngest of her sisters, Kitty and Priscilla. They were to arrive mid November for a week or two. But on 7 November tradition compelled them to receive a travelling Friend from Philadelphia who would make their home his headquarters for six weeks. A stranger for six weeks! Shy Elizabeth was horrified at the prospect. She and Nurse Barns had not even finished putting the house to rights.

American Quakers at the time could be difficult too. Fresh from a rougher way of life, their manners often appeared crude and their conversation could centre on denunciation of the comforts of civilisation. Besides, their table manners could be uncouth; William Savery's general good manners had been exceptional.

Elizabeth stalwartly prepared for the impending visit. Any doubts she might have had were confirmed when George

Dilwyn brought to the house an air of restraint and solemnity. Even the arrival later of Kitty and Priscilla, fresh from the laughter, lively quarrelling and eagerness of Earlham, could not improve the atmosphere. Perhaps they were the wrong two to do it, Elizabeth thought: Kitty, too much the anxious motherly sister, and 'our little rosy Priss' at fifteen too young and shy.

Often Elizabeth looked forward to a snug and happy evening with Joseph and her sisters having made the parlour cheerful with candles and a fire. With dinner cleared, William back at Plashet, Dilwyn out visiting, there would be several hours to spend happily reading aloud over sewing, chatting, enjoying each other's company before the supper tray rattled through the hall on the stroke of nine. But it was not always to be. Dilwyn would change his plans at the last minute and not go out but stay home and receive visitors instead. Away with the sewing and books and happy chatter! The young hostess, ignored for the sake of her weighty guest, would sit quietly, her hands folded in her lap. Her sisters escaped to their bedroom if they could. Joseph tried to stifle his yawns as he sat quietly beside his wife. A heavy silence would fall. As fresh arrivals were shown in, they would shuffle quietly to a seat and the evening would turn into a Meeting. So they sat, with Joseph replenishing the fire cautiously when necessary as if in a sick room. After a while, Dilwyn would feel moved to speak, often at length, and other Friends, both men and women, would speak also, or offer a prayer.

At nine o'clock, if a suitable rustle indicated the session was over, the anxious young hostess would hurry to the kitchen to ensure there was sufficient supper for an extra ten or twelve people.

Eventually it was December and Dilwyn's visit came to an end allowing Elizabeth a sigh of relief. Another visitor arrived soon afterwards but this one was welcome and came only for tea. It was her dear friend Amelia Alderson who two years earlier had married the Cornish artist John Opie. Amelia alighted from her sedan chair in the late afternoon as thick fog enveloped the City of London. Mildred's Court was on a turning out of the Poultry, near the City centre and close to the Guildhall; the building is now a bank but carries a plaque commemorating its famous heritage.

Then the house was set back a little from the traffic and noise of the street and had the charm of a quiet harbour. The Frys' warehouse for tea, coffee, spices and other imports of the East India trade, formed one side and an aromatic smell from the many mingled odours wafted through the air. A warm glow shone fuzzily from the counting-house on the ground floor. The lantern over the front door of the mansion cast a dim, moon-like glow, but the link-boy, whose hire the fog had made necessary, lifted his torch to each step in turn as Amelia clung to the curved iron railing and mounted the steps cautiously in her long, furred pelisse. The boy pulled the huge iron bell that hung outside the door and there was a jangling peal.

The huge door opened immediately and a neat footman ushered Mrs Opie into the chilly, lighted hall. Her card instantly admitted her further into the house and Amelia felt her cold nose tingle as she entered the next room where a generous coal fire roared in the fireplace under the Adam mantelpiece. Warm hangings at the windows shut out the fog and dusk. The young hostess, in her Quaker dress, arose with a glad cry and embraced her friend, removing her long cloak and drawing her to a comfortable chair by the hearth. To the constantly homesick Elizabeth, Amelia represented her happy youth to be welcomed warmly. To Amelia, now a respected novelist, such a welcome was normal and she took it in her stride while observing that Elizabeth had lost weight.

Firelight and candlelight gleamed cheerfully on polished oak
and walnut, on fine linen and silver, on the most delicate of
china cups. No one in London could serve a better five o'clock
tea than Mrs Joseph Fry who had the pick of the market from
her husband's warehouse. To her diary Elizabeth explained her
efforts to have everything in her house

> 'handsome though nothing mearly for ornament.'

> Amelia Opie wrote to a friend next day: 'In
> all Quaker houses there is a most comfortable
> appearance of neatness, comfort and affluence.'

Joseph and William came up from the counting-house for
tea. Joseph was in high spirits and was delighted that one of
the old Gurney circle should see his wife in her new setting.
He was proud of his house and of the grace and order that
Elizabeth had introduced. She, on the other hand, found him
unnecessarily loud in this mood, his sense of humour a little
crude and hers entirely absent. Amelia did not mind; she found
Joseph kind and good-natured. Besides she loved to laugh and
her own husband could be even louder.

Returning home through the deepening fog, she reflected that
Elizabeth was well placed as the wife of a young banker and
merchant in an old-established firm with sound capital behind
it. She was happy for her friend. Although happily married for
two years herself, Amelia was aware that her husband's income
depended on the caprice of fashion. She had married beneath
her father's expectations; John Opie, although an increasingly
famous artist, had little money and was divorced from his
first wife. Although Amelia enjoyed her modest home being
the lively centre of a stimulating and delightful life, she and
her husband had little to fall back on. Sir Joshua Reynolds, Sir
James Mackintosh, Lady Caroline Lamb and the other painters,

writers, musicians and aristocrats who flowed in and out of their house provided excellent company. But times were hard and getting harder.

Those who lived in comfort and luxury were fortunate indeed and were not always aware of the suffering around them. A census of the population in December/January 1801 recorded a population of at least fifteen million people in the British Isles, some four million more than anticipated. There had been bread riots in the streets of Norwich during the time of Joseph and Elizabeth's marriage. But her concerns and compassion, her need to attend to 'other duties', were over-shadowed by the immediate demands of her new life.

By March when she realised she must keep open house at Mildred's Court for Friends during Quarterly Meeting, a special meeting to deal with Quaker business, it was evident that she and Joseph were making their own contribution to the population. But the pace did not slacken on account of pregnancy. Social and domestic obligations had to be fulfilled, difficult though she found both.

> 'Household matters are to me a real trial. I feel
> so incapable of commanding my servants from
> a foolish weakness and fear of them. Company
> days [those with visitors], even with those I like,
> are quite worrying to me; inclination I believe
> would lead me hardly ever to go out or have
> company. I feel so flat with people.'

At last, in April, she had the respite of a visit to Earlham. She was sad leaving Joseph but even the journey through the spring countryside proved a joy. 'Violets and primroses quite decorated the hedges.' And her beloved Earlham was at its best with green lawns, birds nesting, trees tasselled with pale green and the

Wensum running with spring water. The tender care of Kitty and Rachel and the respectful interest of the younger 'four' wrapped her in comfort. She rested in the deep self-content of maternity and wondered why she had ever worried about brother-in-law William, or William the slack footman, or the difficult housekeeper Jane King, or any of the other flurries of domestic life. For now, they seemed unimportant and far away.

Too soon she was back in London in the thick of her domestic duties and all thoughts of Earlham were put on hold. Yearly Meeting, that most important of Quaker meetings, was upon her. This annual Meeting for Business went on for about a fortnight and Friends came to its various events from all over the country. The meetings were held at Devonshire House on the east side of Bishopsgate near Liverpool Street. So it was tradition for the conveniently-placed Mildred's Court to keep open house all day and every day while meetings lasted. The Savorys, Hoares, Barclays and others did likewise but had the advantage of distance, so the bulk of hospitality fell upon the Frys.

Some 40 or 60 hungry Friends might arrive for dinner, an experience in catering and accommodation which Elizabeth had never known at hospitable Earlham. Any reservations Elizabeth might have had about Jane King were put aside as she proved invaluable, having experienced the Yearly Meeting crush for many years. Elizabeth, barely 21, found it all a nightmare at a time when any extra company was such a burden. And the visitors did not hurry away when they had eaten. Such numbers, even in a large house, required dinner to be served in two or three shifts. Those who ate first, then swarmed upstairs to rest, or 'take a lay'. Beds and floors disappeared under billows of resting Friends; every piece of furniture was submerged beneath a tide of bonnets and shawls; snores, stuffiness and confusion filled the house. The domestic staff was thoroughly overworked; all water for washing had to be carried in pitchers to the bedrooms. And there were other even worse tasks as sanitation was still quite primitive.

Finally strangers and acquaintances alike surged out of the house but there was still no rest for Elizabeth. She had to go too. She had to do her duty by sitting wearily for hours on a hard bench in a crowded room listening to lengthy sermons or to the conduct of tedious business. The women and men met separately in their meetings and the interesting work, if any, was done in the men's meetings. Occasionally deputations passed from one meeting to another, to communicate items of business or to exchange religious concerns. Elizabeth found it time-consuming and boring. At the Yearly Meeting he attended in 1797, William Savery recorded that the men's meeting spent three hours discussing whether or not to receive a deputation from the women's meeting. Another day was spent discussing men's hat brims. As 'plain' dress was not a uniform, variations of it were constantly under discussion.

Elizabeth had been plunged into the most religious circle she had ever lived in, yet she had difficulty retaining her faith. The overwhelming burden of her domestic situation was one thing. But the boredom of Yearly Meeting was another. Exhaustion was probably part of it but it lay deeper than any physical cause. Where was the girl who received such inspiration from William Savery? Where was the girl who had maintained her own line against the lack of sympathy, even opposition, of those she loved the best when she turned 'plain'?

She lived among people who thought and talked much of religion. Yet they regarded religion as a state of mind, displayed in certain peculiar habits of dress and speech and in avoiding frivolous and worldly things. They did not, like Savery, and like Elizabeth herself, find in it an irresistible need for activity, for a hands-on approach. Savery had such a passion for international peace that he had lost no opportunity to interview the rulers of Europe on the matter, including royalty, and he had huge sympathy with human suffering. As a young man, visiting a wealthy American family in the Deep South, he had rushed from the breakfast table on hearing the distant cries of a slave being beaten. He stood between the victim and the whip until he had obtained the rescinding of the punishment. From that day on, he worked tirelessly to abolish slavery.

To Elizabeth, the rank and file of English Quakers were turned in on themselves. Their utmost effort was to travel in the ministry to other groups of Quakers. Yet in 1801 there were many problems in England which needed attention. Street riots among the starving in London and other large cities reminded people of the French Revolution and the danger of repetition. Elizabeth, new to housekeeping, had ample funds and never seemed to notice the price of food. But the cost of living had multiplied itself five times since 1773. Bread, ever the staple food of the poor, cost one-and-fivepence for a quarter loaf.

The London mob, believing all price rises were because of greed, would surround and yell at the King's coach and would pelt merchants and brokers in the street. When they found a man in a Quaker coat, they would roll him in the mud. Such was the somewhat unfair reputation of wealthy 'plain' Quakers at the time for being selfish, narrow-minded and tight-fisted. Their coats were outward signs of religion. Although similar to the fashions of the day, the Quaker versions were simplified and unadorned, free of braid, ornate buttons, ribbons, plumes and lace so as to avoid the suggestion of vanity or luxury. The favoured colours were subdued and inconspicuous, grey or brown.

Elizabeth was physically well-fed but spiritually starved. With

Yearly Meeting finally over, the mere relief felt for a short time like peace.

> '*June 5th* I had most of this morning in quietness, which was quite a treat to me. I wrote my journal, settled my accounts, and was not destitute of a wish to do right.'

Quiet intervals were few. Days were hot and languorous and her baby was now heavy and active within her. She wrote in July:

> 'We are so much from home and in such continued bustles I just have time enough to keep things in order; engagement follows engagement so rapidly, day after day, week after week, owing principally to our number of near connections, that we appear to live for others rather than ourselves. Our plan of sleeping out so often I by no means like and yet it appears impossible to prevent it. To spend one's life in visiting and being visited seems sad.'

The delicate relationship between husband and wife was endangered by this endless lack of privacy. It was a tribute to Joseph Fry that his wife was happiest when alone with him, and increasingly as their first year of marriage drew to a close.

> 'I value being alone with my husband: it is a quiet I have not lately enjoyed and it does seem to me, at this time, one of the great blessings of life.'

Sadly for Joseph he didn't recognise this. When his influence

with her was at its height, her softness towards him greatest, he
didn't recognise his opportunities. The fog of continual visitors
confused them. And he lost the chance he might have had to
share with her, and to win her sympathy in some of the things
that he cared about.

> 'It is quite a serious thing,' she wrote 'our being
> so constantly liable to interruptions as we are. I
> do not think, since we were married, we have had
> one-fourth of our meals alone. I long for more
> retirement, but it appears out of our power to
> procure it, and therefore it is best to be as patient
> under interruptions as we can; but I think it is a
> serious disadvantage to young people setting out
> in life.'

She found herself becoming irritated sometimes.

> 'I rather fear'd my beloved husband and myself
> had not been on those sympathetic and happy
> terms I feel so desirable, almost necessary, to
> the comfort of married life. His reading and
> continual humming vex'd me when we were so
> seldom alone,' she confided to her diary.

Worse than his humming, she worried that he might be lazy.
He hated getting up early and often made too much fuss about
his headaches. She found herself urging him down to work in
the counting-house.

Joseph's courtship of Elizabeth had proved that he was not
lacking in essential energy or determination. But he was a man
who loved outdoor pursuits yet was tied to an indoor trade.
No wonder he was reluctant to go to work. A man of jovial
and rather careless habits, he was forced into the meticulous

demands of the counting-house. Had he been a free agent, he would not have lived at Mildred's Court at all; it was Plashet that had his heart. And the life of John Gurney at Earlham, farming 160 acres as a hobby and riding into Norwich to direct the bank and the woollen mills, seemed to Joseph ideal. Short of being a country gentleman, that is what he would have liked to do. The daily tedious round of business irked him; and at Mildred's Court there was very little respite.

Yet alone together at night, all misunderstandings were brushed aside, all pains and fears comforted in the affectionate simplicity of their mutual relationship; their love for one another was deep. How quickly Elizabeth turned from irritation to soft, wifely resolve.

> 'May I give up every earthly consideration
> to please my husband and to render ours an
> increasingly happy union.'

The fruit of that union would soon bring to their lives a most welcome addition.

Motherhood

A s her time drew near, Elizabeth became uncomfortably hot and bothered. The summer heat in London was unbearable and she fluctuated between excitement at the thought of her first child and terror at the ordeal which lay ahead.

On their first wedding anniversary in August, her mother-in-law and sister-in-law came for dinner and by the time they left Elizabeth had tired of conversations about labour.

> 'The thought of a little child of my own within me quite excited my feelings,' she recalled. 'How I love it in prospect. I can but admire how providentially everything is ordered, that now my love and hope of having a child comes just at the time I may be looking forward to the trial of bringing it into the world.'

Although the days of 'Betsy's Imps' seemed so far away, her thoughts were often in the nursery now and how best her child's education could be started from the very first years of its life. Married life might be all-consuming at present, but dreams and aspirations lay dormant at the back of her mind.

Her elder sister Rachel arrived for the birth and also young Hannah. Eventually the day came and she went into labour, its terrors surpassing all imagination. Rachel stayed by her side throughout. All that love and money could do was lavishly and fervently done. But effective pain control was in the future so nature followed its course in agony and discomfort. When at long last her proud husband showed her the tiny new-born Katherine, she could only respond with tears.

Far away the rest of her family awaited news impatiently. Sixteen mail coaches left the General Post Office daily and to see them start was one of the great sights of London. They each picked up mail and passengers from an appointed inn along their way before they left the city on the long country journeys.

The Norwich coach started from the Swan With Two Necks, in Lad Lane. Four inside passengers and one outside was the quota [the larger coaches took six inside and four on top] plus a guard who had a little seat at the back with a large blunderbuss and horse pistols to protect the mail from highwaymen. The coach clipped along at an average speed, including stops, of eight miles an hour. And the excitement on its arrival did a coachman's heart good.

Norwich was no exception. Gentlemen's carriages, citizens on foot and little boys turning somersaults greeted the coach with cheers as usual that day, 23 August 1801, when it arrived in the market-place. In it came at a hand-gallop, horn blowing, horses foaming, wheels flashing intermittently in a cloud of dust. The waiting Gurney chariot was conspicuous with those charming girls from Earlham fidgeting and flustering in and out of it with impatience. Would that anxiously awaited letter come today? Was all well with their beloved sister, the first of them to face the ordeal of childbirth?

Yes, there was a letter. From London. They could not wait to take it home but read it immediately in the carriage, all their heads eagerly together to listen to Catherine, the eldest, who read it aloud. A girl! A niece! They were all aunts! Once back home, they raced for pen and paper to write to darling Elizabeth, and to Rachel and to Hannah.

> Louisa wrote: '... between great fear and great joy, Kitty read that the darling girl was born. I longed to fly out of the coach and tell everybody that knew us the news. Then we went round to tell Hannah Scarnell. How I do long to see it! I think thee, Rachel, must feel so satisfied in having been with Betsy through it all, and I hope it has not been too much for thee or Hannah. What Hannah must have felt when she heard the sweet cries of the child! I long to hear more – how dearest Betsy spends every hour, and what she says, and what she feels, and how you all do, now you have reaped the fruit of such pain as you must have gone through.'

Back in London, Elizabeth was suffering from extreme exhaustion way beyond Louisa's comprehension. Her days were spent in almost passionate rest. A whole year of accumulated fatigue seemed to have taken its toll. Her weakness and low spirits were such that the 'sweet' cries of her child only reduced her to tears. It was a month before she could write in her diary:

> 'I have now pretty much recovered... My present feelings for the babe are so acute as to render me at times unhappy from an over-anxiety about her, such as I never felt before for any one.'

A month later, the mail-coaches brought excellent news the length and breadth of England. Each coach bore a placard proclaiming: 'Peace with France' and the coachmen wore sprigs of laurel in their buttonholes. The noise of celebration in London with roaring crowds, rockets and pistols was not one bit welcome to a resting mother with a headache. Elizabeth complained irritably to her diary that this drunkenness was not the correct way to show their joy. But she sympathised a little when she discovered that the price of bread immediately fell 50 per cent and that all foodstuffs became cheap and plentiful owing to the opening of the Baltic ports.

October 1801 was a month of hope and cheer in Britain and nowhere more so than at Earlham where the family waited excitedly for the arrival of the tired mother and her new baby. Joseph Fry, with growing sensitivity, realised that a trip to Norwich to be pampered and adored by her family at Earlham might bring the bloom back to his wife's cheeks. And the family bustled to ensure every comfort and luxury for their dear heroine and her darling baby. They gathered on the doorstep at the first sound of the chaise on the drive. Among the group was young John Gurney's friend, Thomas Fowell Buxton and his sister, Anna. Excitement mounted as the chaise approached along the avenue of golden limes in the mellow evening sunshine. When it stopped, young John sprang forward, opened the door and let down the steps. Proudly Hannah stepped out first, carrying the baby. There she stood in her white dress, her blue pelisse, her pretty bonnet, unconscious of her own sweetness, looking down tenderly at the sleeping infant. Her sisters surrounded her with gestures of delight and cooing cries.

Fowell Buxton, at six feet four was taller than anyone present, and looked over their heads at Hannah. An almost intolerable emotion swept through him as he thought: 'She shall be my wife!' He was hardly sixteen but looked nineteen; Hannah was nineteen but looked sixteen.

The pale Elizabeth was helped out of the chaise by her husband and brother. John Gurney pressed forward to take her in his arms, his darling daughter, bringing his first grandchild to the house. And each sister wanted her cheek. And the servants were not to be forgotten, curtseying and greeting Miss Betsy and wanting a glimpse of the precious lamb, the new Miss Katherine. And dearest Kitty must now hold her namesake. And somehow the travellers were swept indoors to be fed, rested, petted and admired.

The Buxtons were duly presented. And Hannah, making her curtsey to the tall youth, her absent mind upon the baby, looked up at his grave, intent face without in the least suspecting that she had met her fate.

Elizabeth was charmed by all the fuss.

> 'Our reception was delightful; my father and all so much admire our little darling and seemed to love her so dearly that it was delightful to me. It was indeed a striking sight to see them all meet her.'

But in all the sweetness there was a hint of bitterness for Elizabeth. Many a wounded sensibility, philosophically endured, found expression in a quiver of the lip with the reflection:

> 'How much more I am made of here than in London.'

This criticism did not include Joseph. She wrote of him in her diary in a tone of deep, heartfelt content:

> 'I accepted my Joseph more from duty than anything else, and how much I now love him.'

It had taken over a year of marriage for the newlyweds to settle down and begin to understand each other.

The pleasure of being at Earlham, of being looked after and cherished worked wonders; Joseph was right. Soon the colour returned to Elizabeth's cheeks and her spirits soared. But she was a married woman now, a mother and for the first time saw her old home in a new light. She had matured, become more capable and efficient and she found it impossible to fit completely into the old home routine.

It seemed to her that they all wasted too much time. Her sisters were busy all day, yet what did they do? They had an early start and read before breakfast. Afterwards they strolled about the garden in the sunshine and walked down through the little wood to see the autumn colours reflected in the stream. Then they separated for the morning, pursuing a favourite task in their different rooms. In the afternoon there was usually another walk. Then in the evening, Rachel, Richenda and Anna Buxton would read and the others would work at their embroidery and chat. Someone might play the piano which John Gurney had bought his daughters in 1796. Invented by an Italian in 1700, it had replaced the harpsichord in popularity. Indeed Elizabeth found it unsettling that with so many people wanting to practise their playing and singing, the piano was hardly ever silent.

There was little for Elizabeth to do at Earlham now but care for her baby. She sat in luxurious idleness under the trees on a sunny afternoon, or sewed some trifle for the baby in the cheerful great parlour in the evening, surrounded by soft voices and laughter. She should have been content but she remembered with despair the neglected houses of the poor nearby with which she had once been so familiar. And she thought of the forlorn children who had flocked to Earlham and into whose lives she had once brought a ray of cheerfulness and hope. Her sisters regarded playing the piano as a duty. It reaffirmed her 'plain' Quaker view that music distracted one's attention from the things that really mattered. For instance, not one of them had ever thought of taking over 'Betsy's Imps'. But she was happy to see Joseph benefiting so much from the trip. He had gone off with her brothers John and Sam and with Fowell Buxton, known affectionately by his friends as 'the Elephant', on a shooting expedition to Cromer. All were sportsmen and good friends and spent happy days in the bracing sea air. Joseph had neither customers nor his big brother William to worry him; it was exactly what he needed.

As November drew on, her thoughts began to turn happily towards London. That vital reorientation had taken place at last; she no longer said to herself 'home to Earlham' but 'home to Mildred's Court' instead.

> 'I look forward with much interest and pleasure
> to the thoughts of being quietly and comfortably
> settled at Mildred's Court. I do hope we shall
> remain at home and without company for
> some little time after our arrival, for I do long
> to be settled which I have hardly been since we
> married.'

Her wishes were granted for a while. They returned to London and to the familiar situations with which now she was well able to cope. As a young mother, rather than a bride, she was entitled to a little more privacy and excuses such as teething and winter colds offered a protection against outside intrusion. The days flew by in contentment:

> 'I do heartily enjoy our being alone... Not
> being interrupted I appear naturally to fall into

employment, and it is so sweet to have quiet
plans at my own dear home. How much I think
my marriage tends to my outward comfort.'

By March 1802 the Peace of Amiens was finally settled and 29
April was set as the official day for the Public Proclamation of
Peace. Over 20,000 French prisoners began to leave England
as fast as transportation would permit. In the old-fashioned
courtesy of war, they had been supported for several years by
the French government. Napoleon's economic reforms required
the English to feed the prisoners themselves, much to the anger
of the English government. The prisoners had not been well fed
under either scheme and were delighted to return home as their
renderings of the Marseillaise on departure bore witness.

By the time of the official celebrations, Elizabeth's home was
in turmoil again. She and Joseph and the baby were staying in
lodgings at the village of Hampstead while Mildred's Court was
renovated. On 22 April, as preparations for the great day were
underway, she had a bad day.

'I felt in a great muddle. My house at M. Court
all in great disorder, company, toothache etc
etc baby rather cross. I sometimes think leaving
off malt liquor and wine might help me, but it
appears almost impossible for me, if I do that,
to be well.'

She took the drinks under doctor's orders, a common remedy at
the time. Her irritable mood made it almost inevitable that the
day would end with a quarrel.

The illuminations for the national celebrations were to be on
a grand scale. As well as transparencies and set-pieces, almost
every window in England would feature a triangular wooden

frame set with candles. Elizabeth did not want their landlady to decorate the house. It was celebrating victory in a war which as a Quaker pacifist she could not condone.

> 'Illuminating our lodgings was mentioned and my Joseph said if I would not let our landlady illuminate, he would leave Hampstead. He spoke rather sharply and I felt rather depressed and said, partly in joke, none of the Frys are so ruled as I am by their husbands, and I was very sorry to have made such a remark. The subject of illuminations has been so much talk'd about.'

Elizabeth lost the argument and the lodgings were illuminated as planned; there was peace at Hampstead too. But the argument was an illustration of the conflicting views of the two 'plain' Quakers. Elizabeth, like her mentor William Savery, felt strongly that people who disapproved of war on principle should not show signs of rejoicing at victory. How ironic that Joseph's family had initially found Elizabeth not 'plain' enough.

The Frys, like the nation, then enjoyed a period of calm. The months were free from strain and Elizabeth's increasing serenity was reflected in her diary entry for her second wedding anniversary in August 1802:

> 'Time slips through quickly, trials and pleasures before unknown have indeed been felt by me, trials and joys of many kinds. The love of a husband, the unity experienced; the love of a child, the maternal feelings, are real and great sources of enjoyment. They are apt to occupy the mind perhaps too much. My family is to me in more comfortable order than it was, at least I feel more mistress of it.'

But she despaired of all the bothersome small responsibilities and how difficult it was to keep her mind on them.

> 'My forgetfulness I find a material hindrance to
> me in many such concerns.'

Might she have had what we now call 'baby brain' in new mothers?

For all her contentment and her struggle to be a good wife, mother and mistress of Mildred's Court, her inner spirit continually reminded her that there were 'other duties' to which she might attend. But as yet, she was unable to concentrate fully on them; the time was not right for her. Within six months of first arriving at Mildred's Court, she had made a visit which, unknown to her at the time, proved another milestone in her life. Recalling her interest in education while at Earlham, a friend invited her to see an educational experiment which was going on in Southwark and had started to attract attention.

In May the previous year, she had recorded casually:

> 'We went in the evening to see a Friend who kept
> a school for poor children.'

The Friend was Joseph Lancaster who was setting in motion an educational revolution of such importance that within 34 years there would be 'Lancasterian schools' throughout England. His school was non-denominational and run on a monitorial system. He had the idea that if he allowed boys to make a noise, they would not consider it such a bore to be taught. He divided his horde into small groups of twelve, each with a monitor to keep order, collect and distribute lesson material, and hear lessons recited. The actual teaching of the younger children was partly done by the older, who first learned a lesson, then taught it. The method was both enlivening and economical and

Elizabeth, remembering her crowded class of 70 'schollers', was inspired.

Her first impression of Lancaster was that he was rather cocksure, and that the flattery and interest of his numerous visitors had gone to his head. But as their acquaintance progressed, she recognised that this was merely the assertiveness of a man with enthusiasm. From then on, she kept in touch with his work and helped him both with friendship and with financial aid when he was in dire straits.

While his work remained on the periphery of her mind, mastering family life continued to be her priority. And she worked hard at this, one of her favourite sayings being 'While it is yet day', there was time for more work to be done. The serenity of 1802 was further enhanced when Joseph took her on a delightful journey. It was a business trip combined with pleasure, the first of many they would take together. Elizabeth accompanied him for the sheer fun and pleasure of travel and the enjoyment of his company. He seemed to come into his own on these trips. He dictated the route, chose the inns, and paid the bills. Elizabeth had nothing to do but be a charming companion. How well she succeeded in this is illustrated by the fact that he never tired of taking her with him.

On this occasion, baby Katherine and a nurse came too. Elizabeth was four months pregnant with their second child yet she recalled that it was more like a honeymoon than their first journey together. They visited Coventry, Stratford-on-Avon, Warwick, Wolverhampton, Coalbrookdale, Rock Ferry, Liverpool, Manchester and Keswick. They went to see Shakespeare's monument at Stratford – 'a sweet country churchyard'. They had breakfast at Warwick and admired the castle inside and out. Coalbrookdale in Shropshire brought back happy memories for Elizabeth and she enjoyed the

'extraordinary' town of Chester where the views from the walls
were beautiful.

Bad weather delayed them at Rock Ferry but they made the most
of it, staying at a cosy inn with a blazing fire and candles and
the windows closed firmly against the wind and rain. Elizabeth
was glad of the rest and again wondered at the contentment of
marriage.

> 'The quiet within was so pleasant, when the
> storms without were so violent, and I enjoyed
> my beloved husband's company. What earthly
> pleasure is equal to the enjoyment of real unity
> with the nearest of all ties, husband and children?'

She was delighted with her bravery when sailing across from
Rock Ferry to Liverpool with the wind still high.

> 'I hardly felt any fear. I do not think I am nearly
> such a coward about some little things as I was
> before I married.'

They spent time in Liverpool and Manchester on business, then
headed to Keswick for some robust outdoor activity. They rode
about on horseback in the rain looking at waterfalls. Damp
mists clung in veils about the hills but when the wind blew the
vapour aside for a moment, glimpses of shining lakes appeared.

> 'There is too much water in this place, too
> much lake, too much barren mountain,' she
> complained.

Riding was uncomfortable but the young pregnant wife was
determined to keep her husband company. As the rain cleared
they took a long ride, part of it:

'over rather frightful roads, on the edge of a precipice without any wall or guard on it.' It got worse. 'This evening my husband and I climbed Skiddaw. When we arrived at the top after some pain and fatigue, we were almost in a whirlwind, and so extremely cold and damp, being in the midst of a cloud, and the wind so violent that it appeared almost impossible to stand against it; however we got down safely.'

She delighted in the growing maturity which helped her survive such a day without fuss.

'This would have appeared to me some time ago rather a frightful day.'

By the middle of November, they were home at Mildred's Court and Elizabeth could recall her visit with pleasure as she read her sister Hannah's account of their family trip to the Lakes that year. They were there long enough to gain a less damp and barren impression and to see it in its glory, softly opalescent under the sun. They had stayed north of Windermere, at Ambleside and had with them a highly distinguished tutor, John Crome. Known as Old Crome to distinguish him from his son, although he was only 34 at the time, he was one of Britain's finest landscape artists. Born in humble circumstances and apprenticed to a sign-writer, his talent singled him out and he founded the Norwich School of Painting. He spent days with the girls, sitting in rustic summer houses and helping them to paint the wonderful views including difficult subjects like waterfalls. Long walks and picnics were the order of the day, wrote Hannah, with many vigorous quarrels over plans.

'We three, Fowell and Sam and I, had a very
pleasant and droll ride home in a countryman's
cart, which passed us on our return to Ambleside,
after we had been climbing up a hill at Grasmere
and walking a long way when there. We are all,
even Kitty, capital walkers.'

Fowell Buxton, having been captivated by Hannah as she held
Elizabeth's infant at Earlham, was pursuing his prey albeit
innocently. They were young and forming happy memories
together, the scent of damp thyme, the rush of falling water,
gentle fatigue on a warm hillside and a fun ride home in a cart.
Hannah, had she known it, had no time to develop a life of
her own. She was captured from the beginning by a stronger
personality and woven into the web of his life.

Meanwhile in London, Elizabeth tried to build her strength for
the arrival of another child. She told herself:

'Suffer we must in this world: and the less we
kick against the pricks, the happier for us.'

She was comforted that Joseph's boisterousness was subdued by
his anxiety for her. A pleasing melancholy was a substitute in
him for the deep-seated seriousness that lay dormant in even
the liveliest Gurney. Elizabeth sometimes missed that note of
seriousness in his free and easy, jovial, good-humoured nature.

'My Joseph appears low and not very comfortable
but that is preferable to me to seeing him in an
exhilarated state of mind, as he is more lovable
to me when under a little discouragement, I feel
lowish myself this morning.'

Her sisters, Rachel and the youngest, Priscilla, soon arrived at
Mildred's Court to help her and on 25 March 1803 her second

daughter was born and named after her aunt, Rachel. Two weeks later, Elizabeth wrote:

> 'My heart abounded with joy and gratitude when my dear little girl was born, perfect and lovely. Words are not equal to express my feelings, for I was most mercifully dealt with. My soul was so quiet and so much supported.'

However, she was very ill again after the birth and it was not until June that she recorded in her diary:

> 'I am once more entering upon my usual occupations.' But added: '... my nerves are in an irritable state, I am soon overcome and overdone.'

Perhaps she had post-natal depression, a diagnosis still so far in the future.

Her sister Kitty, who was staying at Bath, came to see her which was a comfort. Indeed it was during this visit that Kitty attended an Anglican service and started on the path that led her finally to membership of the Church of England.

Elizabeth was too unwell at the time to enjoy the arrival at Mildred's Court of another member of her family, her beloved brother Sam. At seventeen, he was a handsome young man with a fine presence and was eager to learn the banking business from his brother-in-law. The year 1803 was an exciting one in which to start banking and Sam took to it immediately.

As she recovered from the baby's birth, Elizabeth was able at last to appreciate having him around. The tie between them had always been a warm and loving one. She had been the sister to whom he had taken his childish troubles, the one to whom his reticent and sturdy disposition allowed confidence. It was

to her that he had run in the dark night when wakened by a
bad dream. Before she had children of her own, her maternal
feelings had been stirred by this particularly masculine brother,
six years her junior. His escapades with the farm horses and
increasing excellence at manly sports appealed to some secret
streak of daring in Elizabeth herself. She was delighted now to
have him in her household and he added to the happiness of
the domestic circle.

In the counting-house as well as in domestic life, he was loved
by everyone. When at work he was thoroughly industrious
and although no one more enjoyed a break for a drive in
the country, or a game of cricket in the fields at Plashet, on
returning to town he would cheerfully go down after supper
into the counting-house and look over the books for a couple
of hours. His popularity was such that the family was seldom
invited to any friend's house without being asked to bring
young Samuel with them.

His sisters wondered if the 'plain' influence of Joseph and
Elizabeth would rub off on him. Priscilla writing home to
Hannah from Mildred's Court considered:

> 'It is difficult, I think, to be here long without
> feeling the influence of Friends, and Betsy is so
> very nearly [closely] connected with us that it is
> now and then painful not to be able to feel as
> she does.'

It was not long before the gentle Priscilla did indeed 'feel as she
does'. But Sam maintained to the end his middle way. It was
Joseph John, two years his junior, who became the distinguished
Quaker among the men of the Gurney family. And at that time
he was studying at Oxford with a private tutor – nonconformists
were barred from membership of the university.

While the Gurney and Fry families developed and grew, England's peace gradually came to an end. The diplomatic wrangling that had been going on ever since the Peace of Amiens ended in severance of diplomatic relations on 12 May 1803 and England declared war three days later. Nelson sailed from Portsmouth a week later to take command of the fleet. On 22 May, Napoleon outraged all international codes by capturing and interning all English travellers in France and Holland, and laying an embargo on all English vessels in ports under his control.

The unexpectedness of this internment and its tedious duration made it one of the worst in history. Detainees were harassed by being moved from place to place. Mothers were separated from their children, young people were parted from lovers, businessmen were cut off from their offices, boys were prevented from returning to college, and all were held in the misery of exile with little hope for nearly ten years. It was considered a gesture of no military value, just of pure spite. Eventual exile to St Helena for Napoleon was deemed fair retribution.

The lack of easy communication made it possible for people to carry on with their lives in relative normality, unaware of impending danger. The real threat of French invasion seemed remote and as such Elizabeth travelled happily to Earlham with Joseph and the babies for their usual summer visit in late July.

Indeed when the Fry's visit was over, the Gurneys went off for a seaside holiday at Cromer. Napoleon still seemed far away from Norfolk. Many English families travelled serenely to remote sea coasts and concentrated on the innocent and peaceful pleasures of the traditional summer holiday without giving the French emperor a thought.

But while the Frys were at Earlham the problems were brought forcibly to Elizabeth's attention.

'I was quite sorry to see a letter from my brother
[in-law] William that expressed he was so fully
occupied that my Joseph thought it best to
determine to go to London in a few days. This
vexed me much, more particularly as Joseph did
not appear the least to mind leaving me, but
even seemed to wish to go. I felt rather low and
delicate.'

She had been concerned to see Joseph giving way to his love
of music and playing the piano at Earlham, an instrument
kept out of Mildred's Court due to the Fry's strict influence.
Here again was evidence of the continual inner battle between
'gay' and 'plain'. Whether Joseph's wish to cut short his holiday
and return to London to help his busy brother William was
influenced by his irritation on the subject of music, by the
crying babies, or by his sense of the urgency of the situation
in town, is uncertain. But he and Elizabeth set aside their
differences about music and enjoyed some happy family time at
Earlham before he left. Her deepening love for him was evident
in her diary entry:

'Took leave of my dear Joseph. My love for him
is only known to a superior [being] to mortals.'

A combination of her character and his ability to please her
made their arguments easily put aside.

Certainly he was soon made fully aware of the danger of French
invasion. Napoleon had a large army encamped at Boulogne
which he called the Army of England. He was preparing a
flotilla of flat-bottomed boats in which to transport it across
the Channel when the moment arrived to hurl it at England's
shores. Although how well flat-bottomed boats might have
fared in the choppy, uncertain waters of the Channel was

another question. But the threat was real. Fear and fury swept over England and 400,000 volunteers offered themselves in service of their country's defence.

Joseph discovered that plans had been made to flood the marshes of the river Lea and destroy the bridges on the Essex Road. At the first news of a landing, it was planned that the King should be ready to flee from London to Chelmsford, and the Queen and the royal treasure to Worcester. Barrels of tar were put on all the church towers along the south coast to be lit as beacons. Even bigger beacons, each of eight wagon-loads of wood and kindling with four or five tar barrels, were built on strategic hilltops where, in flames by night or smoke by day, they would send warning signals for miles.

England had experienced nothing like this since the threat of the Armada. Napoleon himself, the man of legend, was at Boulogne, and was reported to have said:

> 'Let us be masters of the Channel for six hours and
> we are masters of the world.'

Week after week the state of strain continued. The fleet defended the Channel but the fleet could not be everywhere. Napoleon, using a decoy, might get out of Boulogne and attack England in some other area. Was any coastal stretch safe?

The panic spread. John Gurney ordered that four carriages should be kept constantly ready at Earlham to start at a moment's notice for the Isle of Ely, about 40 miles away, in case the French landed on the Norfolk coast.

Priscilla wrote to Elizabeth in November:

> 'My father is going to Lynn this afternoon. From
> Lynn he will continue his journey to Liverpool
> and, I suppose, will not return for a fortnight.

I think we shall be in a very unprotected state if
the French should land whilst my father is away,
without a single man, or even boy, to take care
of us.'

'We had quite a serious conference about it
yesterday morning: thee would have been
entertained to have heard the various plans that
were proposed. It is, however, now finally settled
that as soon as ever we hear the news of their
arrival, we six [sisters], Danny [aged twelve], and
Nurse, and, if we can manage it, Molly and Anne
[servants] are immediately to set off in the coach-
and-four for Ely where we are to take up our
abode, as my father thinks it is a very safe place,
being so completely surrounded by marshes.'

'I hope, as soon as ever you hear of the French
being landed in Norfolk, that you will imagine
us setting off post-haste for Ely. Mrs Freeman
is to stay to take care of the house, as it will be
necessary for somebody to be here. My father
intends to write down directions for every
individual of the family, so that there may be
no confusion or bustle whenever the moment of
danger arrives, if it ever does arrive.'

There was a sense of excitement in all this – although perhaps
not for the poor housekeeper, Mrs Freeman, who was to be
left behind to fend off the French on her own. She need not
have worried. By March 1804, Napoleon and his flotilla had
become a national joke. Preparations for flight subsided; the
war receded to a comfortable distance.

Love and Death

ELIZABETH HAD little time to worry about the war and instinctively resisted thinking about a problem she could do nothing to solve. She eagerly devoted herself to a more immediate task. Shortly after her return to London from Earlham the previous autumn, her mother-in-law became gravely ill at Plashet and William came in a panic and asked for her help. Bringing a London doctor with her, she hurried to Mrs Fry's bedside:

> 'I was quite sorry to find her so ill, and felt real
> love for her,' she recalled.

She enjoyed nursing perhaps because her own ill health gave her an understanding of those little touches which make a sick person comfortable. It is odd that William's own wife, Eliza, who was already in residence at Plashet, did not step in. She had no children and plenty of free time, whereas Elizabeth ran a complicated household, had a two-year-old baby, another of six months, another on the way and many daily demands on her time and wisdom. But William trusted Elizabeth as the more capable of the two, the woman to whom he naturally turned for help in things which might be seen in those days as 'a woman's business'. Clearly William's doubts about Elizabeth's capabilities when she first came to Mildred's Court as a bride had long gone.

Joseph might have been proud of this display of confidence in his wife's abilities, but it cost him her company. For months Elizabeth's time was divided between the two houses and because she always breast-fed her children and did not, as her mother had done, employ a wet-nurse, baby Rachel came too. Yet she remained remarkably resilient through it all except for a time when she was distraught and recorded in her diary:

> 'My darling babe seriously unwell'.

Childhood illnesses were particularly alarming then when the child mortality rate was high.

Also concerning her were William's medical ideas which she found repugnant.

> 'Animal Magnetism has been a very uppermost,
> and also worrying, subject to me, and when it is
> going on as it has been lately at Plashet, my mind
> cannot be at rest about it. I have so much natural
> dislike to it.'

Animal magnetism, a mixture of faith-healing, 'magnetic' healing and mild hypnotism, had always been of interest to the Fry family and, indeed, had been one of the subjects with which Joseph had entertained Elizabeth in the early days of their courtship. But whereas it might have been an interesting topic of conversation, it was quite another thing to see it put into practice on an ailing mother-in-law.

The Austrian physician, Friedrich Anton Mesmer, had popularised the practice, known as mesmerism, whereby a hypnotic state could be induced over the will and nervous system of the patient. Also, the Italian physicist Alessandro Volta had invented the voltaic pile, the first instrument for producing an electric current. These surprising new ideas had flowered among non-scientific minds into curious superstitions and practices. William, for example, claimed to be able to tell by the power of sympathy what part of a sick person's body was ailing them or had the most pain. Although kindness and sympathy played a huge part in Elizabeth's nursing, she did not consider them a treatment. She was all for common sense, simple remedies and close attention to the orders of a good doctor.

She could not prevent William from entering the sickroom and practising his magnetic arts on his suffering mother but it annoyed her. Eliza, too, would enter the sickroom and fuss about. To Elizabeth's irritation, Mrs Fry, with the perversity and confusion of the very ill, would sometimes prefer the company of her more familiar, although ineffective, daughter-in-law. Eventually Elizabeth would find time to let off steam in her diary, ever a safety valve.

> 'I have... felt moments of a sort of jealousy at her preferring Eliza's nursing to mine; however, think it has generally been a uniting time amongst us all, more particularly for Eliza and me. I never remember feeling so much for her as I have lately... In the first place I have felt a good deal for my poor mother.'

Innovative medical practices were being tried out in high places too. King George III had suffered 'water in the chest of the body' and to treat him they 'scarified his legs'. The following day they needed four doctors instead of two. But the King recovered and on 28 March 1804 was proclaimed 'restored to all his domestic comforts.'

By then Mrs William Storrs Fry had been almost a fortnight in her grave. Her death saddened Elizabeth but enabled her to return home, catch her breath and resume control of her household. With the threat of French invasion on hold, life returned to normal although an undercurrent of unrest continued to rumble in the big cities. As she went about her daily business, Elizabeth could not fail to notice obvious signs of poverty in the London streets. Gradually she returned her thoughts to those 'other duties'.

Often, after business hours on a fine, light evening, she and Joseph would go to a poor district in search of someone who had aroused her sympathy. There were dangers in the narrow, dingy streets in the days of footpads [thieves] and Joseph always wore his unpopular Quaker coat. But he was strong and ready for the unexpected and Elizabeth was unafraid. She dreaded rebuking a servant, was terrified by public speaking but never in her life was she afraid of a robber.

And there was a bonus. No matter how risky and unsavoury the side-streets they walked to reach their sordid destination, the main part of their journey was usually delightful. The Thames was still a river highway and they went and returned by water. Some of their adventures were extraordinary. On one occasion, they searched with difficulty to find a woman who had begged so touchingly of Elizabeth. Eventually they found her living 'almost like a gentlewoman' and she had asked brazenly for £30 to pay her debts.

Worse was the woman who begged carrying a sickly baby, ill with whooping-cough, in her arms. When tracked down, she turned out to be a baby farmer and fled to escape the clutches of the law. Some women today still use babies as sympathy props when they beg. For Elizabeth, these were not the simple, straightforward poor of the Earlham countryside or of the slums of Norwich. But there were many deserving cases and sometimes in looking up a deceiver, they discovered a case of real need and could offer help. At such moments Elizabeth felt truly elated.

She also loved going to the workhouse and reading and talking to the children. The Friends of Gracechurch Street Meeting had appointed her a visitor to the Islington Workhouse and at first she felt all her usual terror. But she gathered her courage, found something for their tea and some books to read to them and set off bravely. Once among them and feeling their forlorn childish need, she forgot all about her shyness. Their response was so eager and so genuine and her natural clarity of mind flowed through her speech. It was like the days of Betsy's Imps again.

When she found time in the bright hours of daylight, she would go on many such errands alone and relished her walks over old London Bridge.

> 'I went to see a poor woman – it is always a cross
> to me leaving my children – but going over the
> bridge I enjoy. The air, sky and water look so
> sweetly.'

Soon it was time for her to endure yet another confinement. Her third baby was due and, as usual, she dreaded the birth. In July 1804 her first son, John ['Johnny'] Gurney Fry, was born. Again the birth was followed by weeks of illness – 'sickness, faintness and nervous irritability'. She was taken to Bath for a cure before returning to Earlham for a complete rest.

As the only married sister, Elizabeth had a powerful claim on her sisters' time. Louisa, almost twenty, had been at Mildred's Court earlier in the year and returned there with Elizabeth from Earlham to help with the new baby. Her sisters loved her dearly but sometimes found life at Mildred's Court dull. Their manners were always perfect but they never tried to amalgamate fully with the Fry circle. Louisa wrote:

> 'We have had a regular Mildred Court day, poor people coming one after another till twelve o'clock, and then no quiet. And each day I have been here we have had the Frys, or my uncle, or someone else at dinner. Dear Betsy gets through her bustles by letting them pass without teasing [upsetting] herself about them: she does feel them, but knows they must be borne.'

The Frys and their friends made it difficult for people more worldly than themselves; oil and water do not mix. They would not practise courtier-like manners and were embarrassed when their bluntness met chilly politeness. Elizabeth resigned herself, willingly and sweetly, to her situation but thought:

> 'We ought to make it an object in conversation and in conduct to oblige those we are with, and rather to make the pleasure of others our object... I am clear it is a great virtue to be able constantly to yield in little things.'

John and Amelia Opie were the only friends from her 'gay' past who remained faithful to Elizabeth; but even they found it heavy going. The Earlham girls found ways to escape. They might drive off in a glass coach to St James's Park and walk about admiring the flowerbeds and the fashions. Sometimes they would forget which gate they came in by and wander about for ages, in gales of laughter, until they found their coach and joyfully clambered aboard. In the evening they would go out into the world to visit friends or go to the theatre. The tales of their adventures enlivened Mildred's Court and brought fun and cheer into that sometimes too serious atmosphere.

For all the moments of boredom, the sisters loved being with Elizabeth and her babies. Louisa wrote to her on New Year's Day in 1805 after returning to Earlham:

> 'I have often thought of thee lately, and imagined thee in thy different offices; and amongst the many other pleasures of having been with thee is that of knowing exactly how thy time goes. I often seem to see thee in thy pink acorn gown attending to all thy flock in the dining-room, drawing-room, and – as I imagine – in the parlour, alternately running after thy servants, children and poor. In short, I never felt before the kind of home interest in all of you in St Mildred's Court which I feel now.'

Louisa's hint of broodiness was the precursor to a run of romance in the family over the next eighteen months. Before long, she would learn the ways of domesticity herself with her childhood admirer and close family friend Sam Hoare who had kissed her when she was twelve years old and had waited patiently for her ever since. But although Louisa was the next sister to be married, the 21-year-old Hannah was next to become engaged. Hannah's love, Thomas Fowell Buxton, three years her junior, was an under-graduate at Dublin University and faced more years of study. But his future appeared secure as heir to considerable estates in Ireland. There was general agreement within the families that his engagement to Hannah should be put on a firm footing.

Rachel's letters to Elizabeth gave a clear picture of the excitement at Earlham where they dined and danced and hoped that an announcement would be made by the end of the young couple's walk the following day. They returned engaged to everyone's delight but it was agreed that the wedding would not take place until Fowell Buxton graduated.

The beautiful Rachel herself had still not recovered from the hurt of Henry Enfield's rebound marriage. John Pitchford, that trusted family friend, had proposed to her sometime after Enfield's departure but had been refused. Pitchford had been distanced from the family but John Gurney was entirely free from religious prejudice, unlike his strict brother Joseph and, valuing Pitchford's company, had drawn him back into the family fold once more.

By the end of the year, England was delighting in Nelson's victory at Trafalgar but mourning his loss in the great battle. The euphoric atmosphere carried on well into the New Year and fanned the flames of romance at Earlham. Sam Hoare, whose prosperous banking business had put him in a position to marry years before, finally obtained a promise from the striking and headstrong Louisa. Did she remember then the words she had written in her diary after that dance many years earlier?

> 'Young Sam Hoare was most disgusting; we were on most good terms the first part of the evening, but at last he went so far as to give me a kiss; it was most disgusting. Still I was very agreeable last night; I felt so both in mind and body; how seldom can I say this of myself.'

Their wedding was arranged for December 1806. This gave Elizabeth six months to recover from the birth of her fourth child, a second son, named William Storrs after his paternal grandfather. Early in December, she arrived at Earlham, with

Joseph and their brood, pale and thin but happy to be present to see the first of her sisters married.

The wedding took place on Christmas Eve at the Friends' Meeting house at Tasborough, just south of Norwich and all the Gurney children were present. Sam Hoare had been studying his beloved Louisa for many years and knew her well. So it was not surprising when, after the newlyweds returned from their honeymoon, Hannah wrote to her beau, Fowell Buxton:

> 'December 31st 1806. Louisa and Sam returned yesterday from Cromer, where they have been spending nearly a week in retirement, so that they have now the effect of married people who have begun their career together. Louisa looks sweetly and Sam truly happy.'

Sam took a house for his bride not far from his old home near Hampstead Heath and Elizabeth was delighted to have a sister living so close to her. One of the first letters Louisa wrote as a married woman described a visit from Elizabeth and her horde. It was to Hannah in January 1807 and was full of advice from a new bride to a sister soon to be married herself. Like Elizabeth before her, she confessed to difficulties adjusting to her husband's family although they were well known to her and she had her house to herself most of the time. Elizabeth's visit was her first 'full company-day' at home.

> 'It was Sam's day out, so I determined to enjoy dear Betsy and all her darling and noisy flock. They arrived in a hack about one...Fowell walked in with Dan [youngest brother Daniel Gurney] at his side a little before three, and soon after that we dined, the children in the drawing-room and we in the dining room.' She was anxious that

her guests would enjoy their meal and visit. 'It was so very strange to me to feel myself in this capacity with all of them. We chatted pleasantly in the afternoon, and after an early tea, Betsy and Catherine and brats left us three to a truly snug and happy evening.'

She added, perhaps a little guilty about the word 'brats':

'But first I must tell you how very sweet the darling children were, and what a treat it was to me to have them routing about the house. They all seemed thoroughly to enjoy the novelty and were quite happy with their exalted ideas of 'Aunt Hoare' and her house which little Rachel said was almost as fine as the King's house... About eight dear Sam came in, looking most sweet and cheerful, rejoicing to be at home and delighted to see Fowell. We all sat round the fire, talking, laughing and easy and happy... Indeed, Hannah, I do think thee has got a delightful husband, I did think what two prizes they were when I saw him and Sam walk off arm-in-arm this morning, both looking so very agreeable, handsome and delightful.'

She finished her letter with more sisterly advice concerning marriage and ended with a somewhat comical warning about mad dogs and the need to make sure one's men folk wore boots 'for they generally bite men's legs.'

Hovering over this seemingly happy atmosphere was a large black cloud. Romance had not been kind to young John Gurney and he suffered terribly after an unhappy love affair. The family tried to comfort him as best they could unaware that their distractions would only make matters worse. In his emotional state, he fell violently in love with his beautiful cousin, Elizabeth Gurney. She lived near Earlham at Keswick Hall, the family home bought by their grandfather in 1747 and inherited by her father, Richard.

John and Elizabeth were determined to be together but the marriage of first cousins was much frowned upon and there was fierce opposition from both families. John, with his father's obstinacy, argued the point. After all, his father had encouraged the affair by thoughtlessly inviting them both on a family tour with 'three chariots, whiskey' and Sam Hoare and Fowell Buxton extolling the joys of betrothal.

Quietly in January 1807, they were married, supported by the kindly attentions of the bridegroom's sisters at home and a long and warm letter from Elizabeth. But the disapproving fathers ostentatiously went for a walk during the ceremony to mark their official disapproval.

Four months later the whole family assembled at Earlham for yet another wedding, this time of Hannah and Fowell Buxton. His hopes of an inheritance had fallen through and although his prospects were uncertain, he went ahead with his wedding once he had taken his degree. His fortunes might have wavered but his self-confidence was fortified by university honours and by the tribute of being asked to sit in the House of Commons as member for Dublin University. Although his mother, a sister of Uncle Richard Gurney's wife, was a Quaker, his late father had not been. The family had been raised as 'churchmen' so he could have accepted the invitation. He declined since now he would have to earn a living for his bride, and MPs were not then paid. But the invitation turned his attention to the possibility of a political career. The seeds had been sown for his distinguished future as a social reformer and anti-slavery campaigner.

Before the year was over, his uncle, Sampson Hanbury, offered him a promising position in the firm of Truman, Hanbury and Co, London brewers, with the prospect of a partnership after three years' probation. So he and Hannah moved to London and Elizabeth delighted at having a second sister within reach of an afternoon visit. The company was immortalised by Mrs Micawber's comments in 'David Copperfield':

> 'I will not conceal from you, my dear Mr Copperfield that I have long felt the brewing business to be particularly adapted to Mr Micawber. Look at Barclay and Perkins! Look at Truman, Hanbury, and Buxton! It is on that extensive footing that Mr Micawber, I know from my own knowledge of him, is calculated to shine; and the profits, I am told, are e-NOR-mous!'

Fowell Buxton certainly found them so.

These weddings within such a short time proved rather overwhelming for those left behind at Earlham. Rachel wrote to her sister:

> 'I daresay, dearest Fowell and Hannah, you do not wonder that, in certain moods the past should rise up mournfully before me. The sight of you all happily married brings some sad regrets…'

Rachel, her eldest sister Catherine, and the youngest, Priscilla, never married.

The melancholy of an emptying house had fallen upon Earlham Hall. Four were now married; Sam was in London; Daniel away at school; and the remaining sisters were often visiting the married homes. Fowell Buxton, like all the other husbands, comforted his new bride's homesickness by spending the last weeks of their honeymoon at Earlham. When they finally drove away with Priscilla who was to be their first guest, the house and grounds became dreadfully quiet.

> 'My father and Joseph [Joseph John, then aged nineteen] and I walked through the garden and along the path towards the violet-grove, all deeply impressed [saddened] by parting with you,' wrote Rachel. 'At last my father burst into tears, which you may be sure affected us not a little. Upon recovering himself he opened his heart to us in the sweetest manner about you... indeed the way in which he spoke of all his children drew tears from me...'

Once they had talked about their feelings and cheered each other up, they walked on towards the river where they discovered some local boys fishing. They brought them home for a feast of strawberries. But they were forlorn again in the morning.

> 'We three were the only Gurneys at Meeting.'

Life continued to be a bustle at Mildred's Court. Elizabeth's previous thoughts had been with the love affairs of Louisa, John and Hannah. But she had one going on under her own wing. Her brother Sam had become acquainted with a charming and suitable girl, Elizabeth Sheppard who lived with her parents at Ham House in Essex, not far from Plashet. The girl's mother was a Gurney, a cousin of the Earlham group, and Elizabeth had probably been indulging in a little matchmaking.

Sam was nearly 21 now and already showing promise of that genius for finance which would make him one of the richest men of his time. His father had recently started him in business with the firm of Richardson and Overend, bill-brokers in Lombard

Street, in close connection with the Norwich bank. He was ambitious and gaining self-confidence. But before Elizabeth Sheppard's shy and gentle beauty, his blossoming confidence vanished. He was 'exceedingly in love.' When he could stand it no further, he wrote to his father seeking approval and to ask for his help. They became engaged that winter and were married in April 1808 at Barking Meeting House in London.

Elizabeth almost missed the wedding due to ill-health following the birth in February 1808 of her fifth baby, daughter Richenda.

> 'Poorly all night, so much so that my attending
> dear Sam's wedding appeared almost out of the
> question, but to the surprise of all that knew my
> state of body I attended this wedding.'

A nursery governess had been added to the Mildred's Court household at Joseph's insistence.

> 'I felt a good deal about Mary Ann Davies coming
> to teach the children and live here, fearing for the
> peace of our nursery establishment,' Elizabeth
> wrote.

But Joseph was adamant that it was for the best by taking pressure off her and helping her regain strength for other matters.

> 'My dear Joseph's truly sweet and amiable state is
> a great comfort to me.'

The following month the family gathered again at Earlham. Scents of spring were in the air and as they arrived each recalled the previous May when the house was overrun with bridesmaids in muslin, roses and straw hats and a wedding-chaise drove gaily down the avenue for Hannah and Fowell Buxton's happy day.

This time it was a hearse that advanced slowly under the pale lime trees; and of the group that waited for it by the doorway all were weeping. Elizabeth's ill health sometimes caused her to feel 'in the valley mentally and bodyly'. She may have felt:

> 'hardly any sense of any good thing or hardly a
> good desire, and also tried with nervous feelings'.

But these feelings passed and good health returned and she had five lively children at home in London as her recompense. She was fortunate. But her brother John was not. For him it was more heartbreak. His beautiful wife and first cousin Elizabeth had died in childbirth. Did he think this was a judgement on them? Perhaps, for he never recovered fully and gradually declined in body and mind until he died six years later aged 33.

As the autumn leaves fell later that year, so too did William Storrs Fry. Avoiding animal magnetism at home, he came to Mildred's Court and put himself in the gentle, caring hands of his dear daughter-in-law. Five weeks of nursing increased their affection for one another. In a moment of consciousness before the end he murmured to her gratefully that he was 'comfortable, comfortable, comfortable'. His words drew tears from Elizabeth who had long forgotten the rough words and ways that used to anger and pain her.

> 'I loved him very dearly, and his memory is sweet
> to me.'

Plashet

J UST WHEN Elizabeth's lifestyle might have permitted more attention to 'other matters', destiny drew her in another direction. The death of her father-in-law caused a dramatic change in their lives. Joseph inherited his beloved Plashet and for the next twenty years she would be mistress of a house and estate as large and beautiful as Earlham Hall.

She longed to give Plashet her full attention but before she could do so her nursing skills were required again. Her sister Hannah fell ill and Fowell Buxton's first thought was to call upon Elizabeth. He had an unmarried sister of his own, and a sister-in-law as yet without children, both close by but he and Hannah wanted Elizabeth. And Elizabeth did not hesitate to respond. Too late they discovered that Hannah had scarlet fever.

Elizabeth as usual was stalwart in the face of danger.

> 'Being the only sister at liberty I have nursed her.
> This I consider a great privilege to be able to do:
> though I have felt it a very serious thing, with
> a young babe, and the mother of so many little
> lambs, to enter so catching a disorder.'

She was half afraid of reckless selfishness. It would have been very wrong to risk the children's health 'to gratify inclination, which leads me to enjoy nursing those I love so dearly.' But justifying her actions, she added:

> 'indeed I had hardly an option, as I was in the first instance brought into it not knowing what the complaint was; and in the second, there was no one else that I thought proper to take my place.'

Luckily no one else caught the deadly disease this time and Hannah recovered. Although quarantine was not yet fully understood, hygiene was improving and Elizabeth's meticulous attention to detail was sure to have helped.

By January 1809, Elizabeth could at last accompany Joseph to Plashet and make plans for taking control of their new home. The estate was in East Ham, Essex, not far from Epping Forest and had a farm as well as extensive gardens. Elizabeth grew to love Plashet every bit as much as Joseph did but before she could put her stamp on the place she became ill with a fever. She felt so terrible that she feared death and begged 'that I might live long enough to do a little more good here'. By the middle of February, she was recovering and had discovered herself pregnant again, an excellent reason for regaining full strength.

> 'I think I feel my present situation almost like a fresh tie to the world. These dear babes do attach me very much here. I think the trying times I mostly have after my confinements are evidently for my good, and prevent my resting in the enjoyments of increasing family as I might otherwise do.'

And then it was spring. Oh, the delights of Plashet in spring! To roam in Epping Forest with the children and dig up violets and primroses to carry back and plant under the trees at Plashet. What joy it was to feed the fish in the ornamental ponds; to watch the birds building nests and rearing their young. What delight it gave to renew the pleasures of her childhood, strengthened by a new freedom and the proud joy of authority. She was mistress of these wide acres. Joseph of course was master and she deferred to him winningly but he was a businessman and had to travel some seven miles up to the city every day. The management of the house, gardens and farm fell increasingly to Elizabeth. And she loved it. In no time she had noted many things to be done in the village beyond. Joseph too was intensely happy to be master of Plashet at last. Elizabeth commented, lyrically:

> 'My beloved Joseph sweetly tendered under a sense of good. I felt him a sweet companion, and that we may be inabled to go hand in hand helping one another and not drawing one another back.'

Soon it was time for a visit to Earlham and Elizabeth was glad that not even spring at Plashet prevented a trip to Norfolk. But it seemed no time until she was back again in London for Yearly Meeting and the demands of hospitality at Mildred's Court. She had barely caught her breath after this major event before an urgent message came from brother Sam who could trust no one but Elizabeth to see his dearest wife through her first confinement. For once, although it was a 'privilege' to be asked, she dreaded it. She knew too much and her own time was drawing near. Nerves, imagination and sympathy were tested and she could only record it as:

> 'a trial… which at one time I felt no strength to
> encounter; but power and courage were given me
> sufficient for the day.'

What astonishing demands young husbands could make on
their sisters when thinking only of the welfare of their wives.

Her own time drew closer but there was little respite. Eliza
Fry broke a blood vessel and became dangerously ill. William,
panic-stricken, threw animal magnetism to the wind and called
for Elizabeth who came, nursed and comforted.

Not surprisingly afterwards Elizabeth did not feel well herself.
She moved about her duties at Plashet or sat out on its spacious
lawns low-spirited and languid and reproached herself for
'nervous complaints'. August was a lovely month and she felt
better. And then came September, and the harvest moon and
blackberries thick in the hedges.

> 'Time runs on apace. I desire my imagination
> may not dwell on that which is before it.'

On 20 September 1809, her sixth child, Joseph, was born.

As if some unkind force wanted to test her strength and courage
to the limit, a barrage of bad news from Earlham hit her before
she had time to recover from the birth. She was at Tunbridge
Wells recuperating when it started. News came that Daniel,
the baby of the family, now aged eighteen and working at the
bank in Lynn, had scarlet fever. Dear old Nurse, beloved of all
the family, in looking after him had caught the disease herself
and had died. Now Priscilla had caught it and was lying ill at
Earlham. And, the final straw, her father was seriously ill after
an operation.

While Elizabeth and Joseph pondered on the seriousness of
these events, further word arrived that her father was in fact

dying. Without delay, they started one of those miserable journeys, so wretched to endure, so forlorn in retrospect, driven on by the desire to be at their destination in time. She longed to see her beloved father once more and was frustrated that they could not get there quicker.

After a night in Mildred's Court on their way from Tunbridge Wells, they made the journey in a day despite Elizabeth's delicate state and Joseph's desire to protect her. They reached Earlham Hall at midnight. As she stepped out under the dark shapes of the trees and saw the pale and tear-stained faces in the shifting light of lanterns, she knew she was carrying her new born son into a house where there was fever. But at that moment her dearest father had first claim.

As if in a dream, someone gently took the baby from her arms and removed her wraps. With Joseph's support and Rachel's arm around her, they went upstairs to her father's room.

> And so 'I once more saw him who has been so inexpressibly dear to me through life, since I knew what love was. He was asleep, but death was strongly marked on his sweet, and to me, beautiful face.'

In that sleep he quietly slipped away at dawn on 28 October 1809. His children were bereft.

The funeral was at Gildencroft, that green and quiet burial ground in the heart of the city of Norwich. The family were all present, including Daniel and Priscilla who came from their sick-beds. Catherine, the eldest, remained composed throughout. She had recently joined the Church of England and marked it by wearing mourning in solitary correctness at her father's funeral. Richenda sobbed throughout. Daniel, scarcely able to stand, leaned on the coffin with one arm and held up the sobbing Priscilla with the other. Joseph John gave a simple, touching address. And it was during the moving silence which followed that it happened.

A sudden flood of emotion overcame Elizabeth; a certainty of God and of life beyond the grave. Without effort, as spontaneously as a child, she opened her lips and spoke. Her sweet, clear voice was heard saying a text in the form of a prayer.

> 'Great and marvellous are thy works, Lord God Almighty: just and true are all thy ways, thou King of saints: be pleased to receive our thanksgiving.'

That was all. But the effect was electric. To her husband, her brothers, sisters, friends and afterwards to herself, it marked an epoch. Since first coming under the influence of William Savery, Elizabeth had contemplated this possibility with dread. Her fear of any form of public speaking was well known. Now it had happened and it brought with it an extraordinary release. She felt quiet and calm yet strangely invigorated both mentally and physically.

The reactions of her family were various. Uncle Joseph was, of course, delighted. Even Catherine felt that it had been appropriate. Brothers Joseph John and Sam were cordial supporters; Elizabeth was a favourite sister and both were markedly Quaker in their outlook, particularly Joseph John who was already an able speaker himself and welcomed his sister into that service. But her brother John, who until his wife died, had been the society man of the family and in constant social demand, held a strong masculine prejudice, unlike most Quaker men, against women speaking in public. And he made his feelings known. Daniel kept quiet but in later life said it was the funerals more than anything that drove him away from the Society of Friends. He disliked the 'public exhibition' of the family with both men and women speaking.

For the moment, however, they encouraged Elizabeth and, above all, she had her husband's approval and was deeply grateful for that. But the trauma of their loss remained; grief was never far away. Whatever one believed of heaven, the earth was sadly changed and they were conscious of 'non-returning Time.' That they would never see their father again was painful.

> 'Now to have father, mother and nurse all taken from us, and to be ourselves occupying the situations they then held and to have children coming on, who are in the same way to succeed us' was a reminder of the relentless march of the generations.

And Earlham, dear as it was and often as they might gather there in future, would never be the same again. It had lost its heart.

Plashet that autumn provided peace and sanctuary for Elizabeth. The smell of burning leaves, the aisles of bare trees, the purple, misty views, restored her health, both in body and mind, after a period of prolonged anguish and pain. Walking with renewed energy along the quiet lanes, meeting occasionally a countryman in white smock-coat, or an old woman in a red cloak, or a scattering of children, bobbing and curtseying, she felt no more the old nostalgia for her childhood at Earlham. This richer, softer country was truly home, was truly hers. She felt herself again taking root and hoped that this time it might be forever. She wanted nothing better than this.

She couldn't say whether she or Joseph or the children were the happiest when they left London and returned to Plashet. The children were exuberant and even the daily commuting was an enjoyment to Joseph. Elizabeth could hardly describe what it meant to her to come out in the morning and smell again wet grass instead of coffee, to watch the darting flight of birds other than sparrows, and to feel around her the wide peace of the country. She liked the feeling that the local people had dwelt here year after year in the same cottages, were born, married and died in the same village and all knew each other well.

With winter on the way, she set to work immediately finding out the needs of the poorest in the village and providing remedies. The vicar, Mr Angelzaark, and his wife were overjoyed to find the new mistress of Plashet in this mood. One never knew with Quakers whether they would help with affairs outside their religion or not. The former master and mistress had stuck very firmly within a narrow Quaker orbit. Mr Angelzaark was delighted to find their heirs very different. Mr Fry was bluff, good-natured and generous. Mrs Fry was not only easy to approach but behind her beautiful manners lurked an actual eagerness to meet him more than half-way, to seek his advice, to use his knowledge, to share in his labours for the improvement of the parish. Mrs Angelzaark was Elizabeth's guide to many a needy home and a warm friendship sprang up between them. Indeed it was to her that Elizabeth, many years later, shared a secret by showing her the text in the Bible that touched her the most:

'Lord, I believe; help thou mine unbelief!'

Elizabeth started a soup kitchen in one of her large barns and when the weather became harsh the villagers came in their droves through the mud and snow. No one went home empty-handed. There were those who thought such lavish and indiscriminate charity encouraged vagrants. But a generation struggling inadequately with unemployment could only reply that even vagrants had to be fed. It was surely cheaper to feed them for free than to let them steal. Elizabeth Fry was not a theorist but she felt that if those who were fortunate enough to have money to spare did their duty for the benefit of the poor, then there would be less misery in the world. She was not a socialist and in later years, when she heard of such people, uttered a few words in their condemnation; as far as she could make out, their chief peculiarity was that they did not believe in God.

Soon the short English winter passed and the slow spring began. The family at Plashet entered a happy new routine which varied with the changing seasons. The children had schemes connected with farm, garden and animals. And Elizabeth loved to garden. She loved to plant, pull up weeds, to neaten and beautify. Some of the best memories her children would treasure in later life revolved around those days gardening with her in the spacious grounds of Plashet. They would fuss about her with their little trowels and forks and had their own individual gardens to attend to as well as helping her with hers. And Joseph too enjoyed improving the estate as well as hunting and fishing when possible.

Other memories were created during those happy days. The children often accompanied their mother on her trips to the village visiting the poor. Each child was encouraged to bring something to give to the children. Afterwards Elizabeth would ask each of her children to explain why they had picked that gift for the particular recipient. About half a mile from Plashet there was a colony of Irish and visiting Irish Row was a particular favourite. The wit and warmth and happy-go-lucky atmosphere where the pigs and chickens actually shared the house helped visitors ignore the dirt and poverty. And the Fry children loved going there. 'Oh Mother, do let's go to Irish Row!'

Elizabeth liked it just as much. It made her laugh to be offered with great ceremony an overturned bucket for a seat. And to be in the midst of a fluster of chickens that her hostess was trying to scurry out of the room. How all the children, Irish included, laughed until the tears poured down their faces! Even the flustered mother would laugh in the midst of her exasperation with the stupid birds!

When they were sad, how deep their grief. Elizabeth would share with the priest the task of comforting them around a rough coffin with the paper cross upon the dead. Quakers had discarded symbols such as crosses in an effort to come closer to that for which the symbol stood. 'There are differences of administration, but the same Lord,' Elizabeth would say, and she would help defray the expense of the funeral, not inquiring too closely as to whether she was paying for a Mass.

For guidance in educating children, she had written in her journal:

> 'Children should be deeply impressed with the belief that the first and great object of their education is to follow Christ and indeed to be true Christians; and those things on which we, the Society of Friends, differ from the world in general, should not, I think, be impressed upon them by only saying, as is often done, 'because Friends do it', but singly and simply as things that the Christian life appears to us to require, and that therefore they must be done. They should also early be taught that all have not seen exactly the same, but that there may be many equally belonging to the Church of Christ who may in other respects be as much stricter than ourselves as we are than they in these matters.'

It was natural that holding such views, she would not only co-operate warmly with Mr Angelzaark, but enlist his help in her own projects. The first and most important of these was, of course, a school. She found a large, empty room close to her house and felt it would serve every purpose as a schoolroom in the days when even Christ's Hospital, with its high standard of scholarship, taught many of its 600 scholars in one large hall. A competent schoolmistress was engaged and trained in the Lancasterian method of her friend Joseph Lancaster. With the vicar's help, some 70 children were enrolled and before long each one could read a real book aloud at night to their astonished parents. As books themselves were very scarce, Elizabeth was quick to give a Bible to proficient readers. Soon the children were writing the family letters when necessary.

The topic of educating the poor was much under discussion in the early nineteenth century. Some argued for a scheme of national education, and some maintained that 'book-learning' would only make labourers, especially their wives, unfit for their jobs. It would give them 'ideas above their station'. Even William Wordsworth, although keen for everyone to be able to read and write, argued that one of the happiest men he knew was illiterate. Was it wise for an infant to learn more than its parents? Would not the child become arrogant and superior and abandon love and obedience? Another person advised: 'Begin your education at the top of society; let the head go in the right course and the tail will follow.'

But Elizabeth Fry of Plashet House did not care about heads and tails, about implications and far-reaching effects, about the labourer or his wife being unfit for their station, or setting the child above the parent. She knew that reading and writing were vital for the soul and she set out to give them, and other benefits of schooling, to every child that she could reach. She did not think in national terms, but in personal ones. Here were John Smith's five children, and the head-gardener's two, and the coachman's seven, and the ten little rowdies of Judy O'Grady, and so on, in a sum of human units as she grew to know her countryside, family by family. Her school flourished and outlived her being eventually absorbed into the scheme for National Education.

The health of everyone around her was of equal concern. She couldn't indulge her passion for nursing with all her sick cottagers, but she could advise and oversee and get her doctors to prescribe. And, above all, she could oversee vaccination and was credited with keeping her neighbourhood free of smallpox.

Her reputation grew. When the gypsies came on their annual round and camped in a leafy lane near Plashet, and a desperate elder brother sought her help for a sick child, she took them under her wing. Each year she went down to their camp with comforts for the frail or ill and advice for the mothers on the care of their babies. Her clear courtesy and friendly dignity appealed to them. She became 'our Madam'. They liked to see her in her Quaker dress kneeling in the green grass among their caravans, her fair face, framed in its dainty muslin cap, bending over one of their dark-skinned children while her cool hands at once diagnosed and comforted. Something adventurous deep inside her responded to them and their carefree lifestyle.

Elizabeth's life might have been privileged but it was not carefree. As her responsibilities grew, she worked harder. And always in the back of her mind were those 'other duties' and a feeling that she had not yet found her life's work. On the day of her father's funeral she had taken a definite step into a new career. She believed she might have found, at last, her life's work. Since meeting William Savery all those years ago, she had felt that no other avenue of service was as valuable and important as his. But timidity had placed an insurmountable barrier in her way. The removal of her fears had seemed like a miracle.

> 'What has appeared almost impossible to flesh
> and blood has been made not only possible but
> easy.' Yet for all her growing confidence she
> still felt it was 'very awful to be thus publicly
> exposed.'

Her husband's opinion was of the greatest importance to her. Had he opposed her, she would have capitulated. But she noted in October 1810 his help and sympathy:

> 'I think the late public service I have been called
> into has very closely united us, and I believe
> proved a stimulant. What a comfort!'

Just months later, in February 1811, her seventh child, Elizabeth, was born. And weeks later she was formally 'recorded' in the books of Meeting as an approved minister. Her sister Priscilla was with her and they were both delighted. The 'recording' was to Elizabeth one of the most important events of her life. It did not appoint her to preach, or require her to preach anywhere at any time but it expressed approval of her speaking and a hope that her gift would continue to be exercised. Priscilla was recorded by the Norwich Meeting a few months later and the same distinction was conferred on Joseph John. Years later the practice of 'recording ministers' was dropped by Friends in England. The practice tended to be misunderstood by other churches and suggested a return to priesthood and sacraments which contradicted the spiritual democracy of the Quaker body.

The Quaker ideal sought awareness in every mind of the possibility of being the channel for Truth. A fresh and lively preaching might arise through different men and women speaking and this was welcomed but did not need to be formalised. Elizabeth Fry's contributions had an immediate appeal because of her singer's voice and slightly different way of putting things. Now almost 31, she still retained her girlish grace albeit with a hint of matronly dignity. She set an important example to other young women. There were many mothers whose domestic cares made them quite indifferent to the needs of Meeting and whose spirits were becoming stifled under piles of cookery and baby linen. Her example encouraged them to take a couple of hours off for peace and contemplation.

It was more than just an escape for Elizabeth. It gave her an opportunity to lay aside her confusing accounts, the matter of little Rachel's pert manners and whether or not baby's gums needed lancing. Another world, a world more real than this, seemed to lie beyond it.

> 'I have renewed evidence that there yet remains a
> God hearing prayer.'

To become, even in the smallest degree, the messenger of God was an overwhelming experience. It deepened in her daily the sense of God's reality that she had so often felt slipping from her. And it seemed to lead her towards that other life of which she had dreamed.

There was an unexpected disadvantage of being a 'recorded minister' as far as Elizabeth was concerned. By sitting on the 'facing benches' or 'minister's gallery', she had to watch, helplessly, the atrocious behaviour of her children. They ranged from ten down and wriggled endlessly and obviously throughout the boredom of two hours silence. No wonder an agitated mother sometimes 'broke up Meeting prematurely … my dear children behaved so badly'. Surely not many children could sit still in silence for two hours.

She knew that her new position entitled people to point the finger and accuse: 'Folk should practise what they preach' or 'Physician, heal thyself'. But when her children grew beyond babyhood, there was no denying that she found them very hard to manage. The fact that she was a 'minister' had nothing whatsoever to do with it. Had she but known it, her sister Louisa's letter to Hannah would have confirmed for her that her children were noisy, troublesome little 'brats' before she undertook any public work.

Often it was when she most wanted them to behave well that they were at their worst – romping, shouting, and quarrelling. She found it distressing but was not sure how to discipline them; she hoped that they would simply grow out of it. In the privacy of home she often found them naughty and trying and felt quite discouraged.

> 'I feel at times deeply pressed down on account
> of my beloved children. Their volatile minds try
> me but I have a secret hope concerning them –
> this all will end well.'

Her family and friends kept their criticism of her children politely under wraps for as long as they could. But when she began to speak more regularly in Meeting and started visiting other Meetings, there was uproar. What! A mother leave her family? 'But, Elizabeth, consider! Look at the results on your children!' Although it seemed okay when she went on an extensive business trip with Joseph and later visited William and Eliza Fry who had moved to Hill House at Rodborough. It was only her absences from home 'in the ministry' which were selected as evidence of neglect.

Nonetheless she was concerned by people's criticism:

'… indeed it is an awful thing to have to preach
when practice is so imperfect. I desire to examine
where I can mend towards my beloved little
ones, but it is not in my power to turn them
or alter their motives, but I must in humility
endeavour to do my best.' After she had spent a
week away with a visiting American Friend, both
Richenda and Louisa spoke to her. 'Dear Chenda
thought the children ought to be under more
subjection… Louisa thought I devoted that time
to Friends that I should devote to them.'

The family continued to criticise. Joseph John, now master
at Earlham, invited her to the inauguration of the Norwich
branch of the Bible Society where the Bishop of Norwich and
other attending clergy were astonished, but charmed, to find
a lady taking vocal part in the proceedings. She stayed some
weeks for a large family gathering and then told her maiden
sisters Rachel and Priscilla that she wanted to stay and attend
the Suffolk Quarterly Meeting.

'They of course did not like it, but dear P. cast
me very low by saying her faith was at times tried
by my so often leaving my family. This was a
home stroke.'

It seemed no one had ever felt her faith was tested when
Elizabeth left her family and rushed to nurse their various
ailments, scarlet fever, broken blood vessels, or dying parents-
in-law. But she never used this defence. She clung fast to her
conviction that she had duties outside her home as well as in
it and that she must somehow find the right balance between
them. After all, she told herself when hurt, life was short and
what did people's opinions of one matter in so short a span?

Yet she did mind. Very much. But she kept on course. She was convinced that she was not always good for her children.

> 'I indulge them too much when young… and perhaps their nurses do so too.'

She felt that occasional absences seemed to readjust her relationship with them and soothe irritated nerves on both sides. It seemed that she was not a good educator of youngsters so wilful, so determined, yet so dear. After much soul-searching, caused especially by Priscilla's upsetting words, she wrote in October 1811:

> 'My beloved children cause me much uneasiness. I fear they suffer much from my not having the knack of managing them. I often feel very low and much try'd by it. I think neither my husband nor myself have the right art with them.'

But what a nurse she was to them if they were ill. Even to her nephews and nieces, as one niece gratefully recorded:

> '… her soft hands, her sweet voice, her delicious company!'

Deplore as she might her shortcomings as a mother, hers was the largest and the most vigorous family of the Earlham stock.

The path of her life continued and she thought she saw clearly the course it was taking. It was a busy life full of opportunity and variety and it was as adventurous in its way although so different to the life of the gypsies. Plashet took up most of her time. There were house parties - 'eighteen in addition to our own family slept here last night' – garden parties, dinners. Every Sunday either Fowell Buxton and Hannah, or Sam and Louisa

Hoare, would arrive from Hampstead to visit. Or brother Sam and his Elizabeth would stroll over from her parents' home, Ham House nearby. Or all of them would turn up at once, with their increasing number of children, and create a family gathering reminiscent of the old days at Earlham.

There were grey days of course such as when the children were ill but on the whole there was an atmosphere of sunny peace which indicated, in the beginning of those middle years, that the pattern of her life was set. But for Elizabeth there were moments of restless discontent when she would write:

> 'I long... not to be a drone... I fear that my life
> is slipping away to little purpose.'

On 12 September 1812, her eighth child, Hannah was born. A month later, Napoleon began his retreat from Moscow and his Grand Army faced destruction. His Russian campaign had widespread repercussions and unsettled finances in England. There was a run on several of the private banks; even the Fry bank found itself in trouble.

When the first hint of trouble reached the peaceful security of Plashet, Elizabeth realised that she was far from indifferent to fortune.

> 'I could desire... that if right for us, we may be
> able through life to live in the open liberal way
> we do now, endeavouring to make all around us
> comfortable, and that we may be able to continue
> generous friends to the poor. I fear to be much
> limited would be very difficult to me.'

Her fear was apparent in a stark diary entry on 18 October:

> 'It appears that without help the banking-house
> must stop payment.' But less than a month

later help came: 'brothers John and Sam and Hudson and J. Overend met at M. Court to look into the real state of affairs which proved very satisfactory, all things being in such nice order and the state of the business in general so good that there appear'd no doubt Gurneys would do what was needful for us and according to human probability we should be safely carried through.'

It was a difficult time for her when she was already feeling low and unwell after Hannah's birth. To have to close Plashet for the winter and return as usual to Mildred's Court was the final straw.

'I am almost surprised at myself, the tears have often risen; very few, I believe none know, how sweet the quiet and the beauties of the country have been to me; it takes hold of some of my tender feelings.'

Destiny required her to be in London that winter. She missed the freedom of Plashet terribly and with prescience compared the greyness of London around the house in Mildred's Court to a prison.

A Spell in Prison

D URING THE winter of 1812-13 one of life's coincidences
set another milestone in Elizabeth's life. Since the
summer, a French émigré Quaker travelling in the ministry
from his home in America, had been in Britain. Stephen Grellet
was a friend of Elizabeth's mentor, William Savery. Indeed it
might well have been Grellet's continental influence which
had encouraged Savery to travel to Europe in the first place.
Although more evangelical than his friend, Grellet resembled
him in charm of address and in a passion for peace, which he
never hesitated to express, even in time of war.

It had all started in 1795 when Elizabeth was a girl of fifteen
learning her lessons, including French, and playing pranks
at Earlham. Etienne de Grellet du Mabillier, a young émigré
from the French Revolution, arrived in New York with his
brother. Their father was the son and heir of wealthy porcelain
manufacturers in Limoges and had been ennobled by Louis
XVI and made comptroller of the Mint. When the revolution
started, the Grellets found themselves on the side of the
aristocrats. Etienne, then sixteen, had served in the reserves of
the army which had hoped to restore the King. He and his
brother escaped to seek their fortune in a new world; their family

estates and fortune were lost. Their father and mother had been imprisoned in France and threatened with the guillotine, but were released the day after Robespierre's death in 1794.

With money enough to last for some time with care, the two boys altered their names to suit their new life – Etienne became Stephen and they dropped the rest of their surname. They realised they could not afford to stay in New York so left the city for Newtown, a quieter and cheaper town on Long Island. There, following their father's maxim of always seeking the best company, they called upon Colonel Corsa, whose wife was a Franklin. Stephen's good looks had been marred by smallpox but his graceful manners and interesting story won him the immediate friendship of these kind Americans who were rather proud that their daughter's French was up to the occasion. The two Grellets soon became close friends of the Corsa household and worked hard on their language skills.

As his English improved, Stephen's curiosity was aroused. He had been brought up an aristocrat, had lived through the French Revolution and was becoming a citizen of the new American republic. He wanted to know more, particularly about the country's theory of government. The intelligent Miss Corsa lent him a book called No Cross, No Crown by William Penn. Perhaps she had not read it herself, but a little work with the dictionary made it clear to Grellet that this book was not a political or social treatise, and he set it aside. Yet something in it had touched his sensitive subconscious.

A few weeks later, when walking alone in some fields, he had what he regarded as a psychic experience, the first of many. He was in a state of vague reverie, deep in thought, not religious in any way, when 'I was suddenly arrested by what seemed to be an awful voice proclaiming the words, "Eternity, Eternity, Eternity"... My whole man shook and it brought me, like Saul, to the ground'.

Once home, he opened No Cross, No Crown and struggled through it with a dictionary – twice. Then he laboured through an English Bible; although a Catholic, packing a French Bible had not been top priority as he and his brother escaped France and the guillotine. The next day a Meeting was to be held nearby and the brothers were invited. The speakers were two visiting English Friends, Rebecca Young and Deborah Darby – the same Deborah Darby of Coalbrookdale in Shropshire who, a few years later, would provide another of Elizabeth's milestones with her 'deep, clear and striking' preaching and her prophecy as to Elizabeth's future.

Deborah had a similar effect on Grellet, although during Meeting it was mainly the silence that affected him. When Friends spoke, he understood little of what was said. But he and his brother were invited to dine at Colonel Corsa's to meet the two ladies. After dinner there was a serious conversation which the eager young Frenchman found impossible to follow.

> 'I could hardly understand a word of what was said, but as D.D. began to address my brother and myself it seemed as if the Lord opened my outward ear and my heart... She seemed like one reading the pages of my heart, with clearness describing how it had been, and how it was with me... No strength to withstand the Divine visitation was left in me... I was like one introduced into a new world... my heart glowed with love to all... to be remembered as long as I have the use of my mental faculties.'

Like Elizabeth with Savery later, Grellet had many more conversations with Deborah, taking the trouble to go to places where he knew she would be found, and always had his first impression confirmed. So Stephen Grellet became a Quaker in the autumn of 1796; speaking and travelling in the ministry followed. He interpreted his extraordinary psychic powers as sensitivity to the direct and immediate 'leadings' of the Spirit of God. Often he spoke in Meeting with piercing accuracy about a person present who was a complete stranger to him. He even impressed President James Madison's wife, Dolley.

These 'leadings' drove him to the right place or person at the right time. He was 'sent' instinctively to help with the yellow fever epidemic in Philadelphia. On another occasion he was 'sent' home suddenly to his wife and family while he was in the middle of a preaching journey. He had no previous contact with them but on arrival discovered them to be seriously ill. People like Grellet, William Savery and Deborah Darby never had a dull moment; their lives were filled with interest and surprise. They were forever engaged in useful activity of which the outcome was not important to them. It was the doing which mattered. Life held no fears for them, so death had no power over them. In such 'obedience' lay a peculiar magic.

It was a fortunate chain of events which 'sent' Stephen Grellet to Elizabeth Fry. If Deborah Darby had not dug herself out of her comfortable home on the borders of Wales and taken the long voyage across the sea in pursuit of an idea, she would not have touched Grellet. He, in turn, might not have touched William Savery who, with Deborah, had touched Elizabeth in England. And now Grellet was in England to complete the circle. The ever practical Elizabeth Fry, who could not experience this mysterious, distinct 'leading' from within, was given the right impetus exactly when she needed it, sometimes from people who came from far away to give it.

As he worked his way towards London, passing from one Friends' Meeting to another, Grellet took every opportunity to

visit French prisoners. Some had been captured recently; others
had been in the country since long before the abortive Treaty
of Amiens.

'Baneful indeed is the scourge of war,' he wrote in his diary in
1812.

> 'With deep anguish of spirit I have visited this
> portion of my fellow-man… Some of them have
> been prisoners for nine years, and many, I find,
> have been brought up tenderly, even in affluence,
> having been conscripts that were forcibly taken
> from their homes, bands of whom I saw in
> France, fifty or more chained together, dragged
> as sheep to the slaughter… Some of them are
> contented in their present bonds, under the
> consideration that were they liberated and sent
> back to France, they would soon be driven again
> into the army and placed in a condition worse
> than the present.'

He told the prisoners that later he would take his message of
peace to France. And so he did, being arrested and almost killed
on a number of occasions. As a Frenchman and an American,
his position in England could have been precarious too. Britain
had been at war with both countries. There were at least two
Acts of Parliament which could have been invoked against him
– the Alien Act of 1793 for the supervision and, if necessary,
removal of aliens, and the Seditious Meetings Act of 1795.

Grellet went on his illuminated way unmolested and was,
anyway, indifferent to the dangers. The majority of his Meetings
were gospel-like and politically inoffensive. But he was a man of
intense, even passionate sympathies and his diary, like Savery's,
was packed with information about social conditions. Born in

wealthy and cultivated circles, and never having known the need for money, first by birth and then by his own ability, he nonetheless understood the wrongs and sorrows of the poor. Many travelling Friends would pass through a country with their eyes exclusively fixed on their own and others' spiritual condition. But not Grellet. He noted that in the Yorkshire and Lancashire dales, in the autumn of 1812, wheat was 22 shillings a bushel and oats twelve shillings, reducing the poor to a diet of potatoes and chaff.

> 'They knit woolen stockings; men and women
> and children, walking in the fields or highways,
> keep on knitting as fast as they can.'

Reaching London in mid-winter, he 'felt deeply for the sufferings of a large portion of the labouring class'. Unemployment was rife because of stagnation caused by war and there was a general shortage of bread throughout the whole country. The import of foodstuffs like wheat and oats had been forbidden in a mistaken effort to maintain the prosperity of agriculture by keeping up the price of home-grown products.

Grellet was deeply concerned by it all and, with the consent of London Friends who were by this time entirely under his spell, he called a Meeting in the Meeting House at St. Martin's Lane for 'thieves, pickpockets and prostitutes'. Since such people were night-hawks, the Meeting was set for seven o'clock on the evening of 19 January 1813. Amazingly, a large number of people turned up. Grellet was moved to see that they were mostly young people: 'I wept bitterly over them.' They had not expected that and it had a dramatic effect.

> 'The lofty heads, the proud looks were brought
> down. I have seldom known such brokenness...'

The Chief Police Magistrate was so impressed that he offered
to collect all the scum of London for Mr Grellet. Mr Grellet
declined, but asked instead for a permit to visit the prisons. He
spent several days at Newgate because it had

> '... religious opportunities in the many separate
> apartments where the miserable inmates are
> confined. Several were under the sentence of
> death...'

At last he had been everywhere except to the women's quarter.

> 'The visit to that part of Newgate which is
> occupied by the women prisoners had very
> nearly been frustrated. The gaoler endeavoured
> to prevent my going there, representing them as
> so unruly and desperate a set that they would
> surely do me some mischief; he had endeavoured
> in vain to reduce them to order, and said he could
> not be responsible for what they might do to me,
> concluding that the very least I might expect was
> to have my clothes torn off.'

Certain, as usual, where his duty lay, Grellet got his way. He
visited not only the women's yard, but the 'sick ones upstairs'.
He had seen much misery in his time, but what he saw there
was so beyond the limits of humanity that it seemed to him
amazing that the very gaolers could bear to leave it as it was.

> 'On going up, I was astonished beyond
> description at the mass of woe and misery I
> beheld. I found many very sick, lying on the
> bare floor or on some old straw, having very
> scanty covering over them, though it was quite

cold; and there were several children born in the
prison among them, almost naked.'

It was a cold January and he was so deeply upset that he left
the prison and went straight away to the one person he felt sure
would help.

'I went to Mildred's Court, to my much valued
friend Elizabeth J. Fry.'

He always inserted her husband's initials into her name in his
diary to distinguish her from her two sisters-in-law – unmarried
Elizabeth Fry and William's wife, Eliza. He told Elizabeth of the
horrors he had seen, stating that something had to be done
immediately for the poor children.

Elizabeth sent for material without delay and then gathered
some friends to help. They set to work with such determination
that the following day, Elizabeth arrived at the prison with a
bundle of made-up garments for the naked children. What
she saw there changed her life forever. So simply, directly and
humanly was she called to what many regarded as her life's
work.

Prison Life

NEWGATE PRISON was considered by many to be one of the most beautiful buildings in London. The prison which stood on the corner of Old Bailey and Newgate Street was burned down during the Gordon Riots of 1780 and rebuilt on the same site with a similar interior plan two years later. The architect George Dance was always bothered by windows so the outer wall of Newgate gaol had none and the building became his architectural masterpiece. The walls rose up to a cornice in plain rusticated blocks of masonry, relieved by deep shadowed niches containing eighteenth-century figures – Liberty with a French cap, and Plenty with her cornucopia. Nothing could have been less prison-like than that façade until a person saw the design of leg-irons, fetters and chains over the doorway.

The prison reformer John Howard, inspecting the place soon after it was finished, commented:

> 'All I will say is that without more than ordinary
> care, the prisoner in it will be in great danger of
> the gaol-fever'.

He himself died a few years later in Russia of gaol-fever, a typhus disease transmitted by ticks and fleas.

The design ignored decent sanitation or ventilation. The window tax prompted several windows originally planned to be sealed. [The window tax introduced in 1696 by William III lasted until 1851 and required owners of properties with over six windows to pay a levy.] Because the outer prison wall had no windows there were no through draughts. There were three quadrangles, the main one in the centre for the men, the small one on the left for debtors, and the one on the right for women. The ground-plan showed six rooms, or wards, surrounding the women's yard, for their use. The chapel, plain but neat, was in the centre of the main building. The punishment cells for difficult prisoners were underneath. Two rooms upstairs were used as infirmaries, one for men and another for women, although neither had any additional conveniences and male gaolers tended both sexes.

Prisoners sentenced to death, whether men or women, sick or well, were confined to the condemned cells. This part of the prison, Old Newgate, had survived the fire and the cells were particularly horrific. They were nine feet by six feet with a vaulted roof almost nine feet to the crown and had a small, double-grated window. The stone walls around each cell were lined with planks studded with broad-headed nails.

> Howard wrote: 'I was told by those who attended them that criminals who had affected an air of boldness during their trial, and appeared quite unconcerned at the pronouncing sentence upon them were struck with horror and shed tears when brought to these darksome solitary abodes.'

Ordinary prisoners, irrespective of age or crime, and usually known simply as 'transports' or 'fines', were locked together in several large rooms at night and allowed the use of both rooms and the yard during the day. Beer was on sale at a tap in the prison and provisions could be bought from the gaolers. Poor prisoners who depended on prison rations did badly.

Attending chapel was not compulsory and the noise of non-attenders in the yard tended to disrupt services anyway. But there was usually 100 per cent attendance at the condemned sermon, a morbid event held on the Sunday before every batch of executions.

> One particularly articulate prisoner wrote: 'Three unfortunate men were ordered for execution. On the Sunday morning they were placed in the condemned pew, with a coffin on a table in the middle. The pew is large enough to contain 30 individuals. It is in the centre of the chapel. Here the condemned are the gazing-blocks of the other prisoners and of those who paid a shilling for admission to the gallery. One of the three, a man of good position condemned for forgery, begged to be spared this final humiliation. He was told it was a necessary part of his punishment. The Chaplain preached on "Be not deceived, God is not mocked, etc"... told them they would in all probability never hear another sermon and scolded the wretches already worn to the bone with misery. Next morning at half-past seven the clergyman's voice was heard in the vaulting passages, "I am the resurrection and the life"... Christianity appears more hateful to me every time I reflect on this circumstance.'
>
> He added: 'I do not believe that there ever yet was an individual possessed of sufficient

fortitude to bear a long imprisonment with
patience. The prisoner from the moment he
enters his dungeon seems to have severed the
last link with human nature. His preconceived
horror of a prison falls far short of that which
overwhelms him when he has been a few days
a prisoner. All the courtesies of civilised society
are laid aside, and human nature, deprived of the
decent mantle of politeness, stalks before him in
naked, horrible deformity... When I first came
here even the sick men, through a whole winter,
had heavy irons about their legs.'

Male and female prisoners awaiting transportation were only
detained at Newgate until the sailing of the next available
ship to Australia. But even those under short sentences were
uncertain of the length of their stay. At the expiry of the term
set by the judge, they had to pay a fee to the gaoler before they
could be released. If they had no money they might not be
released.

This confusion added to the intense depression and tense
irritability which prevailed. There was no kindness, no humour,
no order, even of meals, and nothing to do. The only diversions
were gambling, fighting and drunkenness. Those who were
dead drunk were happiest. A nineteenth century gentleman, in
a letter to the London Chronicle, recorded:

'Sir, Of all the seats of woe on this side of hell,
few, I suppose, exceed or equal Newgate.'

So the keeper and turnkeys were understandably astonished
when Elizabeth and her friend, Anna Buxton, laden with
bundles, entered the prison and walked purposefully through
vaulted passages until at last they came to the women's yard at

the extreme southern end of the building.

Elizabeth Fry's first impression of Newgate from outside might have been one of a certain architectural beauty. But inside she found gloom, bad smells, and overwhelming pandemonium. The sounds which echoed down the vaulted passages and grew louder as she approached were hardly human. Stephen Grellet had described the women's quarters:

> 'They occupied two long rooms, where they slept in three tiers, some on the floor and two tiers of hammocks over one another... When I first entered, the foulness of the air was almost insupportable; and everything that is base and depraved was so strongly depicted on the faces of the women who stood crowded before me with looks of effrontery, boldness and wantonness of expression that for a while my soul was greatly dismayed.'

Following their guide, Elizabeth and Anna passed the barred gateway of the women's yard and were compelled to stop and look. The women, seeing visitors, pressed to the bars, stretching out desperate hands, whining, begging for pence to spend on beer at the prison tap. Those in front were fought by those behind; hands snatched them back by the hair, pinched them and punched them in the ribs with fists and elbows.

Elizabeth's wise eyes missed nothing. She had seen drunken Irish, gypsies in the extremes of poverty, the squalor of the London slums but she had never before seen a mass of women, by the hundreds, reduced to the level of wild beasts.

Even the male prisoners were shocked at the depravity they saw in the women. One of them described going to the partition dividing the men's from the women's yard.

'We looked over, and the scene was even more disgusting than in the other yards. Their manners, gestures, language, were alike indicative of vice and ignorance. One of them had blackened her face and was dancing for the amusements of her companions. Oh, my happier, more enlightened countrywomen, while you are subscribing your thousands and tens of thousands for the propagation of Christianity, little do you think what misery exists in your own land and among your own sex.'

Elizabeth gazed thoughtfully and moved on. She was there to visit the infirmary upstairs where she found all that Grellet had described. Here dwelt misery itself. Elizabeth set to work; it was just the sort of challenge she relished. After an hour or two, she and Anna had every baby snugly wrapped, every mother a little comforted, and all the sick given at least the relief of thick, clean straw between them and the bare boards.

The guards brought what Elizabeth and Anna paid for.

'You see, lady, straw an't allowed here free, nor in most prisons it an't. Prisoners gets it as pays for it. If we gave it we'd have to pay for it ourselves, and it would soon mount up, ye see.'

Elizabeth knew that there was too much to be done here, even for the immediate emergency, in one visit. The prisoners themselves needed proper winter clothing and her medical eye detected that in general soup was needed more than medicine. She had made three return visits before mentioning Newgate in her diary in February. Then, when their task was completed to the best of their ability, they said farewell and left the tearful women to their fate.

Domestic Change

B ACK ELIZABETH went to the complicated demands of her domestic life with two houses to run, her unruly children to love and increasing speaking in Meeting and travelling in the ministry. Mildred's Court had become more difficult to run since William and Eliza had moved to Gloucestershire in the hope of improving Eliza's health; her brother-in-law had provided a valuable extra pair of hands out of office hours. While the Frys were in the country at Plashet, the clerks from the business, and their staff, used Mildred's Court as a sort of dormitory so when the family was in London too, it was a double household. Her diary was filled with all these demands on her time. An entry for 15 February 1813 records:

> '... laudable persuits, more particularly seeing after the prisoners in Newgate, with Anna Buxton.'

In April the Frys returned joyfully to Plashet and country life, leaving Mildred's Court again in possession of the clerks. The children were thrilled to be back and raced wildly about the lawns and dug happily in their gardens. They rode about the countryside on their ponies just as their mother and indeed, their sometimes critical aunts had done as children at Earlham. So long as they were not rebelling against lessons or Meeting, their parents rejoiced in their various activities and high spirits.

Elizabeth sometimes found it discouraging to visit her sister Louisa at Hampstead and see how orderly and obedient her children were. Louisa had turned into an expert on juvenile education and was writing a book about it. Elizabeth, while admiring her sister's ability and the wonderful results, could not help secretly hoping, even believing, that her children would turn out just as well 'in the end'. She abhorred corporal punishment, which was widespread at the time, and would not let tutors or governesses beat her children. At one time, she visited Plashet Cottage where her spinster sister-in-law, Elizabeth, lived.

> 'Much grieved, nay shocked, so as not to have yet got over it, by an apparent accident when at the cottage to overhear sad screams from poor Johnny and to find that he had been whip'd or was whipping in a manner truly unmerciful which I stop'd, but it has left a painful remembrance.'

After all, she had not been fond of lessons herself; and Joseph was not fond of Meeting, a point which had been raised with him by the Elders much to their disquiet. But they were hardly 'whipping' matters.

Soon it was September and apple time and Elizabeth should have been in the best of spirits but she was anxious.

> 'I begin to think another child is on the way. This has also laid me low from my fearful mind, but I look upon it as one of the services of my life to bear children. The prospect of more children

is sweet at times, very sweet, but my weak nature
sadly flinches at suffering.'

To make matters worse, the Frys' financial difficulties were
far from over. Joseph came home from the city, his normally
happy face strained with worry. And although he could enjoy
a game of cricket with his boys in the fine, light evenings, he
sank into serious reflection when the children were in bed.
Alone with his wife, who always found his moods of depression
rather endearing, he confided in her his worries. He drew not
only upon her womanly comfort but also on her clear, cool
Gurney mind and talked things over with her frankly. She
offered comfort and advice but her expansive and generous
temperament hated a pettifogging economy.

> 'To cut down expenses?' She is willing, she longs
> to, but how? She feels burdened by worries. '...
> but I hope to get through: a feeling as if our
> expenses exceeded what they ought is at times
> painful... being thought much richer than we
> really are.'

As if to add to her burden, winter arrived bringing snow and
freezing temperatures. The children were delighted not to be at
Mildred's Court and to be able to skate and throw snowballs.
But Elizabeth was increasingly concerned about the poor. The
weather was so harsh and the soup being made for them in her
barn was not as thick as in former, more affluent years. She was
horrified to see one woman pour out some soup to share with
her pigs. Perhaps she misinterpreted this because even valuable
pigs have to be fed. She no longer had an unlimited store of
warm blankets and things to give away. Her thoughts returned
to the poor creatures in Newgate whom she had helped the
previous winter. But her hands were tied now in all directions.

There was so much to do, yet she could not do it. Domestic duties and financial limitations hampered her on every side. She found release occasionally by visiting Meetings.

Soon it was spring 1814 and her 34th birthday drew near. 'Thus my time slips away.' Her ninth child, Louisa, was born in June and again Rachel came to be with her:

> 'A tenderly beloved friend, a most watchful and
> valuable nurse, and a most loving sister.'

For Rachel, being part of this happy marriage and growing family opened old wounds and by the time she left she was quite depressed which made Elizabeth anxious. But she had little time to dwell on her sister's low spirits. She had a household of 'nine children, governess, tutor, eight indoor servants beside many outdoor' to administer. No wonder cutting expenses seemed prudent.

In August there was yet more sadness for the family when her brother John succumbed to the grief which had consumed him since his wife's death six years earlier and died. By December, Elizabeth was:

> '... much engaged in attending our dear Sam
> and Elizabeth's little Catherine, who has been
> dangerously ill.'

What hope was there for the remote claims of prisoners, however wretched, to compete for her attention when her life was already so full? Yet again fate was to intervene. It was drastic financial cuts which eventually freed Elizabeth for the work which even she did not yet realise would make her a household name.

In June the following year, the battle of Waterloo ended the French wars in a blaze of glory. But rather than stabilising the economy, it unsettled it more. Soldiers flooding back into the country further upset the social conditions at a time when unusually high demands for arms, munitions and manufactured goods for the war had stopped overnight. The problem was viewed later by some as proportionately as great as the aftermath of the First World War in 1918. Sir John Fortescue, the military historian, writing in The Times of 30 July 1932, said:

> 'Between 1804 and 1814 the proportion of men under arms, afloat and ashore, to the total population of Great Britain, was exactly the same as in the last war, one in fourteen.'

It seemed strange that while Fry's Bank was in difficulties, Gurneys' remained unaffected as did Overend, Gurney and Co, 'the bankers's banker'. William Fry was either unlucky or unwise in some of the firm's speculations. Joseph Fry's abilities were highly respected despite his preference for a life on the land; Sam Gurney regarded the sound training he received from his brother-in-law as the foundation for his own fortunes.

Whatever the reasons, drastic measures became necessary for many people involved in investments abroad or in manufacturing at home. Joseph told Elizabeth that they could no longer continue to support their large household. There was even talk of giving up Plashet, but neither of them could bear to do that if any other way could be found. They thought desperately of a plan which would not harm their children's present and future prospects. To compound matters, a tenth child was on the way.

My attached and obliged friend Elizth Fry

Elizabeth Fry

From a portrait by Mrs Charles Pearson

Engraved by J.J. Hinchcliff

Thomas Fowe

Elizabeth's brot

From an engraving a   *ait*
by George Ri

The young Elizabeth
Aged about nineteen
From a drawing by her friend Amelia Alderson

Earlham Hall, Norfolk (1780 - 1800)
From a lithograph after a drawing by Mrs. F. Cunningham

Mildred's Court, London (1800 - 1809)
A plaque where Mildred's Court once stood in London.

Plashet House, Essex (1809 - 1829)
From a drawing by Katherine Fry
(eldest daughter of Joseph and Elizabeth Fry)

Upton Lane House (1829 - 1845)
From a woodcut also by Katherine Fry

Joseph John Gurney
Elizabeth's brother
From an engraving after the portrait
by George Richmond

Elizabeth Fry reading to the prisoners in Newgate, 1823

From an engraving after Jerry Barrett

Joseph Fry
Elizabeth's Husband
From a portrait by C.R. Leslie, 1923

Anguish and Loneliness

A LL FINANCIAL worries were laid aside that dark winter of 1815 when their beloved, delicate daughter little Betsy fell seriously ill. Hymns and stories mixed in the lively chatter of the child's feverish state as her mother's experienced eye saw, with growing concern, increasing signs of danger. Elizabeth prayed passionately that her little one might be spared and if not, at least be spared suffering. The doctor could do no more. Joseph stayed home from the City and sat with his wife hour by hour, supporting her with his loyal devotion, his own dumb sorrow, as helplessly they watched the little ebbing life. After only seven days and yet another sleepless night, with the child in their room,

> 'Her breath grew more and more seldom and gentle till she ceased to breathe.'

The family was distraught, none more so than Elizabeth who learned the true meaning of all-consuming grief. Tears fell upon her journal for this child who died just three months before her fifth birthday: 'for losing so sweet, so kind a child... But surely not a real evil.' At least her prayers had been answered in one respect and her child had been spared suffering. Was there not a Heavenly Father who had shown 'His unutterable loving kindness to my tenderly beloved little one, who had so sweet and easy a life and so tranquil a death?' She added:

> 'Liable to the frailty of childhood, at times she would differ with the little ones, and rather loved her own way; but she was very easy to lead, though not one to be driven. She had most tender affections, a good understanding for her years, a remarkably staid and solid mind. Her love very strong to her father and me, and her little attentions great; and remarkable in her kindness to servants, poor people, and animals.'

Try as she might to come to terms with the loss, Elizabeth was heartbroken. Every morning there was a fresh stab of human agony:

> '... to awake and find my much and so tenderly beloved little girl so totally fled from my view...' Her greatest comfort was Joseph. 'My much-loved husband and I have drunk this cup together, in close sympathy and unity of feeling. It has at times been very bitter to us both... but we have in measure been each other's joy and helper.'

Spring brought new growth and new life and on 18 April 1816, Elizabeth's tenth child and fourth son, Samuel Gurney Fry was born. He would be known always as Gurney, to distinguish him from his uncle Sam Gurney, and Elizabeth was delighted with him. But little Betsy's vacancy was never filled in her mother's heart. After the sadness and finality of this loss, she found it easier to endure their comparatively trivial money worries.

Two months after Gurney's birth, she wrote in her diary:

> 'It is often the prayer of my heart that we may get
> through our difficulties and trials without others
> in any way suffering through us.' And added:
> 'My husband left me on 7th day under a heavy
> cloud, business going on so very seriously. My
> brother [in-law] William coming here to consult
> my brothers. What will be the result I know not,
> and I desire to leave it. As for our own poverty
> or our children's, though I enter into and feel its
> great seriousness, and poor Wm. and Eliza's, yet
> this is with me a very secondary consideration.'

At last plans were made. And Elizabeth found them drastic and
heart-breaking. Her two elder girls, were to go to Northrepps,
near Cromer, where unmarried sister Rachel was keeping house
for their youngest brother Daniel, then aged 25. Her two elder
boys were to stay at Earlham until after Christmas and then
go to boarding school. The next two, Richenda and Joseph,
were to be cared for by Sam and Elizabeth at Ham House and
join the disciplined schoolroom of their little cousins. That left
four-year-old Hannah, two-year-old Louisa and baby Gurney
to keep Elizabeth company.

Elizabeth was devastated at this further loss and suffered aching
loneliness. In August 1816, she wrote:

> 'I have been to Northrepps to settle my beloved
> girls with Aunt Rachel and Uncle Dan. I can
> hardly express what I feel in thus giving them
> up at so critical an age. Owing to our loss of
> property I cannot keep them at home and have
> them attended to as may be required at their
> age, either as to their heads or hearts. I should

say, give up almost any show or indulgence to have them under my wing, but this cannot be in justice and honour because we are obliged to keep up appearances for the sake of business and, situated as we are, almost every optional expense appears a breach of honesty...'

She continued: 'This should be esteem'd a providential opening for us – a truly valuable and tender sister, one who loves good and follows it – a dear brother just out of serious illness with his heart opened towards good and towards me and mine in our adversity, and these offering to take them, feed them, clothe them and educate them for nothing – I see no way but to fall in with it.'

The following month she wrote to her girls from Plashet:

'My dearest girls, After drinking tea alone in your father's little dressing-room, and taking a solitary walk, and sitting in the rustic portico at the end of the green walk, I am come to write to you, as I cannot have your company. Only think! This evening I have neither husband nor child to speak to, little Hannah being gone to tea at the cottage. I found it even pleasant to go and stand by poor old Isaac the horse, and the cows and sheep in the field, that I might see some living thing to enliven poor Plashet. The grounds look sweetly, but the cherry tree by the dining room window is cut down, which I think quite a loss. The poor little school-children, when I see them, look very smiling at me, and I suppose fancy that they will soon see you home. Poor Jones's little boy is still living; such an object of skin and bone I have hardly ever seen. I fear she is greatly distressed. Our house looks charmingly, as far I think as a house can – so clean, neat and lively – but it wants its inhabitants very much. Your most nearly [closely] attached mother, E.F.'

In her next letter she was making plans for their return the following spring 1817 if all went well. 'I mean that you shall have a certain department to fill in the house among the children and the poor, as well as your own studies and enjoyments; I think there was not often a brighter opening for two girls... Your little room is almost a temptation to me to take it for a sitting-room for myself, it is so pretty and so snug; it is newly furnished and looks very pleasant indeed... And I shall be glad to have the day come when I can introduce you into prisons and hospitals.'

For her sons she could not resist writing out a set of 'Rules for a Boy at Boarding School', something which no doubt they hoped to ignore.

Something which Elizabeth could not ignore was the bleak prospect of winter at Mildred's Court without the comfort of her own bustling household. But by Christmas she and Joseph had settled into town life again. Elizabeth Fry's critics have accused her of getting rid of her children in order to get on with her public work. But it seems that events conspired to leave a woman used to being active and extraordinarily busy with time on her hands. Apart from family and domestic matters, and visiting Meetings, she had done little public work for the past few years. But as winter drew on, she found her thoughts returning constantly to the troubled women of Newgate.

The benevolent nineteenth century was blossoming and theories of the perfect social order were bandied to and fro. Her brothers-in-law Sam Hoare and Fowell Buxton and others could see the magnitude of the evils; could inquire into the causes; could see that legislation was necessary. She listened enthusiastically to their views, particularly to Fowell Buxton's intelligent arguments and had high hopes of his entering parliament. Over a period of three years they had invited Elizabeth on separate occasions to accompany them on visits to various prisons in London. Indeed, on one occasion she took two of her children and discovered afterwards to her horror that there had been scarlet fever in the prison. It was a lesson well learned. But she had gained as good a glimpse of the magnitude of prison problems as Hoare and Fowell Buxton who, during 1816, helped to form the Society for the Reformation of Prison Discipline.

The increase in crime, the horrors of prison and transportation, and of the death penalty, were frequent topics of conversation on family Sundays at Mildred's Court or Plashet. But where to begin in all this evil? The far-seeing theorist sometimes overlooked the small beginning. Elizabeth respected men but had confided in her diary many years previously that although she thought men were cleverer than women she felt women's judgement was equal to that of men 'in most if not all cases'. She accepted that prison reform, indeed social reform in general, was a matter for parliament. But her quiet opinions, backed by fact and observation, had their influence. And while the arguments and discussions flowed around her, she decided to take action.

Return to Newgate

S O IT was that she went down to Newgate prison that cold
January day in 1817, four years after her first visit, not
because she had decided to take up prison reform, but because
she had thought, at last, of something practical which she could
do to help. She went to make human contact with the prisoners;
to take a hands-on approach.

She was not afraid when she went into the women's yard and
the turnkeys could see only the tip of her white cap. Curiosity
might be as dangerous as violence in a rough crowd but no one
was snatching. Quaker dress was not provocative. There were no
feathers, no flying fancy scarves to tempt mischievous or greedy
fingers. It was an outward and visible mark of religion and these
women, like most prisoners, respected religion whether or not
they were believers themselves.

Elizabeth knew she was in danger, particularly if she showed
fear or said or did the wrong thing. But she had never been
less afraid in her life. She picked up a scruffy little child who
immediately started to finger her watch chain. She lifted her
hand for attention and there was silence.

> 'Friends, many of you are mothers. I too am a
> mother. I am distressed for your children. Is there

not something we can do for these innocent little
ones? Do you want them to grow up to become
prisoners themselves? Are they to learn to be
thieves and worse?'

She had gained their attention. Save their children? Sobs and
tears answered her appeal. They gave her a chair, and brought
their children to show her. What tales they told in their simple
way of wickedness, remorse, injustice and despair. Elizabeth
remained with them for hours. She tried to cheer them as
best she could. When at last she was ready to leave and the
barred gate was opened for her, she left behind a strange new
inhabitant at Newgate, one usually abandoned at its doors; that
reviver of human spirit, hope.

What was behind Elizabeth Fry's determined visit to Newgate
that winter's day? It was very simple. Hardly anyone could
possibly have disagreed with it. It required no Act of Parliament,
nor any great outlay of money. She wanted simply to start a
school in Newgate for the children of prisoners and for juvenile
criminals. The idea appeared to her so natural, so modest that
she didn't think it necessary to get help from her eminent
brothers-in-law or the Prison Reform Committee. With clarity
of vision, common sense and practical simplicity, she took
the shortest way to achieve her aim. She sought help from the
women themselves and initiated the most genuine 'reform'
of that period, putting herself light years ahead of the most
advanced thinkers of her time.

When she returned to the prison she was already welcomed as an
old friend. Lost manners returned to the women in response to
her serene courtesy. Proudly they introduced the schoolmistress
they had chosen from among their number, a young woman
called Mary Connor, recently convicted of stealing a watch, but
in other respects well qualified to teach the children. Elizabeth

praised their progress and discussed with them in detail the
necessary rules that would have to be established for the school.
She couldn't proceed without a promise of their complete
cooperation. Armed with this assurance and with a list of
suggestions and regulations, she approached the authorities.

The two Sheriffs of London, the Chaplain, or Ordinary of
Newgate and the Governor met her at Governor's House. It was
one of those occasions when Elizabeth felt it was an advantage
to be regarded as 'richer than we really are'. Only a lady of
wealth and standing could have got access to these important
men. As it was, they listened politely but with the usual official
attitude: her plan was a very nice one – it did both her heart
and mind credit but alas Mrs Fry did not know Newgate as they
did. These bad women were incorrigible, irretrievable. It simply
would not work. Mrs Fry remained serene and suggested an
experimental trial. The badgered gentlemen promised to look
into it and to see her again.

At their second meeting, they expressed their regret but the
experiment was impossible; after a thorough examination of
the prison, they were assured that there was not a single room
which could be spared. With astuteness and a display of her
childhood obstinacy, Elizabeth persuaded the gentlemen to
stand by their statement that the lack of a room was their only
objection. Then, politely, she withdrew and went straight to
her allies, the women prisoners. To state her problem to them
was to solve it. They felt they had space to spare. One of the
smaller rooms was considered, by common consent, to be
suitable. Elizabeth returned serenely to the Sheriffs and was
told she could take the room if she liked and try her benevolent
but surely hopeless experiment.

The following day the little room became Newgate's first school.
Elizabeth was as impatient to begin as the prisoners themselves;

she could never see the virtue of delay! She left the women busily tidying and preparing their children and themselves for their big chance. The next day she returned with her friend Mary Sanderson; both laden with old school-books. Mary Connor was installed as teacher and the school was opened formally.

In this casual way, Elizabeth Fry began a simple project which within a few months had grown to a dimension that made her famous. Within three years, it put her in correspondence, as a prison advisor, with most of the crowned heads of Europe. And after her death, it secured her place as one of the most remarkable women of history.

It was typical of her that when she finally found time to mention it in her diary on 24 February, she wrote about a concern rather than her achievements.

> 'I have lately been much occupied in forming a school in Newgate for the children of the poor prisoners, as well as the young criminals which has brought much peace and satisfaction with it; but my mind has been deeply affected in attending a poor woman who was executed this morning. I visited her twice. This event has brought me into much feeling, attended by some distressingly nervous sensations in the night... This poor creature murdered her baby: and how inexpressibly awful to have her life taken away! The whole affair has been truly afflicting to me: to see what poor mortals may be driven to, through sin and transgression, and how hard the heart becomes, even to the most tender affections. How should we watch and pray, that we fall not by little and little, and become hardened and commit greater sins.'

She rarely gave much space in her journal to her practical activities. She wrote either because 'my mind is full and wants relief' or because she wanted to induce in herself a particular state of mind. As such, without the diaries of others, there would be little information about what she did in Newgate. It was Mary Sanderson's report to Fowell Buxton which mentioned that even on the very first day of school, another, larger, problem presented itself.

Thirty pupils, mostly children of seven and under, were enrolled; the size of the room prevented more. But the door was besieged with girls in their teens and women in their twenties and older, beseeching with tears to be allowed in and taught. It was heart-breaking to dash their hopes and deny what seemed to Elizabeth to be so basic a right, and so necessary. She comforted herself – and them – by promising that this problem, caused by lack of space, would be temporary. She would try to do something for them, if they would be patient and help her to plan. In her daily visits to the school, with various friends, she witnessed the appalling life of the prison yard from many angles. There was no question now of danger; she was known by all, respected by everybody and loved by many. But she saw and heard everything and was acutely aware of all kinds of filth, drunkenness and degradation. She knew that, under the care of men gaolers, the utmost abuses were rife. She knew that male prisoners were let into the women's quarters at night. She knew things 'too bad to tell' so that she never dared take any young people there. But she was neither apathetic towards nor afraid of horror. And she neither despised nor despaired. Her eyes and ears, her heart and mind, were wide open; the question that she asked herself, and the women, was: 'What can be done?'

The more intelligent ones told her the very first day what they needed – employment. And that they wanted to be taught to read and to sew. A third of the women prisoners were unable to read at all; another third could read a little. The enforced idleness, the dreadful boredom of prison was worse to them than its other miseries. It was itself a direct incentive to vicious behaviour as a relief from intolerable monotony.

She wanted to start a school for the women but there were difficulties to be overcome. They wished to sew – admirable. But sew what? Clothes for their children and for themselves. But then what? None of them had thought beyond that. Elizabeth decided they should sew things to sell. And being herself of the merchant class, her next questions were: sell to whom, and by what means? Money would be needed to buy the initial materials. Where was that money going to come from?

This time she turned initially to family. She spoke to Fowell Buxton and Sam Hoare but to her distress they threw cold water on the whole idea. Quite, quite impossible. All materials given out to prisoners for such work would be stolen. The women, even if they did a little work at first, would soon be tired of it. Countrywomen, accustomed to labour, might persevere but most of these Newgate prisoners were the very scum of the city. They had been prostitutes and thieves from their young days, whose every friend, connection and influence was of the lowest criminal description. Old habits and violent passions would soon assert themselves. Elizabeth and her friends would only waste their time and money and get their feelings hurt by attempting such an extraordinary experiment. What authority would they use against creatures who had already defied the laws of the land? What punishment could they appeal to in order to subdue beings already under penalty?

No punishment at all, said Elizabeth, upset but defiant. It was no use even Fowell Buxton speaking to her in his large, noble and emphatic way about female felons. She regarded them as women, as human beings. If Fowell Buxton and his Prison Reform Committee could not help her, she would form her own committee and find the money themselves. Several of her friends had already become actively interested in the Newgate school. She summoned ten of them, all of them Quakers except for her friend Mrs Angelzaark, the clergyman's wife from Plashet, and explained her predicament. Under her leadership, the ten ladies formed the Ladies' Association for the Improvement of Female Prisoners in Newgate, shortened to the Ladies Newgate Committee.

They agreed to take turns in going daily to Newgate to supervise and instruct the women, to provide funds for the necessary work materials until the authorities could be persuaded to help, and to arrange the sale of the women's work. Also they agreed to pay the salary of a matron who would be on duty night and day.

Elizabeth had her plans fully shaped before she approached the entrenched conservatism of authority. She wanted to be sure that she was fully prepared for each likely objection. But now that she had to take that further step and actually approach the authorities, she dreaded it.

> 'My mind and time have been much taken up by Newgate and its concerns. I have been encouraged about our school, but I find my weak nature and proneness to be so much affected by the opinions of man brings me into some peculiar trials and temptations: in the first place our Newgate visiting could no longer be kept secret, which I endeavoured that it should be, and therefore I am exposed to praise that I do not the least deserve; also to some unpleasant humiliations – for in trying to obtain helpers I must be subject to their various opinions! And also, being obliged to confer at times with strangers and men in authority is to me a very unpleasant necessity.'

It was Joseph who came to the rescue. He alone knew that beneath the stately air, the slower movement of the handsome woman of 37, there beat a heart that was still subject to girlish terror. When it became evident that the development of affairs in Newgate would require further sanction and co-operation from the Governor and Sheriffs, he invited the daunting officials to meet his wife in the wealthy atmosphere of his own house and under the dignity of his protection.

Not that Joseph Fry was a dignified man in the same way as the Gurneys or Fowell Buxton. They had natural elegance. But Joseph was a man of consequence. His stocky figure was well known in the City, and it meant money. It meant credit and honesty and success. Fry's Bank, backed by Gurneys', was to weather the storm for some time yet. And in those days it gave a wife authority when her husband showed openly that he favoured her activities.

So it was at home at Mildred's Court where she once thought herself reduced to 'a careworn wife and mother' that Elizabeth Fry finally embraced her new career. The gentlemen came for the meeting. They listened, they argued, they discouraged; and then they consented. Allowing the children's school in the first place had been the thin edge of the wedge. Elizabeth's new proposals were driving the wedge in a little further. Soon prison administration would be altered forever.

Shortly after the meeting, at Elizabeth's suggestion, the gentlemen met the ladies at Newgate. Over 70 women prisoners gathered and Elizabeth spoke to them. She reminded them that only by their co-operation could their wishes be fulfilled, and that if they were to be taught and employed as she hoped, they had to keep to certain rules so that everything could be organised for the good of everyone. She told them that the ladies who proposed to come and help to teach them and provide them with work would do so without any authority over them. It was not intended that they should order and the prisoners obey, but that everyone should work together. Rules had to be set and monitors appointed by unanimous agreement and these rules had to be read aloud and put to the vote. She invited the women to ask questions and comment freely. Then she read the rules, which they had discussed beforehand during many visits, and each rule was voted on separately by a show of hands. They were all unanimously adopted. The Governor made a brief speech of confirmation, reminding the prisoners that this innovation was an experiment and only their good conduct would justify its future. He then turned to Mrs Fry and her committee with a shrug and a gesture – 'Well, ladies, you see your materials!' One of the ladies replied and then closed the proceedings by reading the parable of the Prodigal Son.

The rules mainly concerned organisation. A matron was to be appointed for general supervision. The women were to be provided with materials and instruction in needlework, knitting and other suitable employment. Following the Lancasterian method, they were to be divided into classes or small groups of twelve or less with a monitor over each. The monitors were to be chosen by the women themselves from those among them who could read and who showed themselves capable of responsibility. A yard keeper was to be elected by the women to inform them when their friends came to visit them and to accompany them to the grating and ensure they only spent time there with their friends. This was to enforce the rule that begging, drinking and other bad habits should be given up.

At 9am and 6pm the women were to assemble in the workroom for a short Bible reading by one of the visiting ladies, and to have the work for the day distributed or collected. The monitors were to keep a check on the work of their groups and the matron was to double-check this by an exact account of all the work done by the women, and of their conduct. The monitors had to ensure that their women arrived with clean hands and faces and behaved quietly while at work. Any monitor found to be unsuitable was to be changed and a more suitable member of the group elected in her place.

No penalties were attached to these rules. Any infringement was reported to the matron but Elizabeth and her ladies had no power to punish and the matron was, from the outset, their employee. Later, Elizabeth introduced a system of rewards for good behaviour, the loss of these rewards being the only punishment. Governor Newman, by now completely under Elizabeth Fry's gentle spell, sent his carpenters to clean, whitewash and fit up the prison laundry as a workroom. And it was here that Elizabeth started another of her schools and in this one she certainly had some 'imps'! It was a strange parallel that this school, her most famous, and her first school at Earlham, relatively unknown, each had about 70 pupils.

It was an indication of prison hygiene at Newgate that the laundry should have been made available so readily as a school room. There was no bedding or table linen to be laundered and the prisoners wore their own clothes, such as they were. Large houses such as those Elizabeth had known had much higher standards of cleanliness and considerable amounts of laundry. However in many large country houses at the time, it was the custom to have a major washing week once in every five. Hence, the laundry room would be free for weeks at a time and this may have been partly the case at Newgate.

After a month, the Lord Mayor of London, the Sheriffs and several Aldermen were invited to the laundry to see how Mrs Fry's school was progressing. Many knew Newgate, had visited it a few months earlier and had not forgotten the painful impressions made by scenes of misery and depravation.

What they saw now, without exaggeration, could be called a transformation. Gone were the abandoned, shameless creatures, half naked and half drunk, demanding rather than requesting charity. Instead the 'hell on earth' seemed like an industrious group or a well-regulated family. The gentlemen immediately adopted the whole plan as part of the system of Newgate, empowered the ladies to punish wrong-doers with a short detention, undertook part of the expense of the matron and said very flattering and enthusiastic things to Elizabeth and her helpers.

The grand jury of the City of London drew up the following memorandum in February 1818:

> 'They cannot conclude their report without expressing in an especial manner the peculiar gratification they experience in observing the important service rendered by Mrs Fry and her friends, and the habits of religion, order, industry and cleanliness which her humane, benevolent and praiseworthy exertions have introduced among the female prisoners; and that if the principles which govern her regulations were adopted towards the males, as well as the females, it would be the means of converting a prison into a school of reform; and instead of sending criminals back into the world hardened in vice and depravity, they would be restored to it repentant and probably become useful members of society.'

Patchwork was the first commercial sewing stitched by the women of Newgate. Once their own sewing needs, and those of their children, had been satisfied, they launched into the new work with relish. Thousands of scraps of material in various cloths and textures were given freely by Quaker merchants in the drapery trade, led by Francis Eveleigh who had married Elizabeth's friend Anna Savory. Patchwork was good work for beginners, it was bright and cheerful in the prison, was inexpensive to provide and found a ready market.

There was a demand for it in the remote colony of New South Wales. It seemed ironic that prisoners in a major convict settlement the other side of the world should have their needs supplied by prisoners at Newgate in London. Perhaps the exiles in a strange and different world were comforted by the homeliness of a patchwork quilt, the colours and patterns taking them back to their childhood in England.

Dixon and Co of Fenchurch Street handled most of this trade. When Elizabeth visited them they had given at once a ready guarantee to purchase all that the prisoners could supply. Knitted goods, especially stockings, were saleable too. In directing the Newgate prisoners' products to New South Wales, she was trying to avoid competition at home while at the same time sending the work to what she considered to be a logical destination. The money earned by the prisoners was mostly saved for them for the day of their release or transportation. But Elizabeth knew well the value of the immediate and the tangible. To prisoners, as to children, a penny in the hand was worth many in a bank. Some payment for their work while still in prison would be a fair reward as well as a powerful incentive to work. Let them especially be allowed to buy tea and sugar. Within two years she would record:

> 'There is now a little shop in Newgate for harmless articles of food and other useful articles for the prisoners to buy.'

Elizabeth was conscious of possible problems arising from paying prisoners for their work during a period of serious unemployment outside the prison walls. She was the daughter, sister and wife of able businessmen and had sharp instincts. It was before the days of trade unions but she was wary of competing with local manufacturers and undercutting local rates. Her views held firm all the same.

> '... the benefit which society derives from the employment of criminals greatly outweighs the inconvenience which can possibly arise to the mass of our labouring population from the small proportion of work done in our prisons.'

The speed with which her reforms became established was quite astonishing. On 12 April 1817, she wrote:

> 'I have found in my late attention to Newgate a peace and prosperity in the undertaking that I seldom, if ever, remember to have felt before. A way has been opened for us beyond all expectations to bring into order the poor prisoners: those who are in power are so very willing to help us – in short the time appears to be come to work among them. Already, from being wild beasts, they appear harmless and kind.'

A vivid account of the changes within the prison came from a gentleman visitor:

> 'I obtained permission to see Mrs Fry, and was taken to the entrance of the women's wards. On my approach, no loud or angry voices indicated

that I was about to enter a place which had long been known as "Hell above ground". The courtyard into which I was admitted, instead of being peopled with beings scarcely human... presented a scene where stillness and propriety reigned. I was conducted by a decently dressed person, the newly appointed yards-woman, to the door of a ward, where, at the head of a long table, sat a lady belonging to the Society of Friends. She was reading aloud to about sixteen women prisoners, who were engaged in needlework around it. Each wore a clean-looking blue apron and bib, with a ticket having a number on it suspended from her neck by a red tape... Instead of a scowl or ill-suppressed laugh, their countenances wore an air of self-respect and gravity, a sort of consciousness of their improved character and the altered position in which they were placed. I afterwards visited the other wards, which were counterparts of the first.'

Elizabeth was delighted to find she had ample funds for her work. Joseph had always been a generous provider for her private, household and charitable concerns, but now that his resources were limited, she hesitated to ask him for money. Instead her cousin Hudson Gurney, her uncle Robert Barclay and, above all, her wealthy brothers came to her help. Even the Sheriffs in their new enthusiasm subscribed £80.

Family Interlude

E LIZABETH FELT that things were going smoothly at Newgate enough for her to have a break. It was spring and the stagnant air of the prison was becoming claustrophobic. The flower-sellers of London were hawking primroses at the street corners and Joseph and Elizabeth were filled with nostalgia for Plashet and for their children.

First there was Yearly Meeting to be attended. Mildred's Court had to offer its usual hospitality in spite of the Frys' straightened means. Afterwards Elizabeth felt low and discouraged from all the criticism by Friends as to the questionable wisdom of her public duties. But there were joys to come.

> 'We have been daily watching with some anxiety for a letter to say when we were to expect you... Indeed we long to have you all once more around us. We are a little like children at school, counting the days till the holidays,' wrote the eager mother.

Plashet was open and ready in early June when the dog-roses bloomed and the happy parents welcomed their children home. Elizabeth's life swung back into its domestic orbit with greater

demands than usual because of fewer servants and no governess.
It may even have crossed her mind that it was easier to run a
prison than to run a boisterous family.

> 'June 28ᵗʰ [1817], I am alone at home with my
> nine children, a great and very precious charge;
> at times they appear too much for me, at others
> I greatly enjoy them; I desire that the anxiety for
> their welfare and to have them in order, should
> not prevent my enjoying thankfully the blessing
> of being surrounded by so sweet a flock.'

There was further joy in September when the family gathered
at Earlham for the marriage of Joseph John, then aged 29, to
Jane Birkbeck. The previous year, Elizabeth's sister Richenda
had married her handsome clergyman, Francis Cunningham.
They had a church wedding and Richenda had been given
away by cousin Hudson Gurney – all quite unsettling for her
impressionable young nieces. The more the family came to
love the charming Reverend Cunningham, the more difficult
it became to keep rebellious young Quakers in line. Already
Elizabeth had noticed a change in her daughters Katherine
and Rachel who were living within visiting distance of the
Cunninghams and were under the non-Quaker influences of
guardians Uncle Dan and Aunt Rachel.

By Christmas, the Frys were back at Mildred's Court and
Elizabeth was once more in the thick of things at Newgate. But
she was concerned about her children.

> 'A remarkable blessing still appears to accompany
> my prison concerns; perhaps the greatest
> apparent blessing on my deeds that ever attended
> me... but my beloved children do not appear

sufficiently under the influence of religion.
I am ready to say, oh! That I could prosper at
home in my labours as I appear to do abroad.
Others appear to fear for me that I am too much
divided.'

But as many a modern working mother has found, that
division preserved a balance in her life. For Elizabeth, it kept
her incurably and triumphantly an amateur. She never became
a professional reformer. Efficient though she was, her husband
and her children preserved her softness. To the end of her life
people felt her fascination before they felt her ability. And when
a tug of duties presented itself, the public duty gave way to the
personal. Indeed what may have preserved her gentleness and
her spontaneity in the first flush of her success at Newgate was
that she had to keep returning to Mildred's Court to breast feed
her baby, Gurney.

That winter, a storm of publicity began to bombard her. What
a comfort then that her erstwhile naughty little daughters,
un-Quakerly though they may have felt, were proud and glad
to help their mother with the mass of correspondence which
poured in from every side. Katherine and Rachel were seventeen
and fifteen years old respectively and proved to be very efficient
secretaries. No doubt their father helped set up a system in a
business-like way and may even, in an overwhelming emergency,
have released a clerk to help. Letters came from dignitaries all
over the British Isles, and from the Continent, asking 'How?'

Newgate was suddenly on the map of Europe.

Further Reform

JUST A year after she founded her school at Newgate, Elizabeth received an historic summons. She was called to give evidence before a Committee of the House of Commons on the Prisons of the Metropolis. She was the first woman other than a queen to be called into the councils of the government in an official manner to advise them on matters of public concern.

It was February 1818 and King George III, although in declining health, was still on the throne; his son had been Prince Regent since 1811. The only respectable paid occupation open to an educated woman was that of governess. The right to vote was still limited to the higher taxpayers among men and the dream of ever granting it to women had hardly dawned in the boldest minds.

Yet the early nineteenth century was remarkable for the growing influence of women on national affairs. Elizabeth Fry, Caroline Norton, Harriet Martineau and Florence Nightingale each left her mark indelibly on the course of English law. The beautiful Caroline Norton fought for and won the legal right of a mother to share in the company and education of her children after separation from a brutal husband. While Harriet Martineau, through her journalism and writing, proved an ardent advocate of social reform. On the whole, these women used intelligence and information, clarity of mind and a firm purpose as their weapons, rather than beauty or charm.

Elizabeth Fry was the forerunner of these women and was the most shy although she was learning to manage her timidity. She took her parliamentary summons in a spirit of typical simplicity. She was nervous; she dreaded it, but when the time came she found, as before, that nerves calmed and poise and self-confidence took over. She had no fear of being caught out. She knew what she had done, what she wanted to do and what had to be done in future. She had moved from the particular to the general. And she viewed this meeting with representatives of the House of Commons as an opportunity.

How much she knew of past efforts at prison reform was unclear. John Howard, her immediate predecessor in prison reform, had died when Elizabeth was just ten. He left behind a book as large as a dictionary, a sort of encyclopaedia of prisons. In 1774 he had given evidence before the Bar of the House of Commons and some of his reforms had been incorporated into law already, though not enforced. Strangely his name is not mentioned in Elizabeth's journals and his book was not among her lists of reading. But she must have known about him and had probably discussed his work with her brothers-in-law. There were similarities in some respects between their recommendations although there were also sharp differences. For a start, Elizabeth was only concerned with women prisoners whose needs clearly were so different from men's. Also, although an advocate of the value of occasional solitude and privacy, she disapproved strongly of solitary confinement for prisoners.

Howard believed in separate cells for each prisoner, both day and night. He believed in the value of silence, solitude and meditation to enable contemplation and reform. Indeed he

practised them with disastrous effect on his only son. He left
this principle as a terrible legacy to the boys of Christ's Hospital
whose solitary punishment dungeons, instigated by Howard,
were responsible for cases of hysteria and insanity. His system of
solitary confinement continued throughout history to be one
of the most dreaded and dehumanising punishments in prisons
and elsewhere.

One problem that Elizabeth did not have when the day arrived
to visit Westminster was what to wear. Current fashions were
extravagant – hugely puffed out sleeves, feathered bonnets,
and elaborate hair styles. Thank heaven for Quaker dress. It
was restful, un-provocative, neutral, sometimes pretty in its
simplicity. The type of Quaker cap she wore was described by
a contemporary as being like a Phrygian bonnet. They were
conical shaped and also called Liberty Caps as worn by the US
and French revolutionaries.

Elizabeth's cap was no doubt a simple, if distinctive affair and
she entered parliament feeling, on the whole, self-possessed.
She was described later that year by a Scotswoman meeting her
for the first time as:

> 'Tall – thin – sedate with a physiognomy gentle
> but very observant… [Her] voice and manners are
> delightful… free and unembarrassed… Really,
> I never before felt anything like inspiration or
> enchantment.'

And so she must have appeared to the austere committee which
greeted her in a large room warmed by a glowing coal fire.
There she sat, with her free and gracious manners, in the simple
dignity of her dress, and answered the gentlemen's questions
and ventured to give her own opinions. Speaking at Meeting
had given her good training. Her answers and remarks were

neither flurried nor wordy; nor could they have been clearer. She wanted women warders for women prisoners and better still, an entirely separate prison for women. The College of Physicians, immediately behind Newgate, was shortly to be sold – and she had her eye on it for just this purpose.

The experiment at Newgate or as Elizabeth called it 'our institution' had been working well.

> 'Our rules have certainly been occasionally broken, but very seldom... I think I may say we have full power amongst them [the women], for one of them said it was more terrible to be brought up before me than before the judge, though we use nothing but kindness. I have never punished a woman during the whole time, or even proposed a punishment to them; and yet I think it is impossible, in a well-regulated house, to have rules more strictly attended to.'

> She continued: 'They knit from about 60 to a 100 pairs of stockings and socks every month; they spin a little... They have made twenty thousand articles of wearing apparel the generality of which is supplied by the slop-shops, which pay very little. The earnings of work, we think, average about 18 pence per week for each person.'

Charles Dickens, in *David Copperfield,* used the word 'slop-shop' for dealers in second-hand clothes. Probably the prisoners' work was mending and repairing as well as making cheap, coarse garments for the poor.

The economic factors of supply and demand, of profiteers and middlemen, were a challenge for Elizabeth and her committee.

But she refused to put a gloss on the facts. It had to be better to be occupied in useful and interesting work than to have nothing to do. It was better to be underpaid than to be paid nothing. She refused to believe that the labour and pay rate of less than 100 prisoners could make that much difference to the unemployment situation or the underpayment of labour in general at that time.

> 'My idea with regard to the employment of women is that it should be a regular thing, undertaken by Government; considering (though I perhaps am not the person to speak of that) that there are so many to provide for; there is the Army and the Navy, and so many things required for them; why should not the Government make use of the prisoners?'

She made it clear that of course the government should pay them a fair rate and allow them the immediate use of part of their earnings. Asked if she thought that any rehabilitation could be accomplished without employment, she replied:

> 'I should believe it impossible. We may instruct as we will but if we allow them their time and they have nothing to do, they naturally must return to their evil practices.'

Another advantage of profitable employment in prison was that it could be continued when prisoners were released; it provided a discharged prisoner with a possible means of living. Elizabeth offered an example:

> '... a poor woman for whom we have obtained a pardon... We taught her to knit in the prison.

She is now living respectably out of it, and in
part gains her livelihood by knitting.'

Classification of prisoners was absolutely necessary to keep
criminals apart from first offenders, and small crimes from
more wicked ones; but above all to segregate the prostitutes.
The crowding of all the prisoners together, night and day was a
very bad practice, especially at night.

'If I may be allowed to state it, I should
prefer a prison where women were allowed
to work together in companies, under proper
superintendence; to have their meals together
under proper superintendence, and their
recreation also. But I would always have them
separated in the night. I believe it would conduce
to the health both of body and mind.'

Solitary confinement? Never, or almost never 'only in very
atrocious cases.' And then not for long. Carefully Elizabeth
returned the gentlemen's thoughts to what she had in mind.

'If there were a prison fitted up for us, which
we might visit as inspectors, if employment were
found for our women, little or no communication
allowed with the city, and room given to class
them,' she said. With only female officers and
wardens, except for doctor and chaplain, and
all well fed and clothed, then – 'if there were a
thousand of the most unruly women, they would
be in excellent order in one week; of that I have
not the least doubt.' And what was more, 'many
of those, now the most profligate and worst
characters, would turn out valuable members of
society.'

The gentlemen were impressed. After Elizabeth left them, they wondered how much of the reform in Newgate was due to admirable ideas applicable anywhere and enforceable by government, and how much was due to the unique personal quality of Mrs Elizabeth Fry. They drew up a cautious minute:

> 'The benevolent exertions of Mrs Fry and her friends in the female department of the Prison have indeed, by the establishment of a school, by providing work and encouraging industrious habits, produced the most gratifying change. But much must be ascribed to unremitting personal attention and influence.'

Meanwhile Elizabeth was concerned that an un-Quakerly vice might return to haunt her. What with all the newspaper publicity, and the letters of admiration and requests for advice, and being consulted by sheriffs and members of parliament, she might become unduly puffed-up.

> 'I fear I make the most of myself and carry myself rather as if I was somebody amongst them.' But it was clear, she comforted herself, that when dealing with these uppish gentlemen 'a degree of this sort of conduct appears almost necessary.'

Convict Ships

THE GOVERNMENT was not too keen to build new prisons; they were costly. Transportation or death were still its favourite, and cheaper, remedies for crime. There had been plenty of room for undesirables in some of the American colonies but American independence had closed that opening. Australia had become the favourite destination; it still had plenty of room and convicts disliked it even more because it was so very far from home.

In 1770, when Captain Cook anchored the *Endeavour* off the coast and took possession of New South Wales in the name of the British Crown, he was touched almost to poetry by its flowers and plant life. 'The great quantity of plants which Mr Banks and Dr Solander collected in this place induced me to give it the name of Botany Bay.' Such a lyrical name became synonymous later with the terror, loneliness and misery of the convicts. None of the world's waters bore so frequently a load of human misery as the broad, shallow waters of that bay, once a paradise of nature.

Some 548 men and 188 women were aboard the eleven ships of the First Fleet which brought Britain's first convicts to colonise this barely explored region in 1787. By 1868 when convict transportation ceased, about 165,000 men, women and children of the so-called 'criminal class' had been exiled to Australia. Colonists and settlers obtained convicts as labourers from the authorities; their state was little better than slavery. Women as well as men were absorbed into this system which so often ended in cruelty and degradation. On the complaint of their masters, against which there was no appeal, men could be sentenced to a flogging by the magistrates. Offences ranged from insubordination and rudeness to negligence in grooming a horse.

There were instances on record of wives who had followed their convict husbands out to the colony and taken up land and had their husbands assigned to them as labourers. These situations could have led to freedom and peace. But sometimes, either corrupted by their new powers, or by greed, or perhaps in a spirit of revenge for former cruelties, the women ordered their own husbands to be flogged.

The British government remained indifferent; it was only interested in getting the wretches out of England. Its interest in prisoners ended at the dock-side or, perhaps, even earlier, in prison. Many convicts were already ill before travelling and needed clothes and bedding. Inevitably, many died during the voyage.

By the time Elizabeth came in contact with convict ships in 1818, the colonisation was well underway. One day she found the Newgate gaolers in a state of nerves. They explained that there was always a riot in the prison the night before a transport. The women all went mad, got drunk, tore things up, broke and set fire to all they could and fought all comers. Only by brute force and putting them in irons could they be loaded into the wagons which were to take them down to the ship. Even putting on the irons could be a dangerous and difficult business, complained the gaolers; they were sensitive to being scratched and spat at.

For the fettered women, a trip to the docks in the open wagons was hellish. Apart from the general fear of a terrifyingly long journey into the unknown, the wagons were often pursued and surrounded by a yelling, jeering, catcalling, mud-flinging mob.

Elizabeth was horrified. Quietly she obtained as many facts as possible and then went to the Governor and asked to be given control of the situation. She stipulated that there should be no irons and no open wagons. The prisoners must be taken to the dockside in closed hackney coaches. The Governor, now her loyal and admiring friend, consented, though with dubious warnings.

The night before the transport, Elizabeth stayed with her women until late, reading to them in her mellifluous voice, comforting them, making plans for the voyage and for their future and, above all, promising to go with them all the way to the ship. Instead of a night of riot and wickedness, it was a night of sad farewells. The women who were to remain made a collection for those who were to go and generously pressed it on them. Friendship and pity had come to dwell at Newgate, along with self-respect.

The next day, Elizabeth and some of her ladies came early to the prison. The 'transports' climbed soberly into the closed hackney coaches, trusting in the protection of their friends, and were driven quietly away. Watching the procession leave the gate of the prison, one turnkey said to another that it was like a funeral.

The convict ship *Maria* to which they were taken remained in dock for six weeks prolonging their agony. Elizabeth paid it frequent visits, even driving in from Plashet during the summer. Before it left, she had established her sway over the unknown convicts brought from other prisons. She had divided the 100 or more women into classes of twelve with their monitors and obtained numbers for them which they greatly valued because it simplified the keeping of their own seats at table and their own few possessions. She had provided them all with the necessary materials for making patchwork on the voyage. She had also established, in the stern, a school for the fourteen children on board and one of the prisoners had agreed to act as schoolmistress. They were well started in industrious and orderly habits before the heart-wrenching day of final farewell.

Before the ship sailed, Elizabeth sat on deck reading calmly to them. Sailors aboard neighbouring vessels climbed their rigging to witness this strange sight on a convict ship. Then, as she and a friend took the little boat to the shore, a prisoner leaned over the side of the vessel and said distinctly and with emotion: 'Our prayers will follow you, and a convict's prayers will be heard.' Little did the women realise that to sit in a boat, even in confined waters such as these, would at one time have struck terror into the heart of their gracious friend with her fear of the sea.

From that time onward, for as long as she could, Elizabeth visited and organised every convict ship that carried women prisoners to the colonies. Some 106 ships and 12,000 convicts are said to have come through her hands. Thankfully the whole system of transportation was doomed by the rising tide of public opinion after the parliamentary report of 1837 although it lingered on through inertia for another 31 years.

But for the present, Elizabeth put her indelible mark on the whole hideous process and eased the way as best she could for the unfortunate 'transports'. One of her earliest experiences was to see twelve women arrive to board a ship having made the journey handcuffed. Eleven others had iron bands around their legs and arms and were chained together so if one stepped down from the wagon, all must. Another woman's fetter around her ankle was so small and tight that it had become deeply embedded in her swollen flesh. The agony caused by its removal was such that the woman fainted. Facts like these had only to be reported to Elizabeth Fry before she took prompt action.

Soon it was made illegal to keep irons on women during their transfer from prison to convict ship. Another government regulation which Elizabeth prompted was that women convicts should be allowed to take with them all their children under seven. And mothers of nursing babies should not have to travel until their children were weaned.

Elizabeth's Ladies' Committee had grown into the British Society of Ladies, with the Duchess of Gloucester as patron. The ladies were well versed in their activities. They knew what to do on board a transport, and what to ask for; and they had a set of gifts for each prisoner ready to be marked with her own number so it was indisputably her own. This gesture was in itself unutterably cheering to people long denied all possessions and rights. The gifts were listed:

> 'One Bible, one Hessian apron, one black stuff ditto, one black cotton cap, one large Hessian bag [to keep clothes in], one small bag containing one piece of tape, one ounce of pins, one hundred needles, one small bodkin fastened on it, two stay-laces, one thimble, one pair of scissors, one pair of spectacles when required, two pounds of patchwork pieces, one comb, one small ditto, knife and fork, and a ball of string.'

When ships docked at Rio de Janeiro, industrious convicts could often sell their patchwork quilts there at a guinea each. If not, they could sell them easily on arrival at Sydney and so obtain ready cash and, just as important, the possibility of future employment. Under such comparatively cheerful influences, it was not surprising that some captains on their return to England reported on the health of the women, their attention to cleanliness and improved appearance during the voyage.

It was not always so. Women on board the earliest transport ships brought with them their city and gaol behaviour. After the initial period of sea-sickness, they resumed quarrelling, stealing and generally destroying each other's few personal possessions. In the cramped conditions, gangs formed. There were bullies and victims. The fighting was as vicious as amongst the men. Foul language was spewed against fellow convicts and crew alike.

Although life on board a ship required a certain degree of order and cleanliness according to the standards of the captain, the smell from the ballast and the stench of the bilge were constant. Worst of all was the overwhelming stench from the women's sleeping quarters every morning. During the day and in calm weather, toilet facilities were relatively clean and efficient but at night the convicts were confined to their quarters on the lowest deck. There were lice, fleas and cockroaches to deal with also which, although unpleasant, were familiar to many of the women. Conditions became intolerable when the ships were becalmed or in harbour for long periods.

It was considered to be the right of every seaman and officer to choose a woman as his 'mate' for the duration of the voyage. No doubt the women and young girls had little choice in the matter; some may have welcomed an escape from the filthy crowded orlop as the lesser of two evils. For others, it was probably what they were used to and only confirmed their feelings towards men as a species. Sometimes disreputable seamen offered the women for sex at ports before bundling them back on board to continue their voyage.

Later, ship-loads of women arrived regularly, wives and children of convicts, 'distressed needle-women' from the poor houses of Britain, and other young women, all seeking new prospects in the colony. Expanding agriculture and the gold rush of the 1850s for instance exacerbated an imbalance of the sexes which the maturing colony was crying out to redress with female immigration schemes.

Whether or not Elizabeth, during her lifetime, was fully aware of all the horrors confronting these women is uncertain. Her intelligence, all-seeing eyes and ability to listen probably recognised some if not all of them. Where she found injustice and hardship, she tried to correct it. Certainly some women benefited from months on board ship. They arrived in New South Wales with colour in their cheeks from the sun, sea breezes, fresh fruit and controlled amounts of alcohol. But for too many, it was hell.

In 1826 Elizabeth was able to remark:

> 'we visited the two female convict ships now in the river, and their order, cleanliness and general appearance delighted me, and made me really struck with the wonderful change wrought since we first undertook them.'

From the very beginning the ladies provided libraries on every transport. As one of the matrons wrote:

> 'The library was of great use, as it was only on condition of good conduct that they were allowed to have a book... At three o'clock we dined, and then they were left at liberty to amuse themselves; and it was very pleasant to see here and there a group seated listening to one of their companions reading aloud.'

The books included travel, biography, history, serious poetry, and religious works, but all 'novels, plays and other improper books' were excluded. Quakers at the time considered these as unsuitable reading matter.

Occasionally a travelling missionary or clergyman would be given free passage on a ship in return for supervising the convicts. Sometimes the ship's surgeon would do the job. On these occasions, the prisoners were fortunate. No longer were they crowded together all the time below deck in stuffiness and seasickness but allowed group activities on the airy spaces of the open deck.

A ship's captain writing from Sydney in December 1834 gave details of his voyage when a Baptist missionary, John Saunders, and his wife were given free passage in return for caring for the convicts. On board were 150 women, 41 children and nine passengers.

The captain said of the missionary:

> 'His kind attention to the unfortunate criminals has been unceasing… Some of them who, when they came into the ship, could neither read nor write, have left here well capable of doing both. His wife, a most amiable young woman, was also very kind and attentive to them. The whole of them will have to acknowledge that the *George Hibbert* has been to them a comfortable home.'

Eight years later the *Rajah* carried a clergyman who was returning to his duties and who assembled the free passengers, the crew and the prisoners on deck each evening for vespers with singing. A female warder from a penitentiary had also obtained passage in return for her services, and she wrote a journal letter on board: 'It was, as you will imagine from our latitude, excessively hot, but an awning was fixed up, and gave the deck much the appearance of a church. Seats were temporarily made of planks and tubs, so that all the women were accommodated in an orderly manner while apart, but in equal order, were arranged all the sailors.

'The women for the first time put on the cool white jackets and checked aprons provided for them, and I cannot tell you how picturesque and neat they looked... It was equalled only by their breathless attention during the service. The congregation so interesting, the circumstance of more than 200 persons assembled in such order on the deck of a ship to worship God... alone on the ocean... produced such feelings as I believe none of us ever before experienced.'

Capital Punishment

I N 1818 when Elizabeth was deeply involved with the 'transports', the government's other remedy, death, had yet to be effectively confronted. Fowell Buxton, now an MP in the House of Commons, seconded a motion by Sir James Mackintosh for a committee to consider the criminal laws.

> 'There are persons living at whose birth the Criminal Code contained less than sixty capital offences and who have seen that number quadrupled – who have seen an Act passed making offences capital by the dozen and by the score; and what is worse bundling up together offences trivial and atrocious.'

The idea that with the liberal killing off of criminals one could stamp out crime was far older than the nineteenth century. In Henry VIII's reign, 72,000 people were hanged for robbery alone; and Sir Thomas More wondered that:

> '... while so many thieves were daily hanged, so many still remained in the country, robbing in all places.'

Over 500 criminals a year were hanged during Queen
Elizabeth's reign, yet she complained bitterly of the lawlessness
of the people.

As Fowell Buxton said in the House in 1821:

> 'We have gone on long enough taking it for
> granted that capital punishment does restrain
> crime, and the time is now arrived in which we
> may fairly ask, does it do so?... Kill your father
> or a rabbit in a warren, the penalty is the same...
> Meet a gypsy on the high-road, keep company
> with him or kill him, the penalty by law is the
> same.'

With over 200 capital crimes on its statutes, the government's
intentions were clear but practice could not keep pace with
theory. Judges and juries would fall short of the letter-of-the-law
ideal. In Fowell Buxton's famous speech on capital punishment
he told parliament that he held in his hand 1,200 cases of juries
who had committed perjury sooner than bring in a verdict of
guilty for a small offence which carried the death penalty.

Another loophole of escape was reprieve. John Howard, in his
passion for facts, collected statistics between the years 1750
and 1772 of the number actually executed in any given year.
The total condemned during that period at, for example, the
Norwich Assizes was 434; but the number executed was 117.
The figures became even more disproportionate as time went
on and especially after forgery became a capital offence in
1807. In 1824, some 1,066 people were sentenced to death in
the whole of England, and 40 were executed; in 1825, 1,036
were condemned and 50 were executed.

It had been a capital offence to steal linen from bleaching-
grounds until the linen-bleachers themselves came to parliament

and begged that the penalty be mitigated. The blood-lust of the lawmakers continued. That same year, 1811, a bill was produced making machine-breaking in the factories a capital offence; it was already punished savagely enough by fourteen years transportation. The bill became law in spite of the passionate protest of Lord Byron, whose plea for the starving machine operatives was one of his three contributions to debate in the House of Lords.

A single session at the Old Bailey in September 1801 recorded:

> 'Sentence of death was passed upon Thomas Fitroy… for breaking and entering the dwelling-house of James Harris in the daytime and stealing a cotton counterpane. Wm. Cooper for stealing a linen cloth, the property of George Singleton, in his dwelling-house. J. Davies for a burglary. Richard Emms for breaking into the dwelling-house of Mary Humphreys in the daytime and stealing a pair of stockings. Magnis Kerner for a burglary and stealing six spoons. Robert Pearce for returning from transportation. Richard Alcorn for stealing a horse. John Goldfried for stealing a blue coat. Joseph Huff for stealing a lamb, and John Pass for stealing two lambs.'

Prisoners were strangled in front of Newgate, witnessed by jostling crowds. Sometimes friends and the executioner himself would hang upon the victim's legs to shorten the suffering. A young woman once said to Elizabeth as she hardened herself to her fate:

> 'Well, if the worst comes to the worst, I shall but have to dance for an hour.'

Elizabeth often found herself in demand by women about to die; and her opinion of capital punishment was clear. A woman who murdered her baby was the first to touch her heart. Another was a woman executed for robbing, or rather of being an accessory to the robbery of a house. A diary entry for 4 March 1817 read:

> 'I have just returned from a most melancholy visit to Newgate, where I have been at the request of Elizabeth Fricker, previous to her execution to-morrow morning at eight o'clock. I found her much hurried, distressed and tormented in mind. Her hands cold, and covered with something like the perspiration preceding death, and in a universal tremor. The women who were with her said she had been so outrageous before our going that they thought a man must be sent for to manage her. However, after a serious time with her, her troubled soul became calmed.'

> 'But is it for man thus to take the prerogative of the Almighty into his own hands? Is it not his place rather to endeavour to reform such, or to restrain them from the commission of further evil? At least to afford poor erring fellow-mortals, whatever may be their offences, an opportunity of proving their repentance by amendment of life. Besides this poor young woman, there are also six men to be hanged, one of whom has a wife near her confinement also condemned [both for forgery] and [they have] seven young children. Since the awful report came down, he has become quite mad, from horror of mind. A strait waistcoat could not keep him within

bounds: he had just bitten the turnkey. I saw the
man come out with his hand bleeding as I passed
the cell. I hear that another, who had been
tolerably educated and brought up, was doing
all he could to harden himself, through un-belief
trying to convince himself that religious truths
were idle tales… He sent to beg for a bottle of
wine, no doubt in the hope of drowning his
misery and the fears that would arise, by a degree
of intoxication.'

Elizabeth Fricker's case was particularly upsetting. The man
convicted with her declared, the night before his execution, that
she was innocent, and that 'a boy concealed had let him into
the house.' But Fricker was executed none the less. And so was
a pregnant woman forger once she had recovered from having
her baby, leaving eight orphans on the hands of the state. One
of Elizabeth Fry's helpers tried to comfort the woman forger
after the birth by reading to her, but in vain.

'So unnatural is her situation that one can hardly
tell how to meet her case. She seems afraid to
love her baby.'

The plight of these prisoners haunted Elizabeth at night. As
she became famous, she used this power to obtain pardons or
reprieves wherever possible.

On one occasion she commented to the
parliamentary committee about 'Lord Sidmouth
having been very kind to us whenever we have
applied for the mitigation of punishment since
our Committee has been formed.'

Whatever was in her mind when she made this comment, it proved a grave mistake. Sidmouth was made of very different stuff from her other new friend, Admiral Sir Byam Martin, Comptroller of the Navy, who helped to put into effect her reforms of the convict ships, and whose loyal confidence, once gained, was gained for life.

Henry Addington, Viscount Sidmouth, could be petty and narrow-minded and was notoriously anti-reform. His first rise in parliament, under the wing of Pitt prompted the famous catchphrase: 'As London is to Paddington, so Pitt is to Addington.' In the early years of Elizabeth's marriage, Sidmouth had been Prime Minister for three years and in 1818 became Home Secretary. As such he was the final court of appeal in matters of life and death. The first appeal Elizabeth made to him after her unwise words to the parliamentary committee was promptly refused.

The case was particularly harrowing. A young woman, Harriet Skelton, had been arbitrarily chosen for execution out of a number condemned for forgery and the whole women's side at Newgate felt the shock. Harriet was not a criminal type. Her charm, her quiet demeanour and good behaviour, her superior refinement and the fact her only crime had been to pass a forged note at the insistence of the man she loved – perhaps not even knowing it was forged – had made all the women certain that she would be one of the large number reprieved.

Elizabeth worked hard on Harriet's behalf. She was shocked to be refused by Sidmouth and pressed the point with all her might knowing that a life was at stake. She did not know her man. She supposed, in the innocence of her heart, that the Home Secretary was trying to judge the case on its merits. Her letters were in vain and he refused to see her.

Time was passing and Elizabeth made one last desperate effort. Her old friend Prince William, the Duke of Gloucester was in

London, married now to his faithful Princess Mary, daughter of King George III. Surely the prince would help her, remembering those old days of heartfelt gaiety at Earlham. Indeed he would. He went with her to Newgate, saw Harriet Skelton and heard her statement. He went with Elizabeth to the directors of the Bank of England and begged for their help. And he went with her to the Home Secretary's office.

It proved useless. Sidmouth had entrenched himself in obstinacy. The constant pressure and the fact that he was being put in the wrong in the eyes of all those who were aware of the circumstances, made him peevish. Not even at the request of the Prince would he see that tiresome and dangerous woman, Mrs Fry. Curtly he refused them an appointment. Elizabeth was humiliated and Harriet Skelton was doomed.

The harsh rebuff encouraged Elizabeth to re-focus her energies. She never lost her interest in individual cases but she could see that greater changes would have to be made. Her influence with the public was huge had she chosen to use it. And it was always behind her, that vague, easily summoned power, in all her dealings with authority. Also she had huge personal influence with Fowell Buxton – far more than his wife, her gentle sister, Hannah. It was Elizabeth who over the years had fuelled her brother-in-law's political aspirations and helped him form his liberal and humanitarian opinions. Not that he would have believed himself vulnerable to 'petticoat government' yet it was clear sometimes that what he said in parliament was what Elizabeth might have said had she been there. It was what she was saying out of parliament in her letters, journals and conversations. But she went further than he did.

Fowell Buxton was acknowledged as having great wisdom and foresight particularly in his proposal for abolishing the death penalty for every crime but murder. But Elizabeth had decided already, and experience had confirmed her opinion, that the death penalty should be scrapped altogether.

She wrote in her 1827 book on prisons that: '... the terror of the example [example being the chief argument for capital punishment] is rendered abortive by the notion vulgarly prevalent among thieves, that 'if they are to be hanged, they are to be hanged, and nothing can prevent it'... It lowers their estimate of the life of man... and has a direct and positive tendency to promote both murder and suicide.'

She calmly enunciated the axiom: 'Punishment is not for revenge, but to lessen crime and reform the criminal.'

Reluctant Celebrity

AFTER HER upset with Sidmouth, Elizabeth recorded in her diary that it had been 'a day of ups and downs in a remarkable degree.' The lady who was rebuffed by the Home Secretary in the morning was in the afternoon presented to the Queen amid bishops, ladies, fans, feathers and jewels.

> 'When under great humiliation in consequence of this [rebuff], Lady Harcourt took me with her to the Mansion House, rather against my will, to meet many of the royal family at the examination of some large schools.'

Her daughter Katherine Fry recorded the occasion in a letter to her aunt Hannah Buxton:

> 'With infinite difficulty we got into the ante-room. In a few minutes some men in very grand liveries came in a great hurry to clear the way and lay down a piece of scarlet cloth; the cry was "The Queen is coming!" We looked through the entrance door and saw mamma (!) with the Bishop of Gloucester (!) and Lady Harcourt with Alderman Wood.

'Silence had been previously ordered as a mark
of respect, but a buzz of "Mrs Fry, Mrs Fry"
ran through the room. It was to our utter
astonishment that we saw them come in and
walk along those spread carpets. Lady Harcourt
in full court-dress on the arm of the Alderman
in his scarlet gown, and secondly the Bishop of
Gloucester in lawn sleeves leading our darling
mother in her plain Friends' cap, one of the light
scarf cloaks worn by plain Friends, and a dark
silk gown – I see her now! Her light flaxen hair, a
little flush on her face from the bustle and noise
she had passed through, and her sweet, lovely,
placid smile. In a few minutes the Queen passed,
followed by the Princesses, the Royal Dukes, the
Lady Mayoress, and other official personages…

'The Lord Major placed us behind the hustings
on which the Queen was. We asked him for
mamma. He burst out laughing: "There she is on
the bench of the Bishops"! There were eight of
them there. We heard people pointing her out to
one another: "That is she, with her hair over her
forehead"… "That must be Mrs Fry, with the
Bishops"… "Look now! You may see Mrs Fry;
she rises to receive the Queen's salute."

'Towards the close, after *God Save the King* had
been sung, everybody began to clap violently,
and we asked the cause. "Why, the Queen is
speaking to Mrs Fry." When Queen Charlotte
rose to go, she paused and passed to the side
where the Bishops sat – of course all had risen
– and Lady Harcourt presented our mother.

The Queen, who is so short, curtseying to our mother, who is so tall, not curtseying, was very awkward. Her Majesty asked our mother if she were not afraid of going into prisons, how far she lived from London, and how many children she had. The shouts in the hall were tremendous, and were caught up by the crowds outside. It was told why they shouted, and it was repeated again and again, till it reached our father, sitting in his office at St. Mildred's Court, that "the Queen is speaking to Mrs Fry".'

Elizabeth Fry was now a celebrity. One of the amusements of fashionable society was to go down to Newgate and see her with the prisoners. The American Ambassador wrote home to say that he had now seen the two greatest sights of London – St Paul's Cathedral, and Mrs Fry reading to the prisoners in Newgate. Bored aristocrats and discouraged bishops found the scheme in the prison strange and very moving; quite a new sensation. And it was all the more valued because only a few could be admitted at a time, and only if they had a permit.

'I accompanied Mrs Fry on two occasions,' wrote the Rev C. B. Tayler in his personal recollections. 'Tier above tier rose the seats at the end of the room, a gallery of wooden steps many feet high extending from wall to wall; and on that gallery the women prisoners... were seated... It was a shocking and most distressing spectacle, that range of about 100 women's faces with... vice and crime written on the lines of almost every one. On some the bleared flatness of face from whence all traces of womanly feeling had disappeared; on others the vulgar snivel, seeming from time to time to twist the lips and nose together... But there they sat in respectful silence, every eye fixed upon the grave sweet countenance of Mrs Fry.

'She read that day the fifty-third chapter of Isaiah, in itself one of the great pieces of prose in the English language. "...All we like sheep have gone astray; we have turned every one to his own way; and the Lord hath laid on him the iniquity of us all..."

'Never till then, and never since then, have I heard anyone read as Elizabeth Fry read that chapter – the solemn reverence of her manner, the articulation, so exquisitely modulated, so distinct, that not a word of that sweet and touching voice could fail to be heard. While she read, her mind seemed to be intensely absorbed in the passage of scripture and in nothing else. She seemed to take to her own soul the words which she read and to apply them to herself; and then she raised her head and after another pause of silence, she spoke to the wretched women before her.

'Her address was short and so simple that it must have been intelligible to the capacities of her hearers... Tears flowed freely from eyes which perhaps had never shed such tears till then... What struck me as remarkable in her speaking, and no doubt that which won its way so powerfully to the hearts of those abandoned women, was that she always seemed to class herself with them; she never said "you" but "us".'

Elizabeth found the crowds distressing. She described it in her
diary as: 'making a show of a good thing.' Reading to prisoners
was one of her pleasures and whenever they heard she was going
to read, they would flock upstairs after her joyfully, 'as if it were
a great pleasure I had to afford them.' So unlike the attitude of
her own dear household.

To most of the prisoners, the Bible was entirely new. They
listened to it with fascination. Bible readings were to them a
theatre and a concert, a church, even a family circle, all rolled
into one. Drama and poetry, exciting stories and extraordinary
thoughts came to their ears and stirred their imagination as they
listened to tales of pillars of fire and cloud, a blast of trumpets
and the shout that brought down the walls of Jericho. They
'saw' the angels' ladder and touched the hem of a seamless robe
whose wearer had shown mercy to the prostitute. In their own
innocent way, they worshipped.

Elizabeth was not happy to have her intimate reading time
with prisoners turned into a show. But she was learning the
importance of publicity. She recognised that it was ultimately
good for the prisoners that the world of rank and power should
come inside the prison and see and hear for itself. It stirred
public opinion which might in turn influence government
thinking. So she accepted the situation, rose to it, used it to
her advantage. Plus a responsive audience brought out the best
in a fine reader. To find noblemen, ladies of fashion in velvets
and furs, a famous author like Maria Edgeworth, a few clergy,
and a foreign ambassador in attendance altered the character
of the assembly. But what it lost in intimacy it gained in vital
publicity.

Sometimes Joseph Fry would look in on his wife when he was on
his way to or from his busy office. He would find her serene and
composed, the centre of a hundred eyes yet unembarrassed and
focused on her task. His dear wife with the 'Guido Madonna

countenance' as Maria Edgeworth once described her. Did he smile and remember those early days of their marriage when even to read to himself and his brother William, plus maybe one visitor, covered her with confusion and she had to hand the Bible to him to finish?

Letter from Down Under

W HILE HER readings at Newgate were the latest talking point at fashionable dinner tables, Elizabeth was concerning herself with another matter. A question she had asked since the night her first transport ship sailed was not being answered. What happened to the women convicts when they arrived at the other side of the world?

It was strange that nobody seemed to know. Members of parliament, people in the Colonial Office, captains of ships, were all equally vague and non-committal. It was a very obvious question which must have been asked before. But all Elizabeth could learn was that there was some arrangement; the women were taken care of in some way; there was some system of hiring them out to work for the settlers and suchlike. But no one seemed to know for certain. Convicts themselves seldom communicated with friends at home. When they were transported they appeared to vanish off the face of the earth as if they had died.

Courteously, Elizabeth persisted in asking her question. She made her felon friends promise to let her know, if they could, what life was like over there under the Southern Cross. Her suspicions were dark, but they were less than the truth.

She received a heartfelt letter from Australia in the spring of 1819 which enlightened her somewhat. It was a long letter in neat handwriting from the Rev Samuel Marsden, an Anglican clergyman who was chaplain at Parramatta, New South Wales.

> 'HONOURED MADAM,
>
> Having learned from the public papers, as well as from my friends in England, the lively interest you have taken in promoting the temporal and eternal welfare of those unhappy females who fall under the sentence of the law, I am induced to address a few lines to you respecting such as visit our distant shores. It may be gratifying to you, madam, to hear that I meet with those wretched exiles who have shared your attentions and who mention your maternal care with gratitude and affection.'

For twenty years, he had been struggling to get government action on behalf of the women transports, if only to the extent of building a barracks for them, he said.

> '... to this day there never has been a place to put the female convicts in when they land from the ships. For the last five-and-twenty years many of the convict women have been driven to vice to obtain a loaf of bread or a bed to lie upon. Many of these have told me with tears, their distress of mind on this account: some would have been glad to have returned to the paths of virtue if they could have found a hut to live in without forming improper connections... Many

do not live out half their days from their habits of vice… When they have been brought before me as a magistrate… I was often at a loss what to answer.'

It was no worse than Elizabeth had feared. But Rev Marsden had more:

'When I am called to visit them upon their dying beds, my mind is greatly pained, my mouth is shut, I know not what to say to them… To tell them of their crimes is to upbraid them with misfortunes. They will say "Sir, you know how I was situated. I did not wish to lead the life I have done… I could not help myself, I must have starved if I had not done as I have"… I rejoice, madam, that you reside near the seat of Government, and may have it in your power to call the attention of his Majesty's Minister to this important subject – a subject on which the entire welfare of these settlements is involved. If proper care is taken of the women, the Colony will prosper, and the expenses of the mother country will be reduced. On the contrary, if the morals of the female convicts are wholly neglected, as they have been hitherto, the Colony will be only a nursery for crime…'

He continued: 'It was the custom for some years, when a ship of female convicts arrived, for soldiers, convicts and settlers to go on board and make their choice. This custom is no longer pursued openly, but the total lack of provision for the women convicts makes the real situation

just as bad as ever. And so it will remain, till they
can be provided with a barrack.'

When back in Europe twelve years earlier, Rev Marsden had
contacted the Archbishop of Canterbury, the Colonial Office,
and several MPs and had received promises of immediate
attention. Returning to Botany Bay in 1810, he had been
surprised to find no change. He waited patiently for five
years and then approached the Governor who denied having
received any instructions to build a barracks. After a further
wait, Marsden suggested to the Governor that he go ahead with
the barracks without formal approval from England. At the risk
of losing his own post and livelihood, he sent a copy of his
suggestion and the Governor's negative reply to England. Still
nothing had been done. Rev Marsden did not know what else
he could do to get the ear of England. Perhaps Mrs Fry could
do it. Her 'good intentions and benevolent labours will be all
abortive' if something was not done at the Australian end.

Elizabeth was cheered to hear good reports of some of her
women who were respectably self-supporting.

> 'Mrs B- who came from Newgate in the
> Friendship often mentions your kindness.
> She lives near me, with her husband. They are
> well and doing well, and conduct themselves
> with much propriety, will be useful members
> of society, and are getting forward very fast in
> worldly comforts,' he reported.

With her usual determination, Elizabeth lost no time in
presenting Marsden's information to the proper quarters. And,
as usual, she had already thought of a plan of action. Could not
the men convicts at once set to work to build a barracks for the
women? Surely delay was impossible.

The authorities were flustered. Marsden was a nobody, a mere voice crying in the wilderness. But, Mrs Fry, well she had the ear of England if and when she chose. As such, she might be dangerous, although no one knew it less than Elizabeth. A scandal such as this, once properly aired, might lose the governor of a colony his post.

Communications were sent immediately to the Governor of New South Wales. Then Elizabeth was assured that her correspondent was out of date. That barracks were indeed being built at Parramatta - a European settlement initially called Rose Hill but renamed after it was proclaimed a town in 1790. She must understand that these things were slow work in the colonies. It seemed strange, however, that Rev Marsden, working and living in Parramatta, should have been unaware of this. Certainly work had been completed in March 1819 on substantial new military barracks in Parramatta; so barracks were indeed built – but, it seems, for the military not for the convicts.

Hyde Park Barracks in Sydney, one of the first convict barracks built, was completed by convict labourers. The parties of convicts, iron gangs, usually worked in chains guarded by armed sentries. Initially Hyde Park sheltered 600 men, later accommodating up to 1,400. But the barracks were not adapted for women until many years later.

Female convicts arrived at Sydney, disembarked and were taken by boat sixteen miles up the river to Parramatta. They were housed in what was effectively a new prison – known as The Factory – until suitable work was found for them. Women who bore a certificate of good conduct from the ships' officers were certain of immediate employment. Difficult prisoners were detained indefinitely. All could be returned to the prison for punishment at the complaint of their employers.

Years later a member of Elizabeth's Newgate Committee visited Australia and was commissioned by her to investigate the state of the women convicts. Armed with a permit from the Governor, the lady took the steamboat from Sydney to Parramatta. In the glory of a late afternoon, she passed through that lovely flower strewn landscape with sunset reflected on the river and a wild peace.

Up on a hill, overlooking the large, straggling town of Parramatta, stood Rev Marsden's house in which the visitor received a cordial reception. The Factory, visited next day, proved to be a large, airy building, well situated and remarkably clean. It contained at that time 700 prisoners, divided into three classes. In the third class, the worst and largest, the lady spoke of Elizabeth Fry and gave a general message from her. It gained the confidence of the prisoners who gathered around and told of wrongs unheeded, of bad masters and cruel mistresses, of being treated 'like dogs', of seldom being spoken to without oaths, of being treated as 'devils' rather than human beings.

Two girls had murdered their master, a captain into whose service they had been assigned. The lady recalled that the girls were 'both young and extremely pretty; one especially lovely.' They were anxious to justify their actions and one told her:

> 'I am not a murderer for I never meant to kill the man. We were in liquor when we did it, but we couldn't help that he died, and we were sorry for it; although he deserved it.'

The prison had a matron and there were several women warders but there was little kindness. There was a spirit of revenge rather than reform, and a row of dark punishment cells which Elizabeth would have abhorred and the like of which she wanted abolished from every prison both at home and abroad.

The lady was worried when she left The Factory and tried to organise a Ladies' Committee to check on the women's complaints and generally keep an eye on things. When she returned to England, she wrote a booklet on Australia's women prisoners in the hope of rousing public opinion.

While the Rev Marsden's initial letter was making its slow journey from Parramatta to London in the spring of 1819, Elizabeth had become seriously ill. After weeks confined to her room, her doctors ordered gentle travel, and she was taken in a bed carriage by easy stages through Petworth and Arundel to Brighton. From there she went to Tunbridge Wells and so back to Plashet for the spring. Joseph was by her side, together with their daughters Katherine and Chenda and various staff to help.

Her symptoms were fatigue and weakness rather than pain and at times she was able to feel almost a holiday spirit in the change of scene. She loved being the centre of Joseph's attention and care, being in the company of their girls, and having a complete rest from responsibility.

> 'I am ready to think that this state of bodily infirmity is permitted for my mental rest – that I may retire a little from the world and its business,' she wrote in her diary. 'I am glad to say that my many outward callings when well, do not trouble my mind when poorly, such as my prisons etc., and my dearest children also I feel great comfort about.'

Her illness ended in a miscarriage – 'the child supposed to have been dead four months'. By August she was almost better. Her unmarried sister Priscilla was overwhelmed when she heard of her beloved sister's illness. 'It casts clouds over everything!' But by the end of the month, it was Priscilla herself who was dangerously ill and Elizabeth, restored, was nursing her. Elizabeth recalled:

> 'Indeed, her dependence was so close upon me
> that I could not leave the house night or day for
> any length of time.'

The symptoms were alarming – 'raising blood from the lungs' – and her recovery slow.

Changing Times

D URING THE harsh winter of 1819 a boy was found frozen to death in the streets of London. Elizabeth was appalled; to have children freezing to death on one's very doorstep. She appealed to Joseph, to her brothers-in-law and to her Ladies Committee. Sam Hoare and Fowell Buxton called a meeting, passed resolutions, and collected money. An extensive warehouse in London Wall was offered by Mr Hick of Cheapside. Mrs Hick, Elizabeth and some other Committee ladies went down to prepare it for occupation. Within six hours a 'nightly shelter for the homeless' was open in London. The men's part was provided with straw, the women's with rough bedding. Soup and bread were given to all comers. The average number admitted nightly was 205; the greatest 799. Hundreds of others were supplied with food and clothing.

With that Gurney determination and impatience to see results, Elizabeth did not stop there. Classes were organised for the women and children, and work found for many of the men, especially in connection with the Merchant Seamen's Society; the merchant ships were poorly served at that time.

Writing to her sons, away at boarding school in January 1820, Elizabeth wrote of her busy London life:

'It is almost like living in a market or a fair, only that I have not merchandise to sell! We see a great variety of company, principally people who are interesting and occupied by subjects of importance. We lately had a gentleman, an East India Missionary, who told us many particulars about the poor Indians. I think in one province about seven hundred poor widows burn themselves every year when their husbands die. We expect soon to see the Persian Ambassador, and I mean to give you an account of him... I much enjoy long letters from you... I like having your poetry. Believe me your nearly attached mother, E. Fry.'

Her thoughts were not just in London and with her children. She and Fowell Buxton worried about the Indian widows and he introduced a bill into parliament to forbid the practice of suttee, or Sati, within the British Empire. It became law in 1829, but the practice was not eradicated. Some women preferred to throw themselves on their husbands' funeral pyres and burn to death rather than face life as widows. There are still occasional reports of women committing suttee today.

The year 1820 proved one of change not just for Elizabeth but for everyone. George III died in January and his son George IV, the Regent, started his ten-year rule. His constant disagreements with his wife and Queen Caroline's abortive attempt later to attend her estranged husband's coronation shocked the country. Unsuccessful in her efforts to reassert her position, the Queen died the following year.

In Italy that spring, the wife of an English country gentleman presented her husband with a daughter. They already had a baby girl named after her mother; so they called the second one after the city of her birth: Florence Nightingale.

A year earlier, also in May, another baby girl had been born, this time to the Duke and Duchess of Kent at Kensington Palace. She was christened Alexandrina Victoria and in eighteen years' time became Queen and served as Britain's longest reigning monarch, giving her name to an era.

Meanwhile in Europe there was increasing demand, including now from the Russian court, for advice regarding prisons, and also lunatic asylums where the insane were housed rather than in workhouses. But throughout her work and visits to various prisons at this time, Elizabeth was distracted. Her thoughts were at home where the family faced great sadness and the increasing illness of Priscilla.

Amidst life there is death and the spring had brought untold tragedy to her sister Hannah and Thomas Fowell Buxton. They lost four children in just five weeks. The first was their eldest son Fowell, aged ten, who came home from boarding school with a lung inflammation. The three others, aged four, three and eighteen months died of simultaneous whooping cough and measles. They were buried at Hampstead in one grave with the simple inscription: 'Eheu. Eheu'. The ultimate sorrow. Oh no! Oh dear!

As if that was not enough heartbreak, Priscilla continued to linger and fade at Earlham and at different health resorts. Later in the year she was moved to the Isle of Wight in the hope of a mild winter and wrote to Elizabeth:

> 'There is a certain understanding which I feel
> with thee that I can hardly feel in the same way
> with any other mortal… What a support and
> stay and refreshment, in short what a mother
> thou has been to us…!'

She returned to Earlham but as autumn approached was moved to Cromer Hall in Norfolk. After their overwhelming loss, Fowell Buxton and Hannah sold their house in Hampstead and moved to Cromer Hall with their two remaining children [in time they had two more]. Here Priscilla's doctors hoped the bracing sea air might help her; and Hannah was keen to nurse their youngest sister. Norfolk held so many happy childhood memories for them all and they hoped being back here might revive her.

But in February 1921 Priscilla called for her favourites – sister Betsy and brother Sam, the two busiest members of the family. Sam left a banking crisis and Elizabeth left a life packed with responsibilities. Writing to his wife, Sam said:

> 'As far as the circumstances of the case admitted, Betsy and I had a very pleasant journey… although leaving London at a critical moment has given me some pain. Not that I doubt the propriety of my coming, under the information I then had; and I must therefore leave matters to take care of themselves. Indeed,' added the financier, 'it sometimes happens they do best by themselves, and work their own way better than we can for them.'

As blossom returned to the trees bringing a promise of spring, family friend Amelia Opie wrote:

> 'I hope that warm weather and great care will make this faint bird of paradise tarry amongst us some time longer.'

But Priscilla did not live to see the spring. The following month, on 25 March, the seven sisters were together for the last time.

Linked as they were, their flying red cloaks just a memory, this was a coach they could not stop and their dearest sister slipped away, aged 36 and unmarried.

Inner Reflection

E LIZABETH NOW had twenty years of girlhood and twenty
years of married life behind her. She was 40 and although
that can be an uncomfortable milestone, Elizabeth had never
felt stronger. She looked back through the years of William
Savery and Deborah Darby, her mentors, and saw them as the
messengers who set her feet on the right path forward. She saw
her recurring dream of usefulness and power coming into a
fulfilment beyond her imagination.

For the moment, her life followed a pattern. It was not the
organised routine of which she dreamed; circumstances
prevented that. But she was focusing on a great public purpose
and knew this to be her major life's work.

The sudden and astonishing success of her reforms combined
her talents, including her clarity of thought and determination,
at a particular moment in time. England was going through all
the acute discomforts of change from one form of civilisation
to another. Reform was in the air. The old guard, bred in the
eighteenth century and looking back with longing to its charm,
its widespread happiness, did not see why, now that the war was
over, things could not return to pre-war conditions. So they
resisted all innovation particularly if it meant new legislation
changing the old order forever.

The death of Napoleon, just before the summer coronation of George IV, marked the end of an era. Napoleon had frightened but united Britain. Now he was dead, the unified nation fell apart into struggling factions. All that war had destroyed gradually became apparent. Plenty, security, contentment and the mutual dependence of class on class were threatened. Even the old authority and soothing consolation of the Church was being questioned by dissenters. One social order was vanishing, another must be found.

Eighteenth century government had been that of an aristocracy; the nineteenth century demanded the governance of a growing democracy. The early years of George IV's reign marked dramatic change. There were attempts to soothe distress and to tackle evil at its root. There were schemes for parliamentary reform, for national education, for the recognition of dissenters and Catholics, and for drastic amendment of the criminal laws. Fowell Buxton and his friends were beginning to form a solid force in the House of Commons, a strong group whose collective vote was worth obtaining.

Elizabeth too was sowing the seeds of change. She was probably one of the first women in history, other than royals, who accepted the demands of marriage and many children yet still maintained an active public life. She was also an example of how difficult it was for a woman at that time to combine those demands. Early in the nineteenth century, some believed that women could not reason. Quakers were different; their women held a privileged position. But even Quakers would admonish a particularly public-spirited lady that her place was at home. Elizabeth may have heard of Mary Wollstonecraft's *Vindication of the Rights of Women* but was unlikely to have read it; it was banned in many circles as the work of an atheist and an immoral person. But her ideas were in the air and could not be contained. Some appeared to rub off on Elizabeth. In the introduction to her book on prison work, she made her views clear.

> 'I wish to make a few general remarks which have long impressed me respecting my own sex and the place which I believe it to be their duty and privilege to fill in the scale of society.'

> 'Far be it from me to attempt to persuade women to forsake their right province. My only desire is that they should fill that province well; and although their calling in many respects materially differs from that of the other sex, and may not perhaps be so exalted a one – yet a minute observation will prove that, if adequately fulfilled, it has nearly, if not quite, an equal influence on society at large.'

> 'No person will deny the importance attached to the character and conduct of a woman in all her domestic and social relations, when she is filling the station of a daughter, a sister, a wife, a mother, or mistress of a family. But it is a dangerous error to suppose that the duties of females end here…'

> 'No persons appear to me to possess so strong a claim on their compassion and on their exertions as the helpless, the ignorant, the afflicted or the depraved of their own sex.'

She felt that women should pay attention to those of their sex who were less fortunate; those in hospitals, asylums, workhouses and prisons. She did not want women to neglect their own homes or the education of their children. But she felt that:

> 'The economical arrangement of time, and more especially a subtle division of labour, will enable them to accomplish without difficulty all their charitable objects.'

The many opportunities which lay before Elizabeth demanded time, attention and vigour. Her life had to swing like a pendulum daily from the large to the small; a parliamentary committee, or the menu for tomorrow's dinner; discussion on public measures with Fowell Buxton, or the reprimanding of a housemaid; receiving deputations from abroad to discuss methods of prison reform, or arbitration of a nursery riot. Fortunately for her she had staff to help, albeit in reduced numbers. Close family and friends still regarded her domestic duties as her real life, the large public matters as less important, at best worthy and admirable leisure time pursuits. And emotionally she felt the same. But in Elizabeth's view:

> 'The prison cause affords a wonderful opening. I believe if I had time I should have enough to do without attending to almost anything else; and what is more the attention paid to this subject brings so much fruit with it.'

Other matters took up much of her time but bore no fruit.

> 'My household cares at times a weighty burden, which peculiarly cast me down, and appear as if they must swallow up much of my powers. It is what I have no natural taste or power for, and therefore it is so difficult to me... Then one almost constant source of anxiety, and may I not say sorrow, are our expenses, as in our reduced circumstances I feel it an absolute duty to spend

moderately, and a real want of knowledge of
economy renders it almost impossible to do it,
but money appears to leek on every side and it
seems almost impossible to prevent it. How I can
feel for those fallen in life.'

What a turmoil of emotions she must have experienced during
those testing times. Throbbing with pain for Priscilla's death
and the deaths of Hannah and Fowell Buxton's children.
Worried about money and the control of household expenses.
And anxious about a continuing disagreement with Joseph.
The root of their disquiet could not have been stranger. It was
that old bugbear – music. She, who had loved music and found
it so difficult to abandon when she became a 'plain' Quaker.
She, who Joseph's family once considered not 'plain' enough
a Quaker. Now it was she who was disturbed again by her
husband's passion for music.

Although close and supportive of each other in most things,
they had separate interests too.

'...my beloved companion in life, to whom I
believe I may say I am increasingly attached...'

Joseph encouraged his wife's activities even if he did not share
her devotion to them. Elizabeth could not encourage Joseph's
love of music and feared:

'We in measure draw two ways, which not only
hurts us but the children that have come to an
age of understanding.'

Unable to listen to music at home, Joseph had fallen into the
habit of going out to find it elsewhere. There were 'music
meetings' at the homes of more worldly friends. Joseph would

even slip off to the opera, disguised in the costume of the world, leaving his Quaker coat to bear mute witness against him in the cupboard.

Did he reflect on the lost opportunities of that first hectic year of their married life so many years ago? If they had enjoyed more time alone back then, might he have been able to win her over to his continuing love of music? Before this Quaker view had become entrenched in Elizabeth, might he have been able to persuade her that their joint love of music could be a good influence if used wisely? She had been so soft and open to him then, so eager to please. But he was never ready with words and he had been brought up in the strictest, narrowest circle of Quakerism where music was banned. How he acquired such a love of it was a mystery. And he was unable to defend music on principle. He was never quite sure that it was right and his wife's opposition to it, compounded by the Quaker Elders' disapproval of it, made him grow to feel that it was indeed wrong. It was a mild sin and he had to have it. He also did not hesitate to take his sons with him, just as he took them on shooting and fishing trips.

The blame for any perceived wrong-doing by her family, from a strict Quaker view, fell on Elizabeth. And the Elders seemed quite often to disapprove . Why was a 'recognised minister' of the Religious Society of Friends tolerating such behaviour within her household? If she stayed at home and paid proper attention to her husband and children they might not go astray like this.

Elizabeth had always been sensitive to criticism. She recognised this as a weakness and struggled with it but she felt it none the less. Little did her children recognise this outside pressure on their mother. They only knew it was mother, not father, who tried to enforce so many of the family rules. They knew it was their mother who set the rules, for example, when a tutor took a 16-year-old son and three other youths abroad on an educational tour.

> 'Never allow the boys to be out alone in the evening; nor to attend any public place of amusement with any person, however pressing they may be. I advise thy seeing that they never talk when going to bed, but retire quietly after reading a portion of the holy scriptures. In the morning that they be as quiet as possible and learn their scripture texts while dressing...'

The children were too young to understand that, with a growing puritanical movement in England at the time, there were many other parents, not just Quakers, who were equally strict. Even the poet William Cowper had believed music to be a debauch – including the oratorios of Handel played in church on a Sunday afternoon. Elizabeth's children were unable to look back into their mother's past and see how her natural easiness over trifles had become controlled by religious discipline.

At that time, the Society of Friends was known to be particularly strict and prone to fault-finding. Ironically their petty interference with the daily life and habits of their members in the early 19th century was reminiscent of the strict discipline of other religions. A young Mrs Fry had often found it difficult, in the early years of her marriage, to take all their criticism kindly. She could not help feeling that, even in those days when all her time was given to home and children, she and her husband were under a special scrutiny.

She was right but never quite knew why; in fact Joseph was suspected of being un-orthodox, of being secretly touched with worldliness. And Elizabeth, extraordinary as it would have seemed to her sisters, fell under a similar suspicion. Why?

Because she was one of the Gurneys of Earlham and, as such, stamped indelibly with an air and manner that was too polished, too elegant for Quaker standards of the day.

Years before, in 1806 when the fourth of Elizabeth's eleven children had arrived, a committee was formed by the Society to visit Friends suspected of being 'delinquent' in the training of their children. Elizabeth was astonished and mortified at being one of those visited. And at the next Monthly Meeting much was said about 'dress and parents dressing their children'. The criticisms were patently directed towards the little Frys and their mother. Elizabeth tried to be grateful to Friends for their watchful care over her youth and inexperience. In her maturity she grew used to it, expectant of it, but never hardened to it.

She was criticised variously for raising her bell-like voice with unwomanly clarity in Meeting, and allowing her husband to take two daughters and nieces for a month's 'far too gay' holiday on the Continent. Joseph and the four girls had the time of their lives wearing non-Quaker clothes, listening to music and enjoying public parks and amusements.

As her workload increased over the years, Elizabeth had to steel herself against regular attacks, even in the press, for neglect of her family. Often her friends would defend her vigorously; just as later her own brother Joseph John would defend the blossoming Florence Nightingale from critics who described her public activities as 'unwomanly'. Indeed Florence, before she attained her freedom, was tantalised by her family telling her that they would have no objection to her undertaking a mission 'like Mrs Fry' provided there was first a Mr Fry to protect her. In one of her passionate outbursts, she wrote:

> 'Where do we see the woman with half her
> powers employed? What is she to do? Her best
> plan would be to have a pursuit of her own; with

her family, if any of them like it; without them if
they don't or can't do it, like Mrs Fry…But then
what a cry the world makes!'

Whatever their differences, Joseph always stood by his wife
and throughout her marriage Elizabeth considered pleasing her
husband to be one of her main aims. Although she dreaded
childbirth and post-natal recovery, she loved her children and
never ceased to be concerned for them. And as always she and
Joseph found travelling, away from the hubbub of home and
work, relaxing and unifying. Time spent with him was precious
to her. So it was with enthusiasm that she accompanied him
on a business trip in the autumn of 1821 with their daughters
Katherine and Rachel. Their innumerable trips, albeit often
on business, were like mini holidays greeted with an almost
childish sense of anticipation.

They visited Nottingham, Lincoln, Wakefield, Sheffield, Leeds,
York, Durham, Newcastle, Carlisle, Lancaster and Liverpool.
Elizabeth, so deeply immersed in her prison work, could not
stop herself from combining a little business with pleasure. She
took the opportunity to visit the prisons in every place they
stayed and was always asked to read to prisoners. She rallied
local ladies to form Ladies' Prison Committees too.

> On their return, she wrote: 'My husband and
> myself have had a very uniting journey together.
> I deeply feel the separations that attach to this
> place [home and work] and desire to make
> pleasing him one of my first objects.'

She made a similar journey through the north of England
with her brother, Joseph John, visiting prisons and Friends'
Meetings. Everywhere she went she attracted interest. The
Quaker lady with the angelic face reading the scriptures in

prisons and having everyone, hardened criminals, fashionable observers and rough prison guards alike, in tears touched the sentimental fancy of the 19th century. Elizabeth Fry became the 'Angel of the Prisons' forever seated with a bible.

Her days were filled with prison visits – Newgate, Milbank Penitentiary, Tothill Fields, Clerkenwell Prison. Even visits to Giltspur Street Compter where, before the advent of a police force, people were locked up by the watch before being sent to jail. Then she might call on the Duchess of Gloucester, be presented to visiting royals, receive Lord and Lady Torrington to tea or be informed that the Princess of Denmark wished to have breakfast with her at Plashet the following morning.

> Her head was not turned by celebrity. 'As far as I know my own heart, never less disposed to exaltation….Several things cast a cloud over me, the first seeing my beloved partner in life so devoted to some things that I am confident are most injurious to his best welfare…then my elder children, sweet as they are and much comfort as I at times have in them and strong marks of principle as I occasionally see, yet there is a want, a great want…And two of them…are induced to treat me and to speak to me at times in a manner that cuts me to the very quick.'

Return to Domesticity

BY THE end of the year, Rachel became the first of Joseph and Elizabeth's children to marry. Her choice of husband brought change to the household for she married 'out', married a man who was not a Quaker. She was 'disowned', dropped from membership of the Society, a destructive practice long since abandoned, but this solved the question of Rachel's Quakerism.

Fortunately, Elizabeth liked her son-in-law Francis Cresswell very much and knew it was a good match. She joined her husband in giving full consent and the young couple were married at Runcton by sister Chenda's husband, Rev Francis Cunningham, vicar of the parish. The strict rules of the Society of Friends at the time prevented Elizabeth from attending the wedding ceremony but she presided at the reception afterwards.

A joyful outcome of the marriage for Elizabeth was that Rachel, as a married woman, matured and was no longer a troublesome, occasionally wounding daughter. She proved to be a delightful friend. Greater joy came a year later on 1 November 1822 when Elizabeth's last child and Rachel's first were born on the same day.

> 'How striking to me it was…R and myself had each a darling boy born. Both of us graciously

and wonderfully helped,' Elizabeth wrote. She
was then 42, Rachel 19.

Elizabeth's eleventh and last child was called Daniel Henry
and was known as Henry, or Harry. As for Rachel's little boy,
he might well have been a cocky child for not many children
could boast a twin uncle! Of Joseph and Elizabeth's children
- six daughters and five sons - all but little Elizabeth grew to
maturity. And most lived to a good age despite the dictum
of the time that 'the general probability is about three to one
that a new-born infant will not live to complete its 50th year.'
Data from the French naturalist, Comte de Buffon, was more
depressing. 'Of a given number of new-born infants, one half,
by the fault of nature or man, is extinguished before the age
of puberty and reason – a melancholy consideration.' Even a
mother who stayed at home all the time with her children could
not protect them any more from these statistics than a mother
who freely and boldly embraced public duties as well.

Elizabeth recovered more easily from Harry's birth than from
the others. By December, she was back at Newgate. She wrote
in her diary on 14 December 1822:

> 'I yesterday for the first time since my lying-
> in went to London and visited Newgate. My
> greeting there was warm from the prisoners,
> friends of the committee, etc. My dearest babe
> who I took with me suffered apparently much by
> the drive to and from town, so that its little crys
> almost overcame me.'

In April, she wrote: 'Newgate, and overdone
with company there, so as greatly to prevent my
usefulness to the prisoners. (There was a sale

of the work of our poor prisoners in Newgate,
many of the great of this world present.)'

Although she must have been tired and feeling some strain
after the birth, the innate nurse and doctor in her could not
resist calls upon on her medical skills. Neither, it seemed, could
desperate relatives resist the temptation to call her away from
her busy life to serve their individual dear ones.

In May, a young cousin's wife was awaiting delivery of her first
baby. Elizabeth wrote:

> 'I have passed through a scene of deep affliction
> in attending dear Mary Hanbury. I was called
> to her on the 6th. She was delivered the next
> morning early of a nice boy, did well at first, and
> after great reduction and illness she died on the
> 16th, leaving her beloved father, husband and
> helpless infant behind her.' She added, simply: 'I
> suckling the babe at times, helped to support it.'
> She believed devoutly in submission to the will
> of God but also put huge value on infant life.
> She hated to see children die: 'You none know
> how good or how great they may live to be.'

The following year Joseph took a small place in Dagenham
where he and the children could go fishing. This brought joy
and confusion to Elizabeth in equal measure; she was concerned
about the children's behaviour and that other constant cloud,
money.

> 'We have lately been much pressed by company,
> which leads to handsome dinners,' she wrote.

This was good although visitors tended to make the children, already wilful, more worldly and might encourage 'frivolous' friendships. Also she was worried because during the previous year money had seemed to 'leek' away and she had struggled to be economical.

Visits to Dagenham became a great joy. She loved its informality and simplicity. They had two cheerful little houses on a piece of land that jutted out into the Thames estuary, among water and boats and willows and the greenest of grass. And it became an economy, not to mention a rest, to close the comparative grandeur of Plashet and holiday for a few quiet weeks down at Dagenham.

In March of that year, another piece of extravagance by Joseph was one for which everyone should be grateful. He commissioned the artist, C. R. Leslie to paint portraits.

> Elizabeth wrote: 'My J. F. appointed Leslie the painter to come and take him and myself, which from peculiar circumstances I have appeared obliged to yield to, as so many likenesses of me have already appear'd and it would be a trial to my family to have only these disagreeable ones to remain instead of a good one…'

Could there have been traces there of that old demon, vanity? Certainly she was aware of her contribution to prison reform and of the fame that it had brought. In later life she made it clear that after her death she wanted information about her life and work to be freely available to everyone. For now she was having her portrait painted.

> 'Sat to the artist, but got forward with letters for Newgate sale.' And by December she was relieved

that they had got through the year without
exceeding 'what we think it right to spend...' and
was grateful to the 'abundant kindness of some
near to us.'

There were still money worries during 1824 but she was living
in hope.

'Money has lately very unexpectedly dropped
in a good deal to myself, many hundreds if not
perhaps £2000, and this of course must excite
much thankfulness and pleasure…really wanted.'
She added: 'a year of much increase in property,
so as to remove many of those distressing fears
that I have often had on the subject of money,
which has come when wanted.'

Thanks to the help of family and perhaps fate, the Frys had
survived. But she was never one to be complacent; she knew
how it felt to be short of money albeit on a vastly different scale
to the poor, the convicts and others she tried to help.

Coastguards and Shepherds

A NOTHER PROBLEM was causing her concern now. A wave
of opposition to prison reform and to the interference by
ladies, was gathering force. Elizabeth found it very troubling;
she was not a debater and shrank from controversy.

> 'The burden and perplexity of the opposition
> in the prison cause is almost too much, it is
> so much against my nature to take my own
> defence, or even that of the cause in which I am
> interesting, into my hands,' she wrote. 'My mind
> feels really worn and as if I were driven by the
> almost innumerable calls upon me almost out
> of measure.' She added: 'Great opposition and
> difficulty in getting committees into prisons.'

She became very ill in April with renewed attacks of weakness
and fainting and was taken to Brighton for a cure. Her presence
there attracted large numbers of poor people to visit her. As
soon as she was well enough, she organised, with the aid of local
clergy and gentry, a District Charity Society for the visiting
and care of the poor. It was the first of its kind and arose out
of a combination of Elizabeth's personal efforts for the poor, at

Earlham, London and Plashet, and her interest in the Provident Societies which were created to encourage the poor to save.

The success of the Brighton District Society led to many others being formed. And, of course, in this as in her other organisations, Elizabeth expected each individual to have her own ardent personal touch and flawless good manners. Sadly, both were often absent and the whole idea of charity later fell into disrepute.

There was another bonus to her visit to Brighton. Because of attacks of faintness at night, she was often carried to an open window for air. Often she noticed on the sky-line the solitary figure of a man pacing the cliffs. She became curious about the man and was told he was a coastguard. His lonely and dangerous life and that of his colleagues intrigued her.

The next time she was out for a drive she stopped to speak to the coastguard on duty but the man told her politely that it was against the rules for him to speak to strangers. The following day, she was called upon by the officer in command of the station. He was at her service to answer all questions. Yes, it was true that the duties of these men, preventing smuggling and remaining clear from bribery and collusion, prevented them ordinary human contact. Elizabeth suggested that what these lonely men needed were books.

The officer agreed and Elizabeth enlisted Joseph's help and began to collect information on which to base a plan. It was clear that because a government department, red tape and a sum of money were involved, nothing could be done in a hurry. But within 10 years every coastguard station along the coast of England had a library. There were 500 of them and Elizabeth estimated the minimum cost at £3 apiece. Bibles were given out at once free by the Bible Society. But a £500 grant was finally made by Sir Robert Peel and a committee formed to raise the extra £1,000 needed to buy and distribute the books. This committee included an admiral and 12 naval captains, as well as Joseph Fry and two or three of the wealthy Barclay cousins.

Each library had 52 books of which 20 were adventure and travel, 10 were religious, four or five were biographies; others included Bunyan's Pilgrim's Progress, and a nature book. While they were about it, observed Elizabeth, why not school-books and other books for the children at the coast guard stations? An application was made to the Chancellor of the Exchequer who granted further cash and the additions were made accordingly. Elizabeth did the same, albeit on a smaller scale, for shepherds on the moors after noticing a lonely shepherd on a trip to Dartmoor.

It was around this time that she began to worry about her increasing fatigue. There was too much going on in her life and too many thoughts crowding her mind.

> She wrote of the 'great press of company and engagements' which multiplied 'so that I am at times almost afraid for my mind and understanding lasting long, the press upon me is so great.'

She was 44 then and beginning to tire easily. Perhaps she also had menopausal symptoms which had not yet been recognised as such in those days.

Gathering Clouds

B Y SUMMER 1825, she was feeling better and delighted in the marriage of her eldest son John to a cousin of the Barclay clan, Rachel Reynolds. They took up residence at Mildred's Court.

All was well until November when, to his mother's dismay, John installed a piano. Like father, like son? What could she do? It was her son's home now, Elizabeth reasoned in her diary. One could not tell people what to put and what not to put in their own rooms. Typically she agonised over the problem, tossing it this way and that in her mind. Finally she found a new path. When one's children became adult, they deserved the same tolerance and courtesy that one would extend to other adults. She was careful not to treat John and his wife as if she had authority in their house. She was putting experience to good use and remembering how Joseph's elder brother William had treated them as newly-weds so many years before.

A piano at Mildred's Court seemed trivial come December when a panic in the money market shook the Frys to the core. Several large banking houses in London and many in the country stopped payment. Many, both strong as well as weak, were in trouble; again Frys' bank was one of them.

Elizabeth recalled that Gurneys' banking house had made it
clear:

> '…they wd do no more'. So without help Frys
> bank was in trouble '…our house must then stop
> in that hour. My brothers Joseph John and Sam
> came to tell me of it and to consult me whether
> they shd run the risk of some thousands to do it
> for that day only. This was taking a great weight
> on myself. Deeply try'd as I was I did not give up
> hope and was still for every effort being made.
> The next morning they came to this conclusion
> that if our house had strength to stand through
> 1st and 2nd day alone (without their aid) they
> would then try to carry us through, if not we
> must fall.'

Fry's was safe for the moment. But the shock-waves reverberated
throughout the country. The shortage of gold at the time was
described by one financier as placing England 'within 24 hours
of barter'. And her brother Sam, if Elizabeth had but known it,
was close to the heart of the matter.

The idea of forming joint-stock companies seemed to some
financiers a way of making quick money. Of these, Sam Gurney,
aged 39, was one of the leaders. The launch of the Alliance
Assurance Company the previous year, under the combined
patronage of Sam with Nathan Rothschild, was an early event
in an exciting speculative time. One of the company's schemes
was to rehabilitate the South American gold and silver mines
and equip them with steam engines to strike for deeper ores.

Sam also had influence in a company which secured grants of
land in South America for mining and for emigrant colonies.
South America gleamed like El Dorado in the imagination of

the British public. Gold and silver had been exported there by the million in the spring of 1824. No one seemed to notice that there was too much money abroad. The private banks went on issuing as many notes as they could until the country was deluged with paper money. By 1825, there was 40 per cent more paper out than in 1822. Bankers were willing to discount bills at very long dates. The fever of speculation reached epic proportions. In the summer, the King's Speech, dismissing parliament for the session, had stated confidently that:

> 'The general and increasing prosperity on which
> His Majesty had the happiness of congratulating
> his Parliament at the opening of the session,
> continued to pervade every part of the kingdom.'

But fortunes were beginning to turn. No returns were coming from the huge speculations in South America. The need to collect debts became urgent. Here and there a commercial house could not meet its liabilities and was declared bankrupt. In vain the leaders of finance tried to suppress the demand for ready money. So many firms failed, one after the other, each spreading disorder in its own sphere of influence, that any kind of property became questionable as security.

Soon the banks began to fail, the securities they held for their rash advances having become, for the time being, little better than waste paper. The run upon the weaker country banks was immediate. In December, an important London bank, Pole's of Lombard Street, failed, dragging with it 44 provincial banks. Another Lombard Street banker failed the next day. Just a few weeks saw the downfall of 100 banks throughout the country.

The Cabinet called in Rothschild, Gurney and other able businessmen for advice. Restoring credit was imperative and for that, gold was the magic ingredient. The mint got to work coining it and gold poured forth at the rate of 150,000 sovereigns a day. The Bank of England agreed to make advances of gold to traders upon deposit of goods. But merchants did not need the gold in their hands so long as they knew they could get it. Trust was restored along with mutual confidence and that intangible necessity called 'credit'. Cautious trading resumed. The immediate crisis was over; the regulation of banking had begun.

The following year, the King's Speech at the opening of parliament confessed that the depression had abated more slowly than His Majesty had anticipated. It had not abated but the King's Speech was always buoyed by optimism.

The banking house of Fry had been saved thanks to Elizabeth's brother. Sam Gurney had survived intact and had helped in the more difficult operation of restoring his own credit – and that of the nation. But he only just saved Frys. In her diary of February 1826, Elizabeth confided:

> 'Sam has given me leave to use 200 pounds of my little remaining property for John and Rachel's bills. Ours are not heavier than we can expect, rather better perhaps. I was near sending out of the house some of our valuable pieces of furniture to get money to pay everyone that which is due.'

There was some comfort in this time of stress. 'Last evening my J.F. brought me a present from dearest little Louisa of 100 pounds sterling. My dearest husband brought me 50 pounds which unexpectedly came in to him, and my sweet dear son Wm. out of his own money saved me five as a little present.'

But Elizabeth felt guilt too. 'The very neat things the children and I had on (though partly presents) were rather a burden to me less those who knew our circumstances should think me extravagant.' And this led her to a quite striking conclusion: 'I fully unite in the Christian duty of true simplicity in dress but I think it is rather too much dwelt upon by us as a Society...I also can hardly bear to hear Friends make us out as of a chosen people above others.'

In the summer, Elizabeth enjoyed a short break by the river at Dagenham. This quiet holiday home always refreshed her but it was impossible to be fully at peace with the 'perplex'd state of our business'. One unexpected bonus was that while under this financial pressure, she found her problems with her children seemed unimportant. Adversity was proving unifying in many respects. And her clearer, maturing vision helped also.

> '...experience has proved in my beloved brothers and sisters that much of the unity of the spirit and the bond of peace may be experienced where we may not see eye to eye.'

Her youngest brother Daniel visited Plashet that summer with his aristocratic wife of three years, Lady Harriet Hay, a daughter of the Earl of Erroll. Elizabeth liked her and recorded that she was glad her brother had 'such a dear companion...He is a dear, kind brother to me, considering his circumstances, difference of age [11 years younger] etc to myself, he might naturally have turned his back upon me in the day of trouble instead of warmly and steadily doing all he can to help us.'

She was deeply grateful for her family's support.

'My other dear brothers are also now actively endeavouring to serve us and set our affairs in order,' she wrote. 'I am well provided for and have been all this year, a good deal through the abundant kindness of my brothers and sisters. I am able to give freely to the poor through the abundant kindness of my dear Uncle Barclay and cousin Hudson Gurney. They nearly kept us one half-year whilst the business was in so trying a state.'

The following year from February to May 1827 she took a break from the huge demands of her responsibilities, and travelled with her brother Joseph John to Ireland visiting prisons and Friends' Meetings. It was not a holiday as such and proved exhausting for Elizabeth. But they achieved much as their *Report of the Prisons of Ireland* bore witness.

Joseph was touchingly glad to have her home. Strolling with her and an Irish Quaker visitor in the garden, he caressed her hand upon his arm and became for once almost courtier-like:

'What pretty hands you have, m'dear!' And to their visitor: 'Did Friends in Ireland remark what pretty hands my wife has?'

Others were glad to have her back too. By mid-summer family matters had once again taken priority. She rushed to Earlham where her sister Rachel was seriously ill. Sitting beside her ailing sister in the Blue Room, shaded against the richly scented August heat, Elizabeth opened her diary so they could reminisce together. Her thoughts about this sister in particular, were poignant. She remembered her early beauty and her sad, lost love. Then she thought about each brother and sister in turn, their virtues and their worth. She did not praise the Quaker ones any more tenderly than the others. They were all, now even more than in the days of childhood, 'formed after my own heart.' Rachel had remained unmarried; she never recovered from losing the love of her life, Henry Enfield, to another. On 17 September, she died aged 48. It is said that the longed-for letter from Enfield saying that he had thought of her every day since they had parted, came while she lay dying. She is believed to have died with the letter clasped in her hand.

Early the following year, childhood memories returned again to haunt Elizabeth, this time in relation to her own past love, James Lloyd. She was called to Birmingham to attend the funeral of his father, Charles Lloyd and found there:

> '…others interesting to me whom in early life were dear to me, particularly James Lloyd to whom I was once engaged to be married in my young and gay days.'

She was accompanied on the trip by her brother Sam and was a speaker at the funeral.

But soon afterwards her thoughts returned to her children as often they did - frequently in the middle of business concerns.

> 'My little Harry has been very poorly, but is now better…I have also had to settle my Gurney in at school again with some anxiety because he has not appeared so happy there. Tried to make my visit pleasant to all the boys by taking them for a walk and giving them oranges.' Harry was now six and Gurney, twelve.

Elizabeth was moving gradually into broader paths. Perhaps renewed contact with the cultivated and academic Lloyd circle combined with her former appreciation of the qualities of 'fine' company into which her public fame increasingly took her, prompted this unusual entry in her diary.

> 'I long, I crave, I desire for more of the spiritual life amongst us, and I should much like more intellectual cultivation and taste amongst us. I think, as a family, it would tend to our profit and our pleasure.'

The Storm Approaches

As 1828 advanced, the attention of the Fry family was forced to concentrate on the physical necessities of life. Poverty of a kind, although still cloaked in outward comfort, was hovering over Plashet.

Elizabeth hated being financially vulnerable.

> 'When I see my own family generally in full prosperity and see myself and my family laid low before them as dependants almost for daily bread, and really in temporal things under their control, I feel almost ready to complain,' she confided to her diary. 'Fowell and Joseph [John] have been kinder than I know how to express to me, and Sam, I am sure, means the same, but from his fearful mind and extreme caution in business he has not in this time of deep distress shown himself so strong and firm a helper as they have, nor did he in 1825, partly I believe, because his judgement is against helping us through, and he is weary of the folly and great imprudence of our house.'

She added: 'However, no brother can be dearer
than he is to me and one of the deep sorrows of
times like these is being wounded in the house
of our friends.' Frank Cresswell, on the other
hand, had been the perfect son-in-law. 'Frank
has behaved delightfully and been a son indeed
to me in every way during the time he has been
with us.'

Joseph had to go on a business trip in the spring and took
Elizabeth with him, an arrangement which as usual boosted
them both with holiday spirit. Their daughter Chenda and
her fiancé, cousin Foster Reynolds, came too. Leicester, Lynn,
Nottingham and Derby provided Joseph with necessary
business contracts and his wife with prisons, asylums and
Friends' Meetings to visit.

They stayed for a short while at Matlock in a quiet, comfortable
inn:

'...on the side of a high hill, the river Dore at
the bottom, full with the late rains, flowing over
rocks.'

The joy and peace of an English spring in the country soothed
their spirits even though the weather was wet. And their visit
to the inn was remembered long after when Foster and Joseph,
with great presence of mind, saved it from burning down after
Elizabeth's cloak, left to dry on a chair, caught fire.

Two months later there was more happiness when Chenda
and Foster married. It was a Quaker wedding although, once
married, Chenda promptly cast aside Quaker dress, but not her
faith.

Try hard as he did, Joseph's efforts to save the family fortune
were not enough. Storm clouds swept nearer. Businesses were

going down on every side and each one that fell dragged
others with it. On 26 August, Elizabeth made her last record –
although she did not know it – of what might be described as a
normal day at Plashet.

> 'I expect this morning – 1st sister El. on
> important business [her unmarried sister-in-law
> Elizabeth Fry who lived at Plashet Cottage] –
> next Josiah Forster perhaps to elderize me – next
> our clergyman to see after our poor – next Foster
> and Chenda and most of our family together.'

> She continued ponderously: 'I have felt, as
> I often do, the various influences to which I
> am peculiarly liable – particularly today, just
> expecting to be closeted hours with dear Josiah
> Forster who I may call one of our most authordox
> friends, and then to be hours in near contact with
> our very authordox high Church Clergyman
> [Rev Angelzaark's successor]; both young men of
> strong minds, views and influence. I have real
> love for dear Josiah and much unity though I
> feel from our very different circumstances and
> education we do not in all things, I believe, see
> eye to eye, and my degree of fear of him arises in
> my mind from the high value I have for the good
> esteem and unity of those in religious profession
> with myself, and apprehension that he does not
> fully understand us.'

> Her day ended with relief as she added to her
> diary: 'I had a satisfactory time with both the
> young men. Dear J. Forster only came from
> friendship.'

Within months, business imprudence combined with the misfortune of companies with which Fry money was entangled brought its inevitable conclusion. On 15 November 1828, she noted hurriedly:

> 'The storm has now entered our own borders. The expenses of the year have been so very heavy that it will be very difficult to make ends meet, my own money not coming in as usual.' On 20 November, she added hopefully: 'Some glimmering of light has arisen on our dark picture as to outward things. I have still money for all private debts, and for the present to live comfortably.' But before long it was another tale.

> 'December 3rd 1828. Here I am in my own room expecting an officer in, who is going round the house to take an inventory of all that we possess for our creditors. Another about the grounds taking an account of all that we have there – another in another part of the house watching over the rest of our property.'

The banking house of Fry had closed its doors on a run. Joseph Fry was bankrupt. The Gurney family once again rallied to help and Elizabeth clutched gratefully at each straw.

> 'Since writing the above, my dearest sister Hoare [Louisa] has given us in the most free and generous manner 286 pounds, brother Buxton [Fowell] 100, Priss 25, and Anna Gurney and Sarah Buxton 50; therefore we are now well provided for…'

Letters of sympathy and loyal friendship poured in from every side. Anti-slavery campaigner William Wilberforce wrote. So too did her brother-in-law Rev Francis Cunningham, the Marquis of Cholmondeley, the committee of the Ladies' Prison Society, her old friend Amelia Opie and many members of the Society of Friends who loved and admired her. Her elder sister Kitty hurried down from Earlham to console her in person.

> Oh,' she wrote in her diary, 'if any read this Journal may it lead them to a most tender compassion for those in perplexed and reduced circumstances.'

If she thought things could get no worse, she was wrong. The Society of Friends had always been concerned with the business integrity of its members. But in those days, they were much more ready to 'disown' on the slightest provocation. So many Quakers were concerned in banking at the time that fear for Quaker credit may have urged more severe disciplinary action than usual upon business failure.

> Elizabeth braced herself. 'To-day the case of my beloved husband will be brought before our Monthly Meeting.'

Joseph was disowned. The judgement seemed unnecessarily harsh and ill-deserved. Both he and Elizabeth bitterly felt the blow to pride and self-respect.

> In March 1829 Elizabeth wrote: 'Now it comes near to the point I feel the prospect of my husband's disownment very much. It is so striking a cut down to our family in so many ways. Yesterday at our Monthly Meeting, whether

from my naughty nature or not I cannot say, but
I could not but observe the wonderful contrast
of my circumstances with some present. Looking
at the dear Upton family, Saml. and Eliz. [her
brother Samuel and wife Elizabeth who lived
at Ham House, Upton, near Plashet] and their
children in the midst of prosperity, spiritually
and materially.'

Finally Elizabeth's children had a valid reason to be 'grieved
with Friends' and they did so vociferously. The fact that in
the long run only one of the Fry children, Chenda Reynolds,
remained a Quaker might well be traced, not to their mother's
public work, but to their father's disownment in his hour of
need. The bitterness which its harshness and injustice aroused
in their young, proud minds crystallised their youthful rebellion
against the restraints of the Society of Friends.

Adapting to Change

J OSEPH AND Elizabeth knew that finally they would have to close their beloved Plashet. They needed a smaller house. But where to start? Perhaps unexpectedly it was her brother Sam, always doubtful of the Frys' ways with money, who came to the rescue.

Sam had been cautious in supporting the fortunes of a sinking house – probably feeling that to do so was simply throwing good money after bad. He was an adventurous man who found it hard to resist exciting business opportunities wherever in the world they might appear but he was known also for his generosity. Once when a City friend, in whose integrity Sam had complete confidence, was put on trial for forgery, although he had no actual evidence to offer he went down and stood beside the man in the dock. That silent weight of confidence ensured the man's acquittal.

The lustre of the name Gurney in the City was reflected 45 years later when Gilbert and Sullivan's *Trial by Jury* was written:

> *At length I became as rich as the Gurneys –*
> *An incubus then I thought her,*
> *So I threw over that rich attorney's*
> *Elderly, ugly daughter*

Sam, although always adept at figures, was never entirely comfortable with his wealth. He would listen quietly when unworldly Friends spoke to him about giving too much time and attention to the pursuit of business.

> 'But what am I to do? I am not bookish, like my brother Joseph [John]!' he would declare.

He gave £20,000 a year to charity and a hundred allotments on his estate were given rent-free to those poor and unemployed of East Ham who had the drive to cultivate them.

He was genuinely concerned about his sister Betsy whom he admired greatly. Now that Frys bank had come to its foreseen and inevitable ruin, he felt he could offer some practical help. He had a house available at Upton Lane and by June 1829 Joseph and Elizabeth were comfortably established in it with their family. Their garden joined the grounds of Ham House into which they could freely overflow enjoying the company of Sam and his family. They were still in the neighbourhood which they loved and had an adequate income. Besides, they were learning how to economise and Elizabeth was well aware how fortunate they were.

Luckily their daughter Katherine at 28, and unmarried, was able to undertake the housekeeping. Joseph and his sons were putting all their energies into their tea business which was still solvent. It was not too uncomfortable to take the stage coach the seven miles into the city instead of enjoying the comfort of one's own carriage. And it was interesting to see the new uniformed policemen patrolling the street; peelers or bobbies they were called after the Home Secretary Sir Robert Peel. The world seemed to be moving at an amazing pace. There were steamers on the Thames now. And Sam joked about some day having a steam-carriage of his own, without horses, in which he would go tearing into London at 10 mph!

Elizabeth simply and graciously adjusted herself to her new situation. From the first, Upton Lane became a place of contentment and simple elegance. Not the old life impoverished, but a new life, simpler and perhaps freer.

> 'We are now nicely settled in this our new abode, and I may say although the house is small, and garden, yet it is pleasant and convenient, and I am fully satisfied and I hope thankful for such a home under such afflicting circumstances as ours are,' she wrote. 'A delightful view of Greenwich Hospital park and the shiping on the river and other parts of Kent, as well as the cattle feeding upon the marshes.'

And she came to understand the views of her brother Sam.

> 'I have since, from what has passed, seen that that which was done by my beloved brother in business was a right and prudent measure, and he had good reason to act as he did, both for our sakes and others, and we should have been saved trouble indeed had our hopes attended to him.'

For many women it might have been easier to leave the neighbourhood in which for 20 years she had been a principal figure, dispenser of charity, and generous mistress. It would have been kinder not to live within walking distance of Plashet and to see it closed and in the hands of caretakers, to watch its lovingly tended garden and grounds become gradually choked with weeds. But Elizabeth had for more than 10 years been experiencing the deep inner satisfaction of successful work. In the world's eye she was not Mrs Fry of Plashet House, but

Elizabeth Fry of Newgate. After the first shock of bankruptcy and the initial move, she found a sense of release in being cut off from a mass of domestic detail and village responsibility.

Her first diaries at Upton Lane were full, not of struggle to make ends meet or of vain regrets or weak submissions, but of her relations with her children and the problems of education. She was gaining sympathy and understanding; maturity and experience were mellowing her.

> 'I feel more hopeful on account of my family…I
> see in many of them, if not all, much that is good.
> Naturally,' she confesses to herself, 'I consider
> them a very favoured family, particularly in
> talent and power of mind, and open, generous
> dispositions.'

Fortunately they were able to retain Dagenham as an inexpensive family retreat. The whole family including married sons and daughters and grandchildren occupied the two roomy cottages all summer long, year after year, freely passing from one to the other in happy family parties; rowing and fishing in the *Elizabeth Fry*, coming home in the early evening over the water, singing to the beat of oars. Grandmother Elizabeth secretly loved to hear the children sing; her grandchildren could do what her children could not.

Although content at Upton Lane, the seesaw of existence continued to pain Elizabeth and she was ever sensitive to criticism. In September 1829, she was elated and recorded in her diary:

> 'My husband is likely to have all his private debts
> paid to the full about the end of this month.'

Later in the year she was low and still smarting from their public disgrace, the constant economising and worse, criticism of herself.

> 'I still hear from different quarters evil reports of me...I have been raised up in no common degree and cast down in no common degree.' She even indulged in a little self-pity: 'I have now had so many real disappointments in life that my hopes, that have so long lived strong that I should see much brighter days in it, begin a little to subside.'

To add to her concerns, her son William decided to discard his Quaker coat. She did not want to be unreasonable and she wondered why she minded so much. Her own loyalty to the Society had been severely tested. She wrote:

> 'The longer I live the more difficult do I see education to be; more particularly as it respects the religious restraints that we put upon our children. To do enough and not too much is a most delicate and important point. I begin seriously to doubt whether as it respects the peculiar scruples of Friends, it is not better quite to leave sober-minded young persons to judge for themselves...I have such a fear that in so much mixing religion with those things that are not delectable, we may turn them from the thing itself. I see, feel, and know that where these scruples are adopted from principle, they bring a blessing with them, but where they are only adopted out of conformity to the views of others, I have very serious doubts whether they are not a stumbling-block.'

Perhaps being called to the bedside of a childhood friend's dying son took her back to the days of her own rebellious girlhood and helped improve her relationship with her children. Certainly her children's love affairs fascinated her. It was no use wanting them all to marry Quakers, of that she was well aware. William, who was 'so kind a son, had so sweet and affectionate a disposition – and such talents' was in love with the daughter of a lord before falling for the daughter of Sir John Henry Pelly, Governor of the Hudson's Bay Company. Both were fashionable young ladies yet as 'sweet, amiable and well-disposed' as any Quakers.

> 'It is my solid judgement,' she considered, 'that any real love is not a thing to be lightly esteemed, and when young persons of a sober mind come to an age like Wm., more than 24 years old, it requires very great care how any undue restraint is laid upon them in these most important matrimonial engagements, and that we are all so short-sighted about them that the parties themselves should after all be principally their own judges of it.'

Although tested, Elizabeth's loyalty to the Society of Friends remained firm. If she, and other liberal-minded Friends, had left the Society, it might have suffocated from its own restrictions in the 19th century. But she remained loyal and by the gentle force of her growing stature helped strengthen and develop it.

At Yearly Meeting in 1830, Elizabeth was free for the first time from the burden of hospitality – never again would Mildred's Court keep open house. She concentrated on the state of the Society and the part she played in the various meetings which are the heart of the Society's policy.

'The state of our Society as it appeared in the
Yearly Meeting, was very satisfactory, and really
very comforting to me: so much less stress laid
upon little things, more upon matters of greater
importance, so much unity, good-will, and what
I felt Christian liberty amongst us,' she wrote.

'I am certainly a thorough Friend, and have
inexpressible unity with the principle, but I
also see room for real improvement amongst
us; may it take place! I want less love of money,
less judging others, less tattling, less dependence
upon external appearance. I want to see more
fruit of the Spirit in all things, more devotion of
heart, more spirit of prayer, more real cultivation
of mind, more enlargement of heart towards
all; more tenderness towards delinquents [those
guilty of minor misdeeds], and above all more
of the rest, peace and liberty of the children of
God.'

Although she might have wished less importance was given to
people's outward appearance, the customs of Friends still had
a strong hold on her. Despite their disgrace, she could not
help clinging to her husband's Quakerism for him, even in its
outward aspects. She met him first, and came to love him, in
his Quaker coat. But like William, Joseph was glad to be rid of
it – when he could afford another.

In late summer, she wrote:

'My dearest husband has been at home, and his
company I have enjoyed, and if it were not that
I deeply lament his intention of entirely casting
off the appearance of a Friend, which he means

to do, and I fear, a good deal of his esteem for the Society and its principles, I should think in other respects I have cause to trust that he is in a happier and even more peaceful state than sometimes.'

It was true. There was a relief from years of strain by knowing the worst. There was almost serenity in Joseph's sturdy acceptance of the worst and in his immediate reconstruction of his life and business on other more moderate lines. The speed with which he cleared his private debts, at any sacrifice – of Plashet, of Dagenham if it had been necessary, and of all that went with them – was evidence of his character. But both bankruptcy and his casting out by the Society of Friends had a profound effect on him.

Royalty and Reform

T HE DISTRESS throughout England continued. Although money was abundant now, the Depression was accompanied by cholera epidemics, riots, rick-burning and machine-breaking. The Combination Acts forbidding trades unions had been repealed in 1824. There were strikes, encouraged by emerging trades unions, and cut-throat competition which exploited child labour and threw grown men into idleness. More modern schemes of employment were instigated such as setting thousands of unemployed men to work on the roads.

The accession of the 64-year-old William IV to the throne in 1830 on the death of George IV had marked out his niece Princess Victoria as Heir Presumptive. Elizabeth called upon the young Princess and her mother to interest them, on Fowell Buxton's behalf, in the question of slavery. She was impressed by Princess Victoria's childish charm.

She was also presented to the King's consort, Queen Adelaide, and was in some demand among the ladies of the nobility as an unofficial spiritual advisor. They would send for her when in trouble and depend upon her common sense, her dispassionate sympathy, and that extra something from beyond which was associated with Quakerism. There can have been few people at the time, apart perhaps from priests, in receipt of more curious secrets than Elizabeth Fry. Yet this side of her life, though well known to her family and close friends, and mentioned often, sometimes with a sigh, in her diary, received no publicity. Indeed Byron in *Don Juan* took her to task for neglecting the upper classes without perhaps knowing all the facts.

Oh, Mrs Fry! Why go to Newgate? Why
Preach to poor rogues? And wherefore not begin
With Carlton, or with other houses? Try
Your head at harden'd and imperial sin.
To mend the people's an absurdity.
A jargon, a mere philanthropic din,
Unless you make their betters better: - Fy!
I thought you had more religion, Mrs Fry.

Teach them the decencies of good threescore;
Cure them of tours, hussar and highland dresses;
Tell them that youth once gone returns no more,
That hired huzzas redeem no land's distresses;
Tell them Sir William Curtis is a bore,
Too dull even for the dullest of excesses,
The witless Falstaff of a hoary Hal,
A fool whose bells have ceased to ring at all.

Tell them, though it may be perhaps too late
On life's worn confine, jaded, bloated, sated,
To set up vain pretences of being great,
'T is not so to be good; and be it stated,
The worthiest kings have ever loved least state;
And tell them — But you won't, and I have prated
Just now enough.
[Canto 10 LXXXV – LXXXVII]

With her simplicity and her beautiful manners, she did just that. She even quietly objected in the highest quarters about the extravagance displayed at royal coronations, weddings and christenings in such a time of widespread poverty. As Lord Ashley, politician and social reformer, later observed, her 'courtly politeness knew no change in the palace of a prince or in the cell of a convict. She respected human nature.'

Although still shaken by her personal circumstances and constantly challenged by obligations and moral dilemmas, Elizabeth continued to juggle her public work and her changing home life. Throughout the turmoil, her work remained constant.

> 'I have felt much comfort in my Newgate visits, and having but little company [guests at home] I have been able more than common to attend to the prisoners.'

Aware of the general unrest around her, she pressed on with her prison reform. Sometimes she was summoned to appear before a committee of the House of Commons, once even before the House of Lords. She was accompanied on these occasions usually by Fowell Buxton, or by her brother Sam. Patiently she would repeat her recommendations for permanent legislative reform: women warders for women prisoners, solitude by night, association by day, paid employment, education, rewards and reformation.

She refused to accept that there was any benefit from solitary confinement. And she disagreed with her brother Joseph John that trouble should be taken to make prison 'irksome and unpopular'. In their joint report on the prisons of Ireland, chiefly written by Joseph John, she could not prevent him encouraging the use of the treadmill for male prisoners. But she immediately inserted a statement that it must not be used for female prisoners. Indeed she was delighted when four years later the first prison with women warders for women prisoners opened in Dublin.

Elizabeth's concern was always for the return of prisoners to society. What would best fit them for that? But sometimes it was a case of swings and roundabouts. With the decline of transportation new prisons had to be built and to her horror the idea of solitary confinement began to loom large again. She told a parliamentary committee in 1832 that:

> '...solitude does not prepare women for returning to social and domestic life, or tend so much to real improvement as carefully arranged intercourse during part of the day with one another, under close superintendence.'

More important than the building of prisons was the question of how to prevent crime? Very early she had come to the conclusion that the chief causes of crime were 'ignorance, irreligion, and poverty.' In her eager, amateur way she attacked these 'evils' whenever they came her way. She refused to recognise that certain crimes - greed, avarice, murder - might never be 'cured'. She wanted Acts of Parliament to deal with crime in a widespread and drastic way and kept a very close eye on all bills of a social nature which came before the House. She considered them to be a woman's business.

So too did Harriet Martineau. Harriet, like Elizabeth, was born in Norwich when the latter was 22. She was the daughter of a manufacturer, a Unitarian, and began her literary career as a writer on religious subjects. She became an ardent advocate of social reform. The same wave of bankruptcy which engulfed the Frys also wiped out the Martineaus. But young Harriet rejoiced to be free at a stroke from the burden of gentility and forced to earn her own living. Fancywork, her mother suggested, indeed even tried to enforce. But Harriet had other ideas.

She was interested in political economy, a subject not yet taught in any university. Since she believed that theory could best be learned by concrete example, she started a series of tales on various aspects of economics. She wrote *Illustrations of Political Economy* [1832-4] and *Poor Law and Paupers Illustrated* [1833]. She was read avidly not only by the public but by members of parliament. Her work was filled with mental stimulus, the clarification of issues, and accurate information which could be used in debate.

Elizabeth read her work with admiration, as did Fowell Buxton and Joseph John. In 1833 an interview took place between the two women which Elizabeth, who instigated the meeting, never mentioned in her diary but which Harriet recorded at length. Omissions such as this in Elizabeth's diaries may have been due to the fact that she wrote primarily for herself. Although at this stage in her life she was aware that her diaries might be used by later biographers, and gave specific permission for it 'even if my weaknesses are acknowledged'. Harriet herself left an 'autobiographical memoir' ready for publication after her death.

To have been a fly on the wall during their meeting would have been interesting. Their discussion shows the importance, to both women, of Elizabeth's conscious influence in parliamentary affairs. They met at Newgate in the Matron's room. Harriet, knowing the conversation would concern politics, brought a clergyman as witness. The trusting and easy going Elizabeth never thought of such a thing.

The two ladies, aged 31 and 55, respected and admired one another which made the conversation easy. Elizabeth had heard that Harriet was informed on some of the measures relating to Poor Law reform that were shortly due before the House.

She wondered if it would be 'honourably possible' for Harriet to pass on some of that information so that 'our section of members might come prepared?' Harriet was able to give useful information on the principles of the proposed measures without betrayal of confidence, and willingly did so.

Elizabeth took notes, thanked her, complimented her on her books, and the ladies parted amiably. The results were excellent:

> 'Our section of members' came well prepared, and one and all 'unflinchingly supported' the reform measures. No doubt Elizabeth, always conscious of intellect when she met it and aware of her own short-comings, regarded Harriet with some envy. But Harriet regarded Mrs Fry as nothing less than 'sublime'.

Visiting the Continent

T HE FOLLOWING year, the Duke of Gloucester died. Elizabeth mourned the death of their Earlham childhood friend, then Prince William. She was a frequent visitor at Gloucester House. So the Duchess described the prince's last hours and peaceful death in minute detail. For Elizabeth it was the loss of an old friend and the breaking of yet another link with Earlham and the past.

She was conscious of time passing and of her life flowing down the generations. Witness the family numbers which collected at Upton Lane for special celebrations these days!

> 'There is very great blessing to look round upon our lovely family – children and children's children…' she wrote. In spite of all, she could feel at last 'the pleasure of having with my children the double tie, not only of mother and children, but a friendship formed upon its own grounds. I certainly think that in no common degree my children feel me their familiar friend.'

There was one house where her fame was not recognised. Where she carried no weight; where she was nobody. And

that was Runcton Hall, near Lynn where her youngest brother
Daniel was master; he had bought the hall and moved there
in the autumn of 1816. She was a sister and a welcome guest
certainly, but nothing more. Dan had very definite ideas about
the place of women; and Elizabeth's reaction to him was rather
surprising.

> 'From [a visit to] Earlham I went to a totally
> different atmosphere...Dan would not even
> allow me to read the Scriptures with himself
> and children. To myself I feel it a previlige and
> an advantage to be for a while where I am not
> looked up to or depended upon for religious help
> in the degree I am at home. I feel it an advantage
> to myself to be thought little of. I think it leads
> to a more watchful and humble deportment
> and a more just view of myself. I delight in the
> quiet and liberty of my own room, and I spent,
> I think, some of the sweetest hours here I spent
> anywhere, not being driven by so many interests
> as at home.'

In the latter years of Daniel's life, the bank at Lynn failed,
and he was endowed £2,000 a year by the wealthy widowed
Hannah, Lady Buxton – a suitably sisterly act which he must,
nonetheless, have found humiliating.

Long before that, however, in the summer of 1837 William IV
died of pneumonia leaving no legitimate children. His niece,
the 18-year-old Princess acceded to the throne and so began
the Victorian era.

Elizabeth was 57 now and Joseph, 60. Over the years she had
put on weight and had the matronly look captured in George
Richmond's portrait of her. She still worried about Joseph,

the lasting effect of bankruptcy and the Society's disownment. During May 1833 he went through an unspecified spiritual experience. Perhaps it was something similar to the one experienced by Elizabeth when, as a young woman at Meeting in Norwich in 1798, she first heard William Savery speak. Perhaps it had something to do with the cholera epidemic which was raging at the time. Either way, it was a 'powerful visitation of Judgment mingled with mercy' and had a lasting influence. Afterwards Joseph kept an occasional diary to keep himself up to the mark. Sometimes there might be just one entry all year, sometimes none.

She was right to be concerned about him because he was distracted too. He continued to have business worries but was deeply concerned about their younger sons, Harry, now 15 and more particularly about Gurney, aged 21. And he was still having trouble with himself. The Society of Friends had accepted him back into the fold. But the damage it had done was irreparable. In May 1837, he made an entry in his occasional diary:

> 'Our Monthly Meeting, which had disowned me (not I think on sound or at all just grounds) at the time of our failure in 1828, my honour or uprightness never having been even called in question or ground given, has, during the past year, re-instated me in membership. I apprehended it my duty to apply for it, although I have never yet believed myself required to conform in outward appearance or speech to the customs of the Society or its peculiarities. My dress is simple and plain...'

The humiliation had cut him deep; all the deeper perhaps because of his wife's celebrity. Something within him died and never raised its head again; certainly his love of music waned.

> '…in all these changing things the most
> remarkable change I have experienced has been
> relative to my great love joined to some taste for
> music, with a correct ear and some cultivation in
> singing, which love seems to have passed away
> like a summer cloud, or died off like the leaves
> in autumn.'

It was more than music troubling their son Gurney. A harassed Joseph came to the conclusion that for his own sake and for the sake of peace and harmony in the household, Elizabeth should stay at home more. He made himself extremely clear and Elizabeth was humbled, astonished and distressed.

> 'June 18th. This morning my dearest husband
> really feelingly expressed his deep feeling of my
> constant engagements – calls of duty from home.
> I deeply felt it, for much as I make a point of
> always dining at home and spending evening
> and morning with him and my family yet my
> mornings are much occupied by public and
> relative duties – ministerial, public, children,
> brothers and sisters, their children and others in
> illness, sorrow, etc etc. I felt greatly cast down at
> his remark, desiring to be a faithful loving wife.'

Ironically it was Joseph who next left home. Gurney's 'sense of sin' and smouldering unhappiness and reticence brought on a condition so serious 'so low and morbid' that both parents realised he needed medical attention. On medical advice, Joseph left shortly afterwards for the Continent with Gurney, and took

Harry along for company. Travel, change and recreation were the doctor's prescription – and a suitable marriage might help. They returned with rosy cheeks, smiles and good news. Gurney had met Sophia Pinkerton; and it ended with an engagement.

While they had been away, Elizabeth had been to Earlham to say farewell to her brother Joseph John, who was setting off to travel in the ministry in America. She and Sam and his wife [Elizabeth] went with him to Liverpool where Elizabeth put flowers in his cabin and wept to see him go.

> 'We made things comfortable for him. I attended to the books, and that a proper library should go out for the crew, passengers and steerage passengers.'

Returning to Lynn and Earlham for a further visit, Elizabeth had her first journey by railway from Liverpool to Birmingham. Nothing could be less enjoyable than this new mode of travel, she felt. It was too fast to see the scenery properly:

> '...and the noise is deafening, the motion jarring, particles of cinders or iron dust get into your eyes and blind you for the time and make your eyes weak for a day or two afterward.'

And the crowd! And those packages! It made her think wistfully of the days when they owned their own carriage. But so many people had no carriages of their own nowadays. And the railway was certainly one of the greatest marvels of the age.

Joseph's trip had rekindled his fondness for travel to the Continent. He had been there several times; Elizabeth, on the other hand, had been no further than Ireland and the Channel Islands. His account of the trip with his sons, the messages he brought from some of her correspondents and his encouragement of her interest made her apply for a certificate to travel in January 1838.

What a time of year to sail! She braved the rough Channel crossing and the rigours of winter to set foot in France for the first time. Her husband escorted her, together with two Quaker friends, a woman companion and Josiah Forster. It seemed an extraordinary lack of judgement to plan such a journey at that time of year. Perhaps Joseph was called to Paris on business and Elizabeth took the opportunity to accompany him. Or perhaps both found they had a rare window, a month or two when each could cut loose from their various commitments at the same time and they seized it.

Inevitably, Elizabeth arrived in Paris feeling ill with a fever and was confined to their hotel for some days. However, she received many distinguished visitors there and later was able to visit various prisons. She and Joseph met the Duchess of Orleans, and were presented to King Louis-Philippe and Queen Marie-Amalie. She wrote a memorandum, an informal diplomatic paper, to the King on the state of the prisons as she found them.

She found the whole visit fascinating. At a dinner given for her at the home of the British Ambassador, Lord Grenville, the conversation became so moving that some of the exalted guests were reduced to tears. Hidden springs of hope and faith were touched on many fashionable occasions, and worldly people went away temporarily aware at least that life was short, that there might be a God, that they could do something, if they tried, to improve suffering in others less fortunate than themselves.

She left for home in April and was determined to return. And so she did - between 1838 and 1843 she made five trips to the Continent. Back home there was trouble: Gurney was trying, low-spirited and irritable. His 22nd birthday did not go well.

'I gave him a beautiful Bible and his father, a
present; but I am sorry to say instead of appearing
pleas'd or much so, he appear'd rather disposed
to complain that the Bible was not something
else and the present of money might be spent
some way different to what his father wished.
How discouraging! but at times for all this I see
kindness, love and gratitude in him, but he is in
a low state this morning.'

His future father-in-law, Dr Pinkerton crossed over
unexpectedly from the Continent early in May and visited
Elizabeth and Joseph. They were quite open with him as to
Gurney's condition, as far as they understood it. And Dr
Pinkerton, forming his own opinion, decided that the marriage
should go ahead.

Gurney 'seemed low' and produced what was to Elizabeth a
very distressing symptom. He announced that in future he
intended to go to church instead of Meeting.

'I thought part arose from bodily infirmity,'
wrote the anxious mother. 'I therefore gave
him quinine, and it is curious to observe his
improvement.'

It would, however, take more than quinine to keep Gurney Fry
a Quaker.

Gurney returned to England with his bride in August after the
wedding at Frankfort-on-the-Main on 12 July 1838. Their
return was awaited:

'With no small anxiety…We were much pleased
at Sophia's appearance, pleasing though not

handsome – gentle, very unaffected, sensible, sweet in her manners to Gurney. Gurney at first appeared an altered man, so very sober, happy and agreeable.'

On her return from a visit to Scotland that autumn to make a report on the horrors of solitary confinement in the prisons there, Elizabeth wrote in her diary, with relief:

'…my dearest husband and Katherine appear'd happy and Gurney and Sophia remarkably so.'

Elizabeth was popular in Scotland partly because she so enjoyed their mountains and flowers. But typically she was unaware of the impression she had made on certain keen-eyed people who had met her in person. One of them, George Douglas Campbell, 8th Duke of Argyll, wrote of her in his memoirs:

'She was the only really very great human being I have ever met with whom it was impossible to be disappointed. She was, in the fullest sense of the word, a majestic woman. She was already advanced in years, and had a very tall and stately figure. But it was her countenance that was so striking. Her features were handsome in the sense of being well-proportioned, but they were not in the usual sense beautiful. They were only calm and wise and steady. But over the whole countenance there was an ineffable expression of sweetness, dignity, and power. It was impossible not to feel some awe before her, as before some superior being. I understood in a moment the story of the prison…It is a rare thing indeed in this poor world of ours to see any man or woman whose personality responds perfectly to the ideal conception of an heroic character and an heroic life.'

The following March, Baron von Bunsen, the Prussian Ambassador, was presented to her in London and went even further.

> 'A tall, large figure, about 60 years of age, with eyes small but sweet and commanding expression – a striking appearance, not plain, but rather grand than handsome. This was Mrs Fry, my favourite saint.'

It was around this time that Elizabeth became increasingly restless. There was so much to do, so many opportunities were open to her, such prompt results occurred in reform wherever she appeared, albeit not within her own obstinate family circle. She felt driven hither and thither in the effort to work - 'while it is yet day'. And constantly she faced a conflict of heart. She didn't want to disregard her husband's protest about being away from home too much; she didn't want to leave him, or her family. But she felt drawn to her work. On many occasions she persuaded Joseph to accompany her. On others, she used the opportunities offered by accompanying him on necessary business trips.

Shortly after meeting Baron von Bunsen, she visited France again accompanied by Joseph, eldest daughter Katherine, and Josiah Forster. Their youngest son, Harry, joined them in Paris. Her reputation was so widespread by this time that at Boulogne she was recognised at once, and almost mobbed in her hotel by people eager to see her. She was not allowed to leave Boulogne until she had visited the prison.

When she reached Paris the hotel staff, who remembered her interest in them on her former visit, beguiled her into the kitchen, and listened eagerly to her broken French as she tried to tell them a little about faith and practice. Then they all wanted to shake hands with her, from the chef down. The efforts of her childhood French tutor, Monsieur Lesage were not, after all, in vain!

From then on there were social events, meetings and prison visits. Elizabeth received a letter from the Minister of the Interior granting her and Joseph and Josiah Forster permission to visit all the prisons in France. They remained for six months and made an extended tour.

Joseph may have felt that these long absences from home were incompatible with business – and family life – for this trip was his last. But since the mysterious day of his spiritual experience in May 1833, he had thrown himself into his wife's work. During this French visit he not only gave her the physical support and care which protected her constantly from unnecessary exhaustion, but also took a definite interest in her prison work. He wrote a long letter, on his wife's behalf, to some of the French authorities on the subject of solitary confinement. He stressed the need for all restraining or disciplinary methods in prison to be used only when necessary in the process of restoring a prisoner to society as an efficient person.

> 'Too much silence is contrary to nature, and physically injurious both to the stomach and lungs. And as regards the faculties, we are credibly informed of the fact (in addition to what we have known at home) that amongst the monks of La Trappe, few attained to the age of sixty years without having suffered an absolute decay of their mental powers, and fallen into

premature childishness,' he wrote. [Monks in a Cistercian order founded in 1664 at La Trappe in Normandy included silence in one of their vows and Trappist monks and nuns around the world today still observe this vow.]

The extent to which practical suggestions from Joseph influenced Elizabeth throughout her career cannot be known. But the daily conversations of a long and affectionate marriage were bound to have had some influence, difficult though the effects of that would be to gauge. No doubt his financial support in the good times proved invaluable to her work and peace of mind. And apart from occasional outbursts, he was relaxed about her absences from home, respecting her right to be absent as almost equal to his own. His business acumen was hugely helpful too. He stood by her when she started the schools at Newgate and supported her coast-guard libraries. He was ever a friend to whom she could bring her ideas and problems for discussion.

Wider Horizons

O N HER third visit to the Continent in 1840 she was accompanied by her brother Sam and his daughter Elizabeth. But before they left, she was summonsed to an audience with the young Queen who was engaged to the German Prince Albert of Saxe-Coburg. Lord Normanby, the Home Secretary, presented her and the Queen asked her about her forthcoming trip. She also asked about the Chelsea Refuge for which she had sent Elizabeth £50. Elizabeth thanked her for the donation and for her continued support of 'various works of charity'.

Soon she and Sam and their party were on their travels and if anything could have exceeded the warm welcome she received in France, it was her reception in Germany. They left England in February and returned in May having visited Ostend, Brussels, Antwerp, Amsterdam and Berlin.

Elizabeth held the childish belief that English only needed to be made into baby talk to become intelligible to the foreigner. She moved graciously among the populace in France, Holland, Germany and Belgium offering little tracts from a well-arranged book store on the floor of the carriage and murmuring 'Booky! Booky!' in her melting voice. Some of her admirers maintained that whatever she said in that voice would have everyone listening, whether they understood it or not. A German prince, translating her words to a group of prisoners, saw the hardened audience gradually melt into tears and, moved himself, exclaimed: 'It is the gift of God.'

Elizabeth's niece proved a perfect companion, helpful and kind, and her brother Sam's extravagance certainly added greatly to the trip. He thought nothing of hiring a room in a hotel large enough for 200 people so that his sister, the remarkable Elizabeth Fry, might be able to hold suitable receptions.

A milestone of the trip was a visit to Kaiserwerth on the Rhine – although this visit received just a mention in Elizabeth's diary. She might not have gone there at all had it not been for Baron von Bunsen; he particularly reminded her not to miss it.

An ancient town six miles south of Dusseldorf, Kaiserwerth's fortunes went into serious decline some 17 years earlier in 1823. The silk mill which employed almost all the inhabitants failed and plunged the whole area into destitution. Fortunately it had a pastor, Theodore Fliedner, who was young, energetic and sensitive. He couldn't watch his people starve nor could he find them alternative employment, so he set off on a journey to Holland and England to raise funds for their relief. In England, the little Princess Victoria had headed his list of subscribers. And various wealthy Quakers such as Gurney, Fry, Hoare and Barclay also figured on it, as well as the non-Quaker Fowell Buxton.

Fliedner had met Elizabeth at Mildred's Court. He heard everywhere of her fame and went down to Newgate to see for himself what was being done. He had several conversations with her on the treatment of criminals in prison and the need for helping them to reinstate themselves in honest ways after their release. These conversations included also her other interests, the establishment of schools and the care of the sick.

The contact with Elizabeth Fry and her ideas and work formed a turning-point in Fliedner's life. He was deeply impressed. When he returned to Kaiserwerth, with his immediate task accomplished, he saw his life's work opening out before him. He lost no time in establishing, on Mrs Fry's lines, the Rhenish-Westphalian Prison Association. His position as a minister made it easy for him to enter the local prisons and gave weight to his steady pressure for reforms. His wife helped him and in 1833, in a tiny summerhouse in their garden, they opened a refuge for the reception of a single discharged prisoner.

The following year Fliedner returned to England, partly to raise more funds and partly to talk over his plans with Elizabeth. She gave him of her best and he spent a day at her house – a visit to be remembered forever by him but to Elizabeth distinguished by nothing whatsoever. She was doing this sort of thing all the time, for the entire civilised world east of the Atlantic. She made no special note of Fliedner's visit and soon forgot about it.

Three years later Fliedner and his wife added, on an equally modest scale at first, an infant school, a hospital in which to train volunteer nurses, and a small training department for teachers. How delighted then was Fliedner when on 8 May 1840 Elizabeth Fry and her party came to visit this little tree of her planting! Was she even aware that she had planted the seed? It was the kind of thing she rarely mentioned in her diary. Fliedner, in his honest enthusiasm, his spirit of humble discipleship, is bound to have mentioned it to her. He certainly did some years later in a letter:

> 'Of all my contemporaries, none has exercised a like influence on my heart and life…Thus may my happiness be estimated when Mrs Fry…came in person to see and rejoice over the growing establishment at Kaiserwerth.'

Naturally, she behaved beautifully. She went into every room, gave motherly advice to the 20 deaconesses and the young probationers and to the 12 young ladies in training as teachers. She inspected the wards of 40 or 50 patients; and went over the rules and regulations of the establishment, eagerly submitted for her inspection, in detail with Fliedner. 'Truly,' said Fliedner, glowing at the recollection, 'God was in the midst of us.'

These simple institutions paved the way, before the First World War, for a series of them: 30 in Germany and others at Jerusalem, Alexandria, Cairo, Beirut, Smyrna [Izmir] in Turkey and Bucharest.

Six years after Elizabeth's visit, Florence Nightingale heard about Kaiserwerth. She might have heard about it from Elizabeth herself in a personal interview during the mid-1840s. Certainly Nightingale greatly admired the famous older lady who lived life to the full unlike so many women at that time. When Florence finally visited Kaiserwerth in 1850, she found much there to inspire the development of her own great career.

Fry's Nursing Sisters

F OR ELIZABETH, the visit to Kaiserwerth reminded her of something she had been meaning to do. Back in 1829, the poet Robert Southey had written to their mutual friend Amelia Opie to:

> 'Engage her sympathies and those of Mrs Fry in the establishment of societies for reforming the internal management of hospitals and infirmaries; so as to do for the hospitals what Mrs Fry has already done for the prisons.'

> Amelia passed this on to Elizabeth who replied: 'I have seen the thing wanted to be done, ever since the days of my youth.'

She had even mentioned it in her Prison book in 1827. But Amelia had other things to do and Elizabeth had never found an opportunity to begin such a huge new project.

On her return from Germany, she made the initial plans for a nurses' training home in London. At first they were called Protestant Sisters of Charity but that was changed to, simply, Nursing Sisters. They were often known as Fry

Nurses. Her brother Sam Gurney's wife, Elizabeth, undertook the organisation once the project was launched. The Queen Dowager agreed to be Patroness and an active committee was promptly formed and funds, of course, were forthcoming. The Bishop of London, approached by Mrs Fry herself, gave his support. But she made it clear that the whole project was to be entirely non-sectarian.

Twenty young women were selected at first, trained for a probation period in one of the larger, better hospitals, and finally admitted as Sisters. They lived in the training home, wore a simple uniform, and received an annual salary. They went out to cases, lived-in or went by the day as required. To the poor they went free of charge. To the well-off they charged a guinea a week which went into the funds of their training home. Every nurse who served a stated number of years was to receive a pension on retirement, and a fund was started for that purpose.

This was the first attempt in England to train nurses and to put nursing on a professional basis. The Fry Nurses were respectable women of what in those days was called the lower class. Many women were already trained by experience, practice, good observation and common sense, and already took on nursing duties. To train more of these women and to make them more readily available, especially to the poor, was Elizabeth's aim. Later, Florence Nightingale would take Fry Nurses with her in the first band that went out to the Crimea.

Elizabeth was now 60. Her health was becoming unpredictable and she was tired when she returned from the Kaiserwerth trip. How wonderful it would be to spend time quietly at Upton Lane with Joseph, visiting and being visited by her children and grandchildren, and ensuring that all her prison reforms became permanent laws of the land through her personal contacts with authority.

But commitments stretched out in front of her. There was May Yearly Meeting, then the annual meeting of the British Ladies' Prison Society. There was the French Ambassador and a large party to entertain at home. And now there was also her new nurses' scheme needing attention.

Her daughter Rachel recalled a typical day:

> 'The morning began with a meeting of Friends in London; afterwards she waited upon the Duchess of Gloucester – had a short interview with the Duke of Sussex – drove from London to Upton with the Duchess of Sutherland and Lord Morpeth to meet, at Ham House, the American Delegates who had come to England on the subject of slavery.'

Newgate and the other London prisons badly needed her attention too. It seemed impossible to escape from this endless list of meetings...But as always in the midst of stress, there were rays of light. Her brother-in-law had been made a baronet and had become Sir Thomas Fowell Buxton. And her son William had reopened the manor house of Plashet and was living there with his wife and family. Her son John and his wife Rachel had built themselves a fine new house and no longer needed her to pay their debts. And she counted 18 children, including spouses, and 26 grandchildren. So long as she remained at Upton, she could snatch the occasional day of domestic peace in between work commitments.

Baron von Bunsen, now a firm friend whose son Ernest would shortly become family, had urged her, for the sake of her work, to stay at home and she knew this would be wise. Had she been able to remain there, she might have preserved her own health and put permanently into place some of her measures which depended so much on her personal input for their final success. But time and the need to stay in one place long enough to apply steady and constant pressure were needed, and this was not possible. The demands on her time seemed endless. She received a regular stream of letters from Europe – from the Queen of Prussia downwards. So of course when her brother Joseph John urged her to accompany him abroad in 1841 she went although hesitant at first because of her health. The journey was to include Holland, Germany, Prussia and Denmark and they had been offered letters of introduction to the King of Prussia. Joseph John, his daughter Anna, her niece Elizabeth Gurney, and her own maid would accompany her. She could not say no but found the 'roughs of the journey' very hard to bear. The best hired carriage in the world could be uncomfortable when it struck a bad road with 'sand up to the axles.'

They were away from the end of July to the beginning of October 1841. Royalty and prisons featured high on their itinerary and she enjoyed much of the trip although in poor health. A highlight was meeting Frederick William IV, recently crowned King of Prussia. From the moment they met, an extraordinary friendship had blossomed between the two. Warmth met warmth; simplicity met simplicity. She remembered an early meeting with him:

> 'The King began easy and pleasant conversation
> with me about my visiting prisons. I told him in a
> short, lively manner, the history of it. He said he
> heard I had so many children, how could I do it?
> This I explained…Our very serious conversation
> was mixed with much cheerfulness…I concluded
> by expressing my earnest desire that the King's
> reign might be marked by the prisons being so
> reformed that punishment might become the
> reformation of criminals; by the lower classes

being religiously educated; and by the slaves in their Colonies being liberated. The King then took me by the hand and said he hoped God would bless me.' From then on they shared a special friendship.

On returning to England, she found the trip to Ostend difficult although the crossing itself was 'calm and beautiful'. For some reason Joseph John wanted to return urgently, possibly to prepare for this third marriage in a few weeks, and they had travelled to the port with six horses for greater speed. Elizabeth's body just could not cope and she had become so stiff all over that it had taken two helpers to get her in and out of the carriage and up and down stairs. And she had told her husband, Joseph in a letter:

> 'I have a board in the carriage, so that when Joseph [John] and Anna are outside, I can quite rest and make a real sofa of it, when I need it, which I do for one or two stages in the day. Mary and Francois [her attendants] are very active and kind. I am indeed yours most faithfully and lovingly, E.F.'

Joseph was waiting at Dover to greet his wife on her return and was shocked by how ill she looked. So shocked that he would not risk the journey home and took her straight to the neighbouring seaside resort of Ramsgate to recuperate. She would never let Joseph John be blamed for her condition.

> 'I might have had the same attack at home,' she said patiently.

All autumn, she rested at one place or another with Joseph and her children looking after her. Her body suffered, but her spirits were serene. She had been taking a little opium and wine to settle her stomach for many years and was convinced her symptoms would be worse without them. Besides she felt it was almost worth being ill to be so well looked after by her husband and family. Her brother Joseph John, filled with remorse, gave her a little carriage and her sons provided her with horses for it. Her son William called at Upton Lane for a few minutes every morning on his way in from Plashet to the City and cheered her, as always, with his pleasant chat. And what a comfort it was to have 'a dear, valuable single daughter [Katherine] at home!'

Her life revolved more around home. Visitors came out to see her rather than inviting her into town. These included the Duchess of Sutherland and Baron von Bunsen and his wife. Daughter Katherine was kept hard at it, writing and answering letters on matters that were vital to the welfare of thousands of the oppressed and the miserable all over the British Isles and Europe. Treat prisoners as if they were redeemable; treat the mentally ill as far as possible as if they were sane; teach children, but do not overwork them or treat them harshly – these, in various contexts and applications, were the tenets of Elizabeth Fry's gospel.

And they carried weight; gradually producing results. In Russia, Germany and Denmark, in Holland, France, Scotland, Ireland and England chains were removed, old cruelties were stopped, men gaolers ceased to control women prisoners, the mentally ill were allowed books and occupations and sunshine and to sit at table for their meals instead of being treated like animals. And all prompted by the word of Elizabeth Fry.

In January 1842 she was well enough to accept an invitation from her friends Sir John and Lady Pirie. Sir John was Lord Mayor of London that year and he and Lady Pirie gave a luncheon at the Mansion House on 17 January at which Elizabeth was the guest of honour.

'I hardly ever had such kindness and respect shown me,' she wrote in her diary with unaffected satisfaction. But there had been difficulties.

'I was at first greatly try'd by the carriage not driving up to the door – my having to get out and walk through the mob, driven about on every hand, exceedingly dirty'd even up to the knees that we were doubtful whether my gown were not ruined. [Other carriages and the curious crowds may have prevented her driver from dropping her directly at the Mansion House.] I knew I was after the time and had the most hurried and confused dressing, the Lord Mayor waiting at the bedroom door for me, sending for me again and again. I much feared this flurry would overwhelm body and mind but as I walked into the drawing-room with the Lord Mayor, on his arm, I felt much quieted and supported and very soon in great degree recovered. And as Prince Albert, Sir Robert Peel, Sir James Graham, Lord Aberdeen, the Bishop of London etc came and spoke to me, I was quite self-collected and enabled I trust to put in the word in season.'

She continued: 'An important conversation with Sir James Graham, our present Secretary of State, on a female Prison being built; upon Patronage, Society, etc...With Lord Aberdeen, Foreign Secretary; I requested his help for anything I want for the continent of Europe. With Lord Stanley, our Colonial Secretary [Secretary of State for War and the Colonies], upon the

state of our Penal Colonies as it respected the
women in them and opened the door for further
communications with him on these subjects.'

The Prime Minister Sir Robert Peel walked her into dinner
and sat one side of her with Prince Albert on her other side. Sir
Robert's ear:

'Appear'd perfectly open to me and the Prince
entirely at home – indeed we both felt I believe
as if we had long been friends. I felt perfectly
easy to rise upon any religious occasions…But
I could not rise for toasts, a mode of showing
rejoicing and good will that I did not approve.'

She therefore refused to rise for any of the toasts, explaining her
reasons to her distinguished neighbours, and gracefully wishing
them health and best wisdom when their health was drunk. She
did rise for a 'solemn grace' and also for *God Save the Queen*:

'Feeling it as a hymn…but I told the Prince I did
not unite in praying for victory, for I wish'd only
for peace and no war, therefore no victory.'

She added: 'Sir Robert Peel proposed a toast for
the Lady Mayoress and at the same time spoke of
me in terms of regard and high esteem and said
there was not a table in Europe that would not
have been honour'd by my presence.' She felt she
ought to have risen to express her unworthiness
but 'I felt silence easyest and I trust it was safest.'

The King of Prussia

A NOTHER HIGHLIGHT of January was a visit to London by Frederick William IV for the christening of the Prince of Wales.

> 'The King of Prussia is come,' wrote Sarah Spencer, Lady Lyttelton in a letter, 'most brilliantly and affectionately received by the people, and magnificently indeed by the Queen…The King is fat and tall, and looks at first sight only plain, like a good-natured farmer; but his eyes, though small, are observant, and he talks like a sensible man.'

Lady Lyttelton later became governess to Queen Victoria's children.

There was someone the King was determined to see during his visit and he soon found out how to approach her. Elizabeth Fry and her husband and daughter must meet him for lunch at the Mansion House, this time on 30 January. This threw Elizabeth into a quandary. Some of the stricter Elders had already cast her 'under a cloud' for her participation in the other banquet barely a fortnight before. Were there not toasts and music? Her presence as the guest of honour might have given the impression that she approved of these un-Quakerly habits. And worse, this party was to be on a Sunday. But she really wanted to see her friend again. And a royal invitation was not to be refused. She tossed the problem in her mind – this way and that it went, 'plain' Quaker versus 'gay' Quaker.

Escorted by her beloved Joseph, who had learned now how to keep appointments by the clock, Elizabeth was in excellent time on this occasion. It was Mrs Fry who waited in the drawing room of the Mansion House and the King of Prussia who was late. He had been attending the service at St Paul's Cathedral, cynosure of hundreds of onlookers. But he came in, attended by the Duke of Cambridge, and greeted Elizabeth with the simple warmth of a plain gentleman – 'My dear friend!'

As they took their seats at the table, Elizabeth quietly asked the Lord Mayor if toasts might be omitted – as a favour to her – since it was Sunday. The Mayor whispered a plea just to drink the Queen's health – and that of their royal guest. But the King, whose mastery of English was perfect, had overheard and said that he was sure Sir John would do exactly as Mrs Fry wished. Elizabeth hoped this would pacify the elders and settled down to enjoy herself. The King also enjoyed himself.

> 'I have seldom seen any person more faithfully
> kind and friendly, than he is,' recalled Elizabeth.
> 'The Duke of Cambridge was also there, and
> many others who accompanied the King. We
> had much deeply interesting conversation on
> various important subjects of mutual interest.
> We spoke of the christening. I dwelt on its pomp
> as undesirable, etc; then upon Episcopacy and
> its dangers; on prisons; on the marriage of the
> Princess Mary of Prussia; on the Sabbath.'

Before they parted, they made two further appointments. They would meet next morning at Newgate where he would hear her read and see the prisoners at work. And he would have lunch at her house at Upton Lane.

Both appointments were kept and Elizabeth handled them with her own regal simplicity. Sam and Elizabeth Gurney, and Lady Pirie supported her at Newgate where the King listened humbly to her reading. Elizabeth reminded the prisoners, and the distinguished company alike, that they were all in the presence of the King of kings. She read verses 4 and 5 from chapter 12 of St Paul the Apostle's epistle to the Romans which expresses the complete and vital democracy of the Christian faith.

> 'For as we have many members in one body, and all members have not the same office: so we, being many, are one body in Christ, and every one members one of another.'

As long as she was there they truly felt it. She made the vital connecting link between the King and the prisoner, and the atmosphere flowed through her from the one to the other. This powerful ability to communicate in such a simple fashion was unique to her; it was her special gift.

Those in charge of the King's visit to England were scandalised that one of the first monarchs in Europe, closely related to the English reigning house, should have lunch in a simple middle-class home. Even Elizabeth became aware that objections were being made. But her account was unselfconscious:

> 'There were difficulties raised about the King's going to Upton, but he chose to persevere. I went with the Lady Mayoress and the Sheriffs, the King with his own people. We arrived first.

I had to hasten to take off my cloak, and then went down to meet the King at the carriage-door, with my husband and seven of our sons and sons-in-law. I then walked with him into the drawing-room, where all was in beautiful order – neat, and adorned with flowers. I presented to the King our eight daughters and daughters-in-law (Rachel only away), our seven sons and eldest grandson, my brother and sister Buxton, Sir Henry and Lady Pelly [daughter Louisa's parents-in-law], and my sister [in-law] Elizabeth Fry – my brother and sister Gurney [Sam and Elizabeth] he had known before – and afterwards presented twenty-five of our grandchildren.'

She continued: 'Our meal was handsome, not extravagant, but fit for a king. I sat by the King, who appeared to enjoy his dinner, perfectly at his ease, and very happy with us. We went into the drawing-room…and found a deputation of Friends with an address to read to him. This was done, and the King appeared to feel it much… We then had to part, and when either he or I said perhaps we may never meet again he wept aloud at parting, and hardly let me leave hold of his arm the whole time he was here, except when at table.'

The unavoidable publicity of this occasion brought great pressure because everybody assumed she had recovered fully and could do 'all most anything' again and so bombarded her with requests 'out of the measure of my strength.' Besides which she felt the cloud of disapproval of the strictest Friends, and received 'a strong and painful judging letter,' accusing her of worldliness in relation to her Mansion House luncheons and the King of Prussia's visit. It hurt her, but it opened her eyes more fully to a fact that she had been considering for some time – the danger of the narrow interpretation of the outward forms of religion.

Quakerism in its inception had represented a breaking away of the spirit into freedom from the bondage of outward forms of religion. But in the 18th and 19th centuries it had created new and straighter bonds of its own. Looking back over her life, Elizabeth confirmed her view that it was an error to attach too much importance to dress and speech and other outward things. These might have their value; and they still did for her. Her Quaker 'air' and dress instantly put people at ease in her company. But she could have helped her children more into what she called 'the liberty' of the true Quaker faith had she made less fuss about the unessential. Of course it was a fine line. At a family gathering of children and grandchildren she warned them against the dangers of over-indulgence:

> Against 'undue love of riches' and 'too much partaking of the indulgences and luxuries of life' and 'extravagance, vanity and immodesty of dress.'

A Sad Farewell

ALTHOUGH PEOPLE may have regarded her health restored, Elizabeth was still very delicate and longed for peace and quiet. In January 1843 she wrote:

> 'Another year is closed and passed never to return. It appears to me that mine is rather a rapid descent into the valley of old age.'

She felt weary but always Joseph's presence was a comfort.

> 'I have much valued my dear husband's company, and feel it sweet that in our declining days we can so thoroughly enjoy being together, and that we unite so much in our principles and tastes...I think a quiet spirit before the Lord, and not always looking out for concerns, but knowing how to be still, is a very great point in the religious life.'

She felt that her temptation in life had always been to take things too easily. It was because of this fear, of not doing enough, of not using her life to the full 'while it is yet day', that the restless energy of her brother Joseph John could reach her. In April, he decided to visit Paris with his third wife, the American Eliza Paul Kirkbride, a recognised minister among Friends. What an introduction to Europe it would be for the new Mrs J. J. Gurney to travel in the company of his famous sister, Elizabeth Fry. The change might be good for Elizabeth and she hoped to be able to complete some of the reforms she had instigated in French prison reform; she felt it was her duty to go.

Although exhausted she went and suffered terribly from the cold and a heavy rolling sea. On the way to Paris they visited the Great Central Prison for women. It was in the charge of a mother superior and 22 nuns all of whom she addressed and saluted warmly 'as sisters in Christ'. When they reached Paris, she received a warm welcome from the King and Queen and other distinguished admirers.

Crowds greeted her carriage in the streets. She visited prisons, and tried to speak to prisoners. But her once-clear voice was becoming faint; the interpreter could hardly distinguish her sentences. Several times she wrote:

> 'I was tired and poorly, my flesh and my heart
> ready to fail, but the Lord strengthened me.'

At home in England, the new model prison at Pentonville had been built on the plan suggested long ago by Howard: solitary confinement, day and night, for every prisoner; silence; dark punishment cells. And even in the ordinary cells the glass was of such a nature that the prisoners could not see the sky. The criminal world of London had christened it 'the Bastille'.

Elizabeth had struggled to change its grim, inhuman defects. By letters to the Home Office, by personal appeal at the Mansion House banquet to Sir Robert Peel and to Prince Albert, she sought to abolish these unnecessary cruelties.

'Let them see the sky! Indeed, I should prefer more
than the sky.' And again, she repeated her firm
beliefs: 'I am certain that separate confinement
produces an unhealthy state both of mind and
body…and that a sinful course of life increases
the tendency to mental derangement as well as
bodily disease.' She added: 'I am certain that an
unhealthy state of mind and body has generally
a demoralising influence; and I consider light,
air and the power of seeing something beyond
the mere monotonous walls of a cell, highly
important…When speaking of health of body
and mind, I also mean health of soul…for I do
not believe that a despairing or stupefied state is
suitable for salvation.'

But Elizabeth was taken away from this struggle just when the
steady influence, reiterated from different quarters, and which
she could utilise to the full, was needed the most. Instead, her
diminishing energy was spent in Paris, an object of interest and
admiration to the French.

She celebrated her 63rd birthday there but again not even the
attentive care of Joseph John could protect his sister's health.
When they returned to England in June, it was clear that she
was becoming seriously ill.

'My complaint is a very distressing one – so
difficult to rest or do anything. As to sitting
Meeting, it is real suffering!' At one point, she
wrote: 'My illness has increased. I very much
keep my bed. I am entirely nursed [often by Fry
Nurses] and it is a very serious compleat illness,
one of a very low description.'

In addition to concern over Pentonville, Elizabeth received worrying news about the state of female prisoners still arriving on transport ships in New South Wales. They were being disposed of as 'domestic slaves'. One correspondent said:

> 'I am over-whelmed with the awful sin of allowing so many wretched beings to perish for lack of instruction.'

Elizabeth immediately contacted Lord Stanley, the Secretary of State for the Colonial Department and straight away steps were taken to remedy the situation in Australia.

All the while her health was deteriorating. She was taken to various places to convalesce - to Sandgate to be with her unmarried sister in law, Elizabeth Fry, who was ill. Then she was moved to Tunbridge Wells and some weeks later in October returned home to Upton Lane where for months her daughters took turns in looking after her.

She continued to suffer throughout 1844 with highs and lows. When she was well enough she made visits, received guests, attended Meeting 'while it is yet day'. She was taken to Bath for a cure and returned home refreshed but was deeply upset to learn of the death of her sister in law and Joseph's only sister, Elizabeth.

She spent time with the family in Walmer, near Dover where it was felt the sea air might strengthen her. But there was a fresh wave of sadness while there as she lost her dear son William from scarlet fever shortly after his little daughter Juliana died of it at Plashet. How she survived the heart-break of frequent deaths within her large and adored family is astonishing 'sorrow upon sorrow'. Her strength of character and of belief carried her through although after a time her family felt her thoughts were more often with the dearly departed than with those on earth.

In February 1845, she suffered more heart-ache when her dear brother-in-law and friend Fowell Buxton died. Some said he had been worn out by his anti-slavery campaign in Africa. It was another bitter blow for Elizabeth. They had campaigned hard together over the years and had become very close. He took over the anti-slavery cause when the great campaigner, William Wilberforce became ill. And in 1833 they delighted when the Slavery Abolition Act became law outlawing slavery throughout the British Empire. Of course it continued in many countries so he continued to campaign. How appalled they would be to know that slavery in various forms still exists today.

Sad and ill, she longed to return to Norfolk, to stay once more at Earlham, to re-visit the home and haunts of so many happy childhood memories. To see those wide lawns and majestic trees and to hear again the rippling River Wensum. With difficulty, the ever-attentive Joseph assisted by a daughter, got her there and she spent weeks enjoying the company of Joseph John and his family, and of her beloved eldest sister Catherine. She attended Meeting at Norwich in a wheeled chair. She spent time with family at North Repps and it was here on 10 April 1845 that she wrote her last ever letter to Joseph.

> 'My dearest husband, I am anxious to express to thee a little of my near love, and to tell thee how often I visit thee in spirit, and how very strong are my desires for thy present and thy everlasting welfare. I feel for thee in my long illness, which so much disqualifies me from being all I desire to thee.'

She returned refreshed, but still gravely ill, to Upton Lane. In May she attended two sittings of the women's Yearly Meeting in London to the delight and astonishment to those in attendance.

June arrived bringing her favourite summer scents with it. She not only attended but took part in another annual meeting of the British Ladies' Society held for her convenience at the Meeting house in Plaistow. Although sitting throughout, her mind was as sharp as ever. Prisons for women, she felt, were on the right track. Newgate, Bridewell, The Millbank Prison, the Giltspur Street Compter, White Cross Street Prison, Tothill Fields Prison, and Cold Bath Fields Prison were all in fair order and most were visited by ladies from the Society. She worried now over the most fallen of womankind and longed to be given strength to establish a refuge for 'repentant' prostitutes. This she did not live to see, but an 'Elizabeth Fry Refuge' was established in her memory although probably not as thorough or comprehensive a project as she might have wished for.

She had a short holiday in Ramsgate with Joseph in July for more therapeutic sea air and returned home to help organise a party at Upton Lane to welcome home their youngest son Harry and his bride Lucy Sheppard from their honeymoon. She received her guests in a room opening into the flower garden and was wheeled from there to the end of the terrace. There was a large gathering of close family and friends and as her daughter recalled:

> 'It was a beautiful scene, - the last social family
> meeting at which she presided; and although
> infirm and broken in health, she looked and
> seemed herself.'

She celebrated another family wedding shortly afterwards on 5 August and a week later was moved to a house on Mount Albion in Ramsgate for more sea air. Her late son William's family joined her. Her young grandson, Willie, so like his beloved dad, was a constant companion, reading the Bible to her, drawing pictures for her, sorting shells with her, chatting incessantly, young and old heads together, each diverted and happy. Arranging her shells, minerals, corals and other natural curiosities was always a pleasure for her. It was an interest she tried to instil in her children and grandchildren.

She made a final entry in her diary, that little friend of her heart, on 16 September 1845 recording precious family events. She always enjoyed having members of the family join her for periods of time. She attended Meeting on Sundays and on one occasion spoke of:

> 'The nearness of death and the necessity of immediate preparation and repentence.'

On 29 September most of the family returned to their homes leaving just Joseph and their eldest daughter Katherine behind. But soon others came back to help as Elizabeth's nursing requirements became more difficult. Her previous routine had seen her carried downstairs around noon after washing and dressing upstairs. She would be wheeled from room to room, sometimes joining the family for meals, occasionally reading and enjoying the visits and conversations of visiting family and friends. Now, although she was walking, eating and sleeping well enough, she had serious headaches which came and went.

She who was used to getting her way, suddenly became meek and submissive 'Just as you like' she would reply to questions about her care. Yet she still attended Meeting and continued to sort out Bible readings, Testaments and tracts. She had applied to the Bible Society for a grant to purchase foreign Bibles and Testaments and these she distributed to the foreign sailors she had noticed in the harbour. She spoke of the need to work 'whilst it is yet day, to be ready for the Master's summons come when He might'. She would add:

'Are we all now ready?...Have we anything left
to do?'

She was 65 now and knew the end was near; she knew that the
dreaded journey into the dark lay before her. Her fear of the
sea had been replaced by joy but her fear of the dark and death
remained although gradually she became less agitated about it.
She believed that:

'In tender mercy to her timid nature' she might
be allowed to 'pass unconsciously through the
dark valley'.

She thought how often she had read suitable, soothing tracts
from the Bible to people. Now when others tried to comfort
her with readings her exhausted brain could only focus on
her aching limbs. The more she failed, the less she found they
helped her.

Still she persevered; this magnificent woman so delicate as a
child found great reserves of strength to keep death at bay.
Joseph sat with her every night, holding her hand. And, clinging
to him fast, she would murmur to herself her old mantra:

'Come what come may, Time and the hour runs
through the roughest day'.

On 9 October she wrote to her youngest daughter Louisa saying
how much she would love to see her and her family:

'...my love is very strong.'

Days later she wrote a note to a friend with some texts for a
young person who wanted her autograph. She had written in
a firm hand without glasses – a new and worrying symptom –

'Oh yes, my eye-sight is so much better'.

On a drive later in the morning, her concentration left her and she became confused and the following morning she had severe headaches and was more confused. By late afternoon she had fallen and needed more than one person to get her into her chair. Once there she could not sit upright and with extreme difficulty she was taken up to bed and the doctor called. But there was nothing to be done; it is likely that she suffered a stroke.

Finally she was in the valley; her family stayed by her. Her beloved Joseph sat with her during the night as he had done throughout her long illness. To his delight she brightened throughout the night and although occasionally confused, her mind returned to her. Passages of the bible were read to her and she appeared to understand and enjoy them. She responded clearly to any comments made to her including earlier questions from the doctor.

Gradually the grey dawn of Sunday 12 October 1845 arrived. Her devoted maid saw a slight stir and bent quickly over the bed to hear her mistress's words:

> 'Oh! Mary, dear Mary, I am very ill!' To which
> she replied: 'I know it dearest ma'am, I know it.'
> Elizabeth added: 'Pray for me - It is a strift, but
> I am safe.'

She continued to speak indistinctly in between dosing as she had done during the night. As one of her daughters sat with her she roused a little and in a slow distinct voice said:

> 'Oh! My dear Lord, help and keep thy servant!'

Those were her last words: afterwards a veil closed between her and the world around her. Those absent members of her family were summoned and everyone waited knowing that the inevitable hour was approaching. By Sunday evening her laboured breathing altered and between three and four, in those fragile hours before dawn, on Monday 13 October it ceased altogether. Silence - she was gone.

—

The night had been long and dark but the morning broke gloriously. The sun rose from the ocean as a globe of living fire giving cheer to the grieving family.

Her eldest son, John, and one of his brothers-in-law, accompanied the hearse carrying Elizabeth Fry from Ramsgate back to Upton Lane. It had been suggested that the hearse be followed through Ramsgate by those 'gentlemen of the place as inclined to do so', with shutters closed and other marks of respect but this proposal was not accepted. So the two men followed the hearse on its slow and lonely journey throughout the night.

In the Friends' Burial Ground at Barking, a grave was prepared for her close to that of her beloved four year old daughter Betsy who died in 1815. On Monday 20 October 1845, Elizabeth's funeral procession passed between the grounds of Plashet House, a happy home so dear to her heart, and those of Plashet Cottage.

There is no prescribed service at a Quaker funeral. A profound stillness fell over the huge gathering as over 1000 people stood in silence during the burial. Elizabeth's brother Joseph John Gurney was the first to break the silence when he offered a solemn prayer. Afterwards a Meeting for Worship was held but the immediate family withdrew in favour of solace and their shared memories at Upton Lane.

Joseph Fry's sister Elizabeth had lived in Plashet Cottage until her death the previous year. It was into her cottage that the grieving Joseph moved with his eldest unmarried daughter, Katharine to live the remaining 16 years of his life. He died in the summer of 1861 aged 84 and joined his wife in the burial ground at Barking.

Their grave remains under a small park there but their grave stone was moved over one hundred years ago to the burial grounds at nearby Wanstead Meeting House. Quakers disapproved of grave stones because only the rich could afford them. They officially permitted them in 1850 on condition there was no distinction in size between stones. This remains the case today.

Inspiration for *While it is yet Day*

WHEN I was a child growing up in a Quaker family in Dublin, my father gave me a copy of Janet Whitney's book about Elizabeth Fry. Janet's interpretation of this remarkable woman, combining fact and a little whimsy, has fascinated me ever since.

Elizabeth was one of the first women in history to achieve fame for her causes within the confines of a nineteenth century marriage. This she did by successfully combining a busy home life and eleven children with hard work, determination and a sense of purpose. Coming from a wealthy family helped.

Recently I have been struck by similarities between her times and our own. So I decided to bring Elizabeth's life – her work, her family, her pacifism, and her difficult choices - to a new generation. It will show how in some surprising ways things have not changed much in the 170 years since her death.

She would be sad that women still struggle to balance their work and home lives satisfactorily and without guilt. The widespread illiteracy around the world would sadden her too. What would she think of the need for a Modern Slavery Act in 2015? She and her friends William Wilberforce and brother in law Sir Thomas Fowell Buxton hoped that servitude would be abolished forever with the Slavery Act of 1833.

And what would she think of prison reform today? She abhorred the cruelty, crowding and filth in the prisons she visited in the early nineteenth century. When she first entered the notorious Newgate Prison in January 1813, she recorded "gloom, bad smells, pandemonium." She had never before seen "a mass of women, by the hundreds, reduced to the level of wild beasts." She felt that prison should be an opportunity for rehabilitation and reform, for education and paid employment. There should be no idleness and no extra punishment.

I have tried to keep her wonderful story light to appeal to young people and those who are not avid readers of history or biography. I hope it inspires a new generation and gets people talking about Elizabeth Fry and wanting to learn more about her and her great achievements.

Averil Douglas Opperman

What Is Quakerism?

QUAKERS ARE members of the Religious Society of Friends founded over 360 years ago. Quakerism is a way of life more than a confirmed set of beliefs. It is based on Christianity and finds inspiration in the Bible and in the life and teachings of Jesus. Quakers also find meaning and value in the teachings of other faiths and accept that Quakerism is not the only way.

Worship takes the form of silent Meetings more often on Sundays but on other occasions too, including weddings and funerals. Silence provides the tranquillity needed for reflection where worshippers can be open to thought. All are welcome to speak or share a prayer. There are neither priests nor hierarchy because Quakers believe that every person can communicate directly with God within themselves. They believe that there is a light, a spirit of God, and goodness within everyone. Quakers ask of themselves and of society in general: uncompromising honesty, sincerity, simplicity of lifestyle, non-violence and justice for all, high born or low.

Anyone can participate in decision-making if they wish and can help run the Society; those appointed to specific roles serve for a limited time after which others take their turn. As well as Meetings for Worship, the society holds regular business meetings. At these meetings births, marriages and burials are registered and other matters discussed.

For years there were separate business meetings for men and for women. And in Meetings for Worship the sexes were segregated too – men sat at one side of the Meeting House and women at the other. But this practice ended over a hundred years ago.

In Elizabeth Fry's day, strict Quakers were regarded as 'plain' because of their solemn dress, speech and life style. Those, like some of Elizabeth's family, who continued to enjoy music and dancing were considered 'gay' in its original sense. The term 'gay' is used throughout this book instead of the more laborious description 'Sunday morning Quakers'.

Also Quakers did not use the names of the months, regarding them as heathen. Instead they referred to them in numbers for example First Month 28th First Day would be Sunday 28th January and so on.

Quakers used the pronouns 'thee' and 'thou' to show that everyone was equal in the eyes of God. These terms were usually used for family and inferiors and the more polite 'you' used for superiors.

A Brief History of Quakerism

T HE FIRST regular 'meetings for worship' were organised by the founder of Quakerism, George Fox at Swarthmore Hall near Ulverston in Westmorland [now Cumbria] in 1652. Fox, a shoemaker's apprentice from Leicestershire, was 25 then and had spent years travelling to find the meaning of religion. He was dissatisfied with organised religion and its abuse within the established Church of England: who should rule the State versus who should rule the Church in the time of Oliver Cromwell. He objected to fine buildings, priests and tithes. He came to realise that neither priest nor puritan could help him for he had discovered an inner light which enabled him to communicate directly with Christ.

This became the grand principle of his life and in due course the grand principle of Quakerism. As he travelled he told people how the Light of Christ had broken into the darkness of his spirit. He and his followers became known as the 'Children of the Light' and they felt free to worship anywhere. Prayers and song were not necessary; it was in the deepest places of the human spirit that people should find their faith. Personal experience was more important than doctrine. There was no need for outward sacraments. Religion – and behaviour -

should be plain and sincere. Clothes too should be simple and unadorned.

George Fox refused to doff his hat because God alone would claim his reverence. While others addressed the great with the polite pronoun 'you', keeping 'thee' and 'thou' for families and inferiors, Fox used 'thee' and 'thou' for everyone rich, poor, great or small. He dropped all titles such as 'sir', 'doctor', 'my lady' etc. He demanded honesty in the courts, in business and in schools.

He refused to take oaths because he spoke the truth at all times. By refusing to swear an oath to the sovereign as head of the church, Quakers were disbarred from entering Parliament and from joining the armed forces. So, many Quakers became businessmen hence such household names as Lloyds and Barclays banks, and food manufacturers such as Frys, Cadburys and Rowntrees.

He refused to pay tithe taxes to the State church and his view on sobriety was clear - quench thirst but do not allow people to become drunk. In those days drinking beer, or cider, was safer than drinking un-purified water. Pacifism was, and still is, a cornerstone of Quakerism; Quakers will not take up arms against fellow human beings. During the First and Second World Wars, Quakers drove ambulances, were doctors and nurses, and helped in any way they could without taking up arms.

Eventually George Fox's travels brought him to Swarthmore Hall in Cumbria where Judge Thomas Fell and his wife, Margaret allowed him to meet with his 'friends' regularly. For as long as he lived, the judge protected Quakers from persecution although he never became one himself. By now they had become known as "Quakers", as well as Friends. There are various theories regarding this nickname. A likely one is that while up before the law for his illegal preaching, George Fox told the magistrate he should quake at the word of God. The magistrate threw the word Quaker back at Fox as an insult and Fox and his followers proudly adopted it. Or it may have come from the way Friends trembled through their doubts and fears as they left the rigidity, and relative safety of formal, State religion. Or maybe it was because they trembled when in the presence of God. Others believe the name evolved from the terror Quakers experienced during persecution.

Legislation had been passed outlawing non conformists and in the late 1660s there were mass arrests. Out of about 50,000 Quakers, 500 died in jail. Their bravery caught the attention of theologian Robert Barclay who in 1678 wrote *"Apology"*, a widely read definitive statement of Quaker beliefs and worship. It also impressed William Penn who, while in prison for his beliefs, had written another definitive book, *"No Cross, No Crown"* [1669]. Penn had a close association with America as his father, Admiral Sir William Penn, was given a massive piece of land there by King Charles II in 1681 to repay a debt. This became Pennsylvania in the Admiral's honour and it was where his son created a haven for persecuted Quakers.

Today the number of Quakers in the world fluctuates and figures vary but 210,000 is a fair estimate. There are probably less than 15,000 Quakers in the UK of whom around 8000 are 'attenders' and regularly attend Meetings for Worship in the 400 Meeting Houses. There are over 100,000 Quakers in North America and about 25,000 in Africa. There are smaller numbers throughout Europe and in Asia, Australia and New Zealand, and around 1500 in the Republic of Ireland.

Acknowledgements

M ANY PEOPLE have given me help and encouragement in bringing Elizabeth Fry before a new generation. My main aim has been to make this account of her life an easy, enjoyable read.

I have researched many books and documents in various libraries for information not just about Elizabeth herself but also about subjects relevant to her story. In addition to the more traditional sources, there is endless information available nowadays – almost too much – via the internet. So I have tried to focus only on the woman I learned about as a child and have admired so much ever since. Janet Whitney's interpretation of her coloured my view of Elizabeth's life and inspired me to find out more.

Family and friends have read drafts of *While It Is Yet Day* and I am indebted to them for their feedback - you will know who you are! I am particularly grateful to Ted Milligan, retired Quaker historian, for his interest, advice and encouragement; meeting him was a joy. Also to Glynn and Shirley Douglas in Ireland for their help and encouragement – and for the introduction to Ted.

Thank you too: Lucy Norment and Adrienne O'Connor Grimes in the USA for research; Catharine Neal for pursuing an idea; and Susanne McDadd for editing an early draft – all time-consuming tasks way beyond the call of friendship. Grateful thanks also to: Kate Beaufoy, Charmian Edgerton, Sue and Jerry Johns, Artemis Cooper, Anne O'Brien, Michael Sissons, Myra Street and Gay O'Neill for their input; Malcolm Douglas for his IT skills and to Donna Bradley for practical as well as moral support.

And special thanks to Helen Bowden for enthusiastically embracing the book, and to all the team at Orphans Publishing for their hard work and patience.

To my husband Michael, for his encouragement and for listening to me prattle on about 'EF' for so long, I give my love and thanks; also to our son David for his level-headed advice and foresight; and to my stepsons Pete and Guy for their constant support.

Orphans Publishing

Orphans has a rich heritage in publishing dating back to the 1870's. Our founder, Henry Stanley Newman, a Quaker and philanthropist, set up an orphanage and then acquired a printing press to support the orphans and give them a trade. He also used this print capability to spread his message by printing and publishing religious tracts and books including the Quaker publication, '*The Friend*', for many years. The printing side became a thriving business named Orphans Press but the publishing side gradually lapsed after his death.

'*While It Is Yet Day*' rekindled our desire to support authors as passionate and eloquent about their subject as Averil Douglas Opperman is about Elizabeth Fry. Where there is a story to be told, particularly with a link to our history, Orphans Publishing will summon the entrepreneurial spirit of Mr Newman to reach the public attention our authors deserve.